The New Pay

Linking Employee and Organizational Performance

Jay R. Schuster
Patricia K. Zingheim

Lexington Books

An Imprint of Macmillan, Inc.

NEW YORK

Maxwell Macmillan Canada

TORONTO

Maxwell Macmillan International

NEW YORK · OXFORD · SINGAPORE · SYDNEY

Library of Congress Cataloging-in-Publication Data

Schuster, Jay P.
　The new pay: linking employee and organizational performance /
Jay R. Schuster, Particia K. Zingheim.
　　　p.　　　cm.
　Includes: bibliographical references and index.
　ISBN 0-669-5358-3
　1. Compensation management.　I. Zingheim, Patricia K.　II. Title.
HF5549.5.C67S38　1992
658.3'225—dc20　　　　　　　　　　　　　　　　　　　　92-3029
　　　　　　　　　　　　　　　　　　　　　　　　　　　　　　　CIP

Lexington Books
An Imprint of Macmillan, Inc.
866 Third Avenue, New York, N.Y. 10022

Maxwell Macmillan Canada, Inc.
1200 Eglinton Avenue East
Suite 200
Don Mills, Ontario M3C 3N1

Macmillan, Inc. is part of the Maxwell Communications Group of Companies.

Printed in the United States of America

printing number

1 2 3 4 5 6 7 8 9 10

The authors and the publisher gratefully acknowledge permission to use material from the
following publications:

E. L. Landon, Jr., 1990, "New Strategies for Bank Profitability." Presentation at Robert Morris
Associates 1990 Spring Conference, San Antonio, TX. Used with permission.
R. E. Litan, R. Z. Lawrence, and C. Schultze, 1988, *America's Living Standards: Threats and
Challenges*. Copyright © 1988 Brookings Institution, Washington, D.C. Used with permission.
J. B. Quinn, J. J. Baruch, and P. Paquette, 1987, "Technology in Services," *Scientific American*,
December, 50–58. Copyright © 1987 by *Scientific American*. Used with permission.
M. A. Verespej, 1990, "Healthcare: Price Is Not the Problem," *Industry Week*, 17 September,
22–30. Copyright © 1990 Penton Publishing, Inc., Cleveland, OH. Used with permission of
Industry Week.

*To Hap and Mick
and all they represent*

Contents

Foreword

Ideas about what constitutes good and bad management are changing rapidly. New organizational designs, new managerial behaviors, and different concepts about how to control and manage the workplace are rapidly gaining acceptance in businesses around the world. The reasons for this are many, but perhaps most important concerns what it takes to be successful in today's business environment. Organizations need to continue to improve in their costs, in the quality of the goods and services they offer, and in how quickly they can deliver products and services to customers. Those organizations that do not improve their speed, costs, and quality are destined for extinction. The old organizational models and the practices that go along with them were never designed to perform in the type of competitive global markets that exist today. Thus, it is hardly surprising that they are frequently found wanting and that they are often being cast aside by today's business organizations.

Basic to the effective functioning of any organization is its pay and reward system. Although there have been significant changes in the way many organizations administer rewards, pay systems have been particularly resistant to change. There are a number of reasons for this, including the fact that once an organization adopts a particular pay practice, it becomes highly institutionalized and indeed often becomes central to the very fabric of the organization. Changing it requires undoing years of commitments and behaviors. Nevertheless, in my recent book *Strategic Pay*, I argue strongly that pay systems must change in dramatic ways if organizations are to perform adequately in today's business environment.

Schuster and Zingheim state the case for change even more strongly than my book did. They call for all organizations to adopt a dramatically different set of pay practices in order to be effective. They draw upon their very impressive histories as consultants to outline a new approach to pay that challenges virtually every organizational practice that has been considered good pay administration for the last fifty years. But they don't stop with just challenging traditional practices; they specify in considerable detail what kind of new practices should be adopted. They talk, for example, about the importance of a much greater focus on pay for performance, about a greater focus on market-based pay, and about abandoning traditional job evaluation practices. I believe all of these changes are major, and I believe all of them are necessary if organizations are going to be competitive in the 1990s business environment.

Once the case is made that new pay is needed, Schuster and Zingheim go into considerable detail about the specific policies and practices that need to make up new pay. The reader should find this particular aspect of the book very helpful. Although readers may disagree with some of the specific policies and practices that are recommended by Schuster and Zingheim, it is important to point out that they present an integrated systems view of pay, and as a result it may be unwise to implement only part of their approach. Indeed, one of the great strengths of this book is that the authors take a total compensation approach to pay and are concerned about the fit between compensation policies and practices and the other parts of the organization. Thus, they do not simply recommend small, discrete changes; they recommend an integrated system of policies and practices that fundamentally change the relationship between individuals and the organizations for which they work. Although this means radical change, in my opinion, in most cases it represents needed change.

Overall, Schuster and Zingheim provide a challenging road map for the future of pay systems in organizations. Their book ought to be read by everyone who impacts total employee compensation in today's business environment, since it contains not just challenges to what is done but specific, usable recommendations about what should be done. Although some of the recommendations may seem radical, there is increasing evidence that most of what they recommend is likely to become standard practice in the future. Practices like gainsharing and flexible benefits have already gained significant footholds in American corporations. Many of the other practices are also likely to gain important footholds, because they are congruent with the business needs of most organizations.

Edward E. Lawler III

University of Southern California

Preface

It was Lawler who gave the name *new pay*[1] to reward programs that reflect an understanding of organizational goals, values, and culture and the challenges of a more competitive global economy. This sounds better than other titles such as *alternative reward strategies, nontraditional pay,* or *contemporary pay,* because *new pay* suggests that it will replace what now exists, rather than be a peculiarity that will pass in time.

New pay is more than just business plan gainsharing, skill-based pay, and employee involvement. The new pay view provides that organizations effectively use all elements of pay—direct pay (cash compensation) and indirect pay (benefits)—to help them form a partnership between the organization and its employees. By means of this partnership, employees can understand the goals of the organization, know where they fit in in accomplishing these goals, become appropriately involved in decisions affecting them, and receive rewards to the extent the organization attains these goals and to the extent they have assisted the organization to do so. New pay helps link the financial success of both the organization and its employees. Customer-focused organizations are interested in forming partnerships with customers and outside suppliers. It is more likely that these organizations will be successful in forming external partnerships once they have solidified a partnership with their employees. This partnership ensures that a "win–win" culture exists that shares the results of organizational performance. The linking of employees and organizations does not occur nearly as vigorously without new pay.

This book is written for a number of audiences. First, it is intended for busy executives who are evaluating new pay as a possible business alternative and need a "ready reference" to follow. Executives will be interested in how to evaluate current pay programs against performance priorities, how to use pay to form employee–organization partnerships, and how to build a practical pay strategy and change pay programs to focus on results.

The second audience we hope to reach is that of more senior human resource, compensation, and benefit practitioners and consultants who want an overview of new pay that includes a total compensation perspective. It is important to supplement this book with others on the subjects of employee involvement, variable pay, skill-based pay, and indirect pay. This audience will find the material on why new pay is important as valuable as they will find the parts about building a total compensation strategy, base pay, variable pay, and indirect pay consistent with the principles of new pay. Making new pay work effectively is of practical value to this audience. These readers will also appreciate that much of new pay is based on our experiences in major U.S. corporations; specific information and examples of experiences are included.

The third audience is that of less experienced compensation, benefit, and human resource practitioners who are interested in a basic under-standing of new pay. Some of the specific examples provided will be of interest to this group. The goal is to influence their views so that they will view new pay as representing the only practical future for total com-pensation management in the United States.

The fourth audience is that of academics who are searching for new factors that contribute to organizational success or lack of success. Although it is unlikely that new pay causes organizations to perform most effectively, it is probable that traditional pay encumbers organizations that might otherwise be better able to achieve.

Overview of the Book

In part I, chapter 1 discusses the many socioeconomic challenges and changes organizations must face. The next twenty years will differ substantially from the last twenty years. Changes will have a major impact on how organizations that compete to succeed will behave to survive. Chapter 2 in part I reviews new management strategies for improved performance and relates this to new pay's role in getting better results.

With all the talk about "strategy," a practical manager or professional will want to see how a total compensation strategy can actually be developed (total compensation includes base pay, variable pay, and indirect pay). Part II suggests how to develop a total compensation strategy effectively and how to turn this into results that have the benefit of matching an organization's tolerance for employee involvement with the need for a new pay program of high technical and qualitative value that is sufficiently flexible to change as the organization adapts to a rapidly fluctuating business environment. Chapter 3 describes the strategic principles of new pay and a process that provides the opportunity to determine whether the principles of new pay better parallel an organization's business and financial plans than do its current pay practices. Chapter 4 gives some examples of new pay strategies. Chapter 5 describes how to move from a total compensation strategy to program implementation by means of a level of employee involvement that matches the organization's tolerance, culture, and experience with involving employees in decisions that affect them.

The chapters in part III describe the implications of new pay in regard to base pay and how new pay practices compare to traditional approaches. Base pay, in the form of market-based pay and skill-based pay, constitutes an important component of new pay. These chapters describe the problems that traditional base pay administration creates for organizations trying to improve financial performance, employee productivity, teamwork, and collaboration, and trying as well to introduce a stronger role for employees in the success of the organization. Also, part III suggests how a new pay view of base pay can supplement a strategy of using pay to help management improve performance and productivity.

Variable pay (cash compensation that does not fold into base pay) is very important to new pay. The chapters in part IV discuss business plan gainsharing, winsharing, group incentives, lump-sum awards, and other forms of new pay. It contrasts variable pay based on group performance with variable pay based on individual performance, since group variable pay is becoming important to the future of many organizations. A group is defined as any association of two or more people in a formal or informal organizational unit where cooperation is required to get the job done. Under this definition, the group may be organizationwide, a division, a department, or a team; may be structured around a product, service, function, or work flow; or may be a temporary group formed to accomplish a specific task. Chapter 11 provides examples of new pay programs to help the reader understand the wide range of available variable pay possibilities. Chapter 12 discusses the issues that need to be addressed in designing a variable pay program.

Indirect pay as an element of new pay is addressed in part V. It is critical to take a view of indirect pay that more closely focuses it on the results the organization obtains rather than on an employee's tenure. The unbridled expansion of employee benefits over the last twenty years as fixed costs of doing business has inhibited the ability of organizations to make "pay for performance" more than a slogan taking the place of a strategy in which pay becomes a true reward.

The results of a survey of new pay practices among some of the best-known companies in America are presented in part VI. These results indicate that the way pay is managed differs in tandem with the financial performance of these organizations, and support the hands-on experience described in this book.

Part VII predicts what might occur in the future concerning pay, and what we would like to see occur. It is clear that the field of employee pay will not be "business as usual" unless we are somehow able to turn back the clock and return to the stability of the 1960s. Executives, managers, and professionals will experiment with and use new pay, since little opportunity exists to do much with traditional pay systems other than to encourage bureaucracy, status quo, and mediocre performance that is rewarded on the same level as excellent performance.

We want to thank all the organizations and people who played a part in helping us gather information for this book. Special thanks go to our clients and other organizations who participated in our studies of pay practices and helped us gain an understanding of how they view the possible role of new pay in the future. Also of special value have been the many client experiences that have helped us understand what works and what does not work. These experiences have provided us with the major substance upon which this book is built. We want to express our appreciation to Delene Smith for many years of high-quality professional association and for her professional and editorial contributions to this book. We also want to thank Nancy Fairchild for her valuable critique and contributions to the indirect pay section. We value the contributions of Rick Mayo, who reviewed the indirect pay section and made important comments and suggestions.

Jay R. Schuster
Patricia K. Zingheim

Los Angeles, California

Introduction

The alarm is ringing—it is a "wake-up call" for American organizations. Even the most dramatic cuts in work-force size and other expenses are not resulting in performance improvements. Organizations are finding that they cannot survive and prosper merely by laying off employees and restructuring.[1] Events are unraveling at a dramatic pace, and our businesses are no longer able to compete internationally. We face structural problems of declining worker income. Employees are becoming increasingly disenfranchised and unwilling to align themselves with their organizations. There is a national crisis of health care coverage and cost burdens that our organizations cannot address. As a result, American organizations must discard management methods and approaches that do not fit with rapid change and adopt practices that help make both the organization and its employees into winners. Pay practices have failed to keep up with the times.[2] It is now time for pay practices to catch up.

Pay programs are visible and powerful communicators of organizational goals, priorities, and values.[3] Proper alignment with what is to be accomplished is essential. We believe that new pay emphasizes pay solutions that reflect the proper organizational directions and omits those practices that are counterproductive. Making pay a positive force in the future of organizations seems inevitable and essential.

The roots of new pay began in the early 1980s when some organizations that were striving for optimal levels of performance and productivity determined that how pay was administered mattered in the overall scheme of things. Because of this, they began to question the tradition of merely copying the pay practices of others without questioning the possible negative impact these practices would have on the key role employees play in making the organization a success. These organizations began abandoning traditional pay practices where they failed to meet their evolving needs. Many top-performing organizations moved to more flexible and responsive pay strategies that matched the circumstances in which the organizations found themselves.[4] The rejection of "one size fits all" traditional pay practices gave birth to new pay.

Since these starts in the early 1980s, much has been written about ensuring that pay programs are developed to provide constructive support for the customer, business, and financial strategies of the organization.[5] While no one can argue with the contention that pay should be linked with strategy and tactics, organizational directions change so frequently that an approach to this linkage that incorporates flexibility and responsiveness is more practical than a hard-and-fast association between pay and a short- or long-term business plan. New pay involves strategy-setting pay methods that change as the situation evolves and that are directed toward attaining measurable results. Arguments that suggest traditional pay programs are appropriate for some organizations are only valid if these organizations do not compete for business and customers.

Under new pay, both direct and indirect pay programs respond to specific business and human resource challenges. If quality is a problem, pay can be focused so that quality improvement is emphasized in variable pay. If labor cost is a problem, base pay and indirect pay programs can be designed to be moderately competitive compared to direct business competition. Variable pay can be added to increase overall pay costs only if the extra costs can be passed on to the customer in terms of improved product or service quality and customer value. Flexibility is essential, and traditional pay planning has historically lacked flexibility. New pay responds to these challenges.

New Pay Is Total Compensation

New pay requires the use of all the possible "ammunition" to hit the proper performance targets. This means base pay, variable pay, and indirect pay. These are the elements of the total compensation perspective that is fundamental to new pay. Each plays a unique role in new pay.

Base Pay

Under new pay, base pay levels are matched as closely as possible to the competitive labor market, given the organization's ability to pay, while at the same time permitting the organization to obtain quality talent. Base pay can be adjusted from the competitive market to emphasize jobs and skills that are strategically important to the organization. Base pay serves as a "platform" for variable pay. This is because it is easier for variable pay to mirror the changing and evolving goals of the organization, link the employees and the organization, and at the same time encourage teamwork and collaboration than it is for base pay to perform this role.

Variable Pay

The centerpiece of new pay is variable pay. Variable pay, in forms such as group variable pay, business plan gainsharing, winsharing, lump-sum awards, and individual variable pay, has the flexibility needed to match dynamic circumstances. Variable pay for broad employee populations is able to respond to changes and complex challenges that employees and organizations face. Variable pay flexibly rewards employees for performance that makes the organization successful and controls pay costs when the organization is less successful. Variable pay facilitates the employee–organization partnership by linking the fortunes of both parties in a positive manner.

Indirect Pay

Flexible benefit planning was an early move to new pay. However, many organizations offer benefit choices only to match what other organizations do, rather than to aid performance and emphasize goals. To address the challenges of the future, however, it will be necessary to innovate beyond following the practices of others. Indirect pay cost management and cost sharing will be necessary for indirect pay to supplement rather than detract from the core elements of new pay—base pay and variable pay.

Assembling New Pay Elements

New pay provides pay planners with the ability to adapt base pay, variable pay, and indirect pay to specific situations. Some combination of competitive base pay and a variable pay plan may be used to implement the cash compensation strategy of the organization. Indirect pay, as well as base pay and variable pay, may have a requirement to be reviewed annually and modified as needed to match situations and experiences.

For example, a defined benefit retirement plan may be replaced by a profit-sharing plan to vary retirement funding based on organizational performance results. The possibilities are limitless with new pay, because the situation dictates the design to be employed. The solution starts with the challenge and works back to effective design.

New pay is about matching pay programs to organizations that are changing either because of a desire to do so or because of forces beyond their control. Some may want to prepare for the future in advance of a crisis. Others must adapt quickly to satisfy customers, survive, and/or succeed before it is too late. The need for actual productivity and performance improvements, the changing work force, and the intensified competition for business have required organizations to include human resource issues in their overall strategic and financial plans. They do this by focusing human resource expenditures on directions that support organizational priorities and challenges. We believe this is best done with the help of new pay.

PART ONE

Employees and Organizations in the 1990s

1

Socioeconomic Foundations of New Pay

The Reasons Why New Pay is Essential

To forecast the role human resource systems in general and pay in particular will play in the future of American organizations, it is essential to consider some of the realities for the United States in the 1990s. We interpret these realities as follows:

- Increased global competition for business in the United States and internationally is creating widespread economic restructuring and is forcing organizations to become measurably more productive or fail.
- New technologies will change how jobs are structured and performed, which will in turn affect job requirements and the types of people that are needed to perform the jobs. Many people will not be qualified for these new jobs unless they measurably improve their current skills.
- Changing technologies and a growing service sector will cause activities relating to supplying and utilizing information increasingly to dominate the nature of work. This will create a major shift in the demand for certain types of labor and create spot labor shortages during the 1990s. In this time of shortage, many workers will not be employable because they are not qualified for the available jobs.
- It will become increasingly difficult for workers to increase real income and maintain a standard of living during the 1990s comparable to that experienced in the 1980s unless productivity improves. Positive opportunities for improving productivity exist.
- Fewer new workers entering the labor force (due to population

declines at the ages of normal work-force entry) and stagnant or falling real income mean that a larger percentage of the working-age population will need to work than in the past.

To survive, American industry must have a new view of the future. This view will substantially and permanently change the traditional relationship between employees and organizations. Change will require modifying many of the attitudes, plans, and approaches to both how we work and how we are paid. Organizations and employees will share the responsibility and rewards for success.

The Focus on Productivity

During the twenty years from the late 1960s to the late 1980s, the U.S. economy increased its real output of goods and services by nearly 70 percent, or a respectable average of 2.6 percent per year. During this period, the civilian labor force grew rapidly, expanding by a little more than 50 percent, or by 2.1 percent per year. But although labor productivity in the United States grew rapidly in the twenty years after World War II, it lagged during the twenty years from the late 1960s to the late 1980s. Over the last two decades, output per employed person has increased by only 11 percent. Comparably, the productivity of the Group of Five economies of Japan, West Germany, Britain, France, and the United States had an unweighted average increase of 71 percent during the same period. Clearly, the United States is lagging in productivity.[1]

Over the last twenty years, U.S. economic growth resulted more from additions to the work force than from increases in productivity. However, productivity increases are needed to keep real income for workers growing. Lagging productivity raises some key issues about what has happened in the United States since the late 1960s. Some contend that the country has been creating an excessive number of "bad" jobs, such as selling hamburgers, and not enough "good" jobs, such as producing quality cars. Since the 1960s, U.S. output and workers have shifted from manufacturing to services. In 1967, manufacturing provided 28 percent of GNP; since that year, manufacturing has declined to less than 20 percent. Service industries have expanded from 60 percent to more than 68 percent of the economy. In the Group of Five countries, manufacturing has declined from 30 percent of GNP to 25 percent during this period, and services have expanded from 56 percent to 63 percent, indicating that the United States is staying relatively even with this comparison group. Thus, the relative lag in productivity improvement in the United States compared to the Group of Five countries cannot be explained by the relative mix of manufacturing and service.[2]

Besides the bad-jobs theory, some contend that lagging productivity is the result of employee skills not matching the increased skills required by U.S. organizations. Others contend that lagging U.S. productivity is a result of failing to develop new technology or to utilize current technology fully.[3] Still others contend that it is due to ineffective management practices.[4] Available information and data lend support to the skills contention and to the technology contention. The lack of hard data makes substantiation of the management practices contention difficult, but many believe this is an important element in the productivity gap.

Quality of Jobs

Global competition has placed severe economic pressures on manufacturing and has affected America's semiskilled workers by the millions. Layoffs, plant closings, and wage concessions threaten their middle-class way of life. These workers combine low skills with relatively high pay and living standard expectations; thus, it has not been possible for them to meet their economic needs as the manufacturing sector has changed.[5]

Middle managers have also been affected as cost pressures, competitive concerns, and a wave of mergers have resulted in organizations gutting their management ranks.[6] However, in some instances, the remaining middle managers have greater autonomy and influence. Sometimes these middle managers have placed workers in charge of designing their own jobs, including keeping track of cost and quality. In some instances, this has improved productivity and cost management.

However, despite a few opportunities, economic pressures have had a negative effect on wages. Average real earnings of U.S. workers have declined to the 1961 level.[7] Eight million jobs were created between the late 1970s and mid-1980s; almost three-fifths of these jobs paid less than $7,000 a year in dollars adjusted to 1984 levels, according to a study commissioned by the Congressional Joint Economic Committee. White male wage earners, once the highest-paid workers, have been affected the most by wage changes. According to the study, 97 percent of the new jobs filled by white men in the early 1980s paid less than an adjusted

$7,000 per year. Black males' wages, which increased significantly during the 1970s, have decreased in real dollars.[8] This seems to confirm that there is a slow drift toward industries that pay lower wages. Even though the move is small now, it is there, and it is growing.[9]

This information, combined with the fact that hourly wages of U.S. workers are lower in the service sector than in the manufacturing sector, suggests that the change to a service economy has created more bad jobs and, as a result, decreased earnings. However, real earnings in the manufacturing sector have been almost static over the last twenty years. Also, given current rates of relative wage growth, it is predicted that about one-half of the service industries will close the mean wage gap with the manufacturing sector in the next five years.[10] The speed with which the wage gap narrows depends on the service sector's productivity and utilization of technology.

Further examination of wage patterns is needed to determine the reason for changes in wages. According to Litan in *America's Living Standards*,[11] from the early 1970s to the late 1980s the proportion of U.S. workers with earnings of less than $20,000 in constant 1987 dollars increased from 51 percent to 55 percent, while the proportion of workers with earnings of more than $50,000 also increased from 5 percent to 7 percent. The proportion earning from $20,000 to $50,000—those generally identified as holding middle-class jobs—decreased to 38 percent from 44 percent.

Fewer male workers earn between $20,000 and $50,000 per year in constant 1987 dollars than in the early 1970s. Also, a larger portion of the male population earns less than $20,000. Conversely, the proportion of women earning from $20,000 to $50,000 has increased, and the proportion earning less than $20,000 has decreased. The earnings gap between women and men decreased significantly between 1979 and 1987 due to increases in earnings rather than in hours worked.[12] Thus, women have fared better than men. In addition, older, well-educated workers have fared better than younger, less-educated workers. Most of the decline in the middle of the earnings distribution is due to the falling earnings of young men with no more than high school educations. Sixty-four percent of men from ages 24 to 34 with only a high school education earned more than $20,000 in 1973 (adjusted to 1987 dollars); this dropped to 40 percent by the late 1980s.

Change in real wages varies by earnings level. From 1979 to 1987, the real wages of male employees in the 25–64 age group fell by 2 percent a year for the lowest fifth of wage earners. At the same time, real wages for male employees among the top fifth of earners rose by 0.5 percent per year. The Brookings Institution suggests that this change is caused by a surplus of workers with fewer skills than the labor market now requires. The top 20 percent of American workers are becoming more competitive in world commerce (e.g., workers involved in advanced marketing, strategic planning, computers and electronics, architecture, and law).[13]

Although the value of education varies by industry, education pays. The *Economic Commentary*[14] of the Federal Reserve Bank of Cleveland reports that a one-year increase in education raises average wages by 8.1 percent in service occupations and by 4.6 percent in manufacturing occupations. And not only does education pay, but the return on education has been increasing. In 1983, a one-year increase in education resulted in a 6.3 percent higher wage than the mean of all workers; by 1987, the figure had increased to 7.4 percent. Those with an education are winning during competitive times, while others are not. Since more jobs will be available in the service sector than in the manufacturing sector, education is important. Entry-level skills required by service occupations tend to be higher than those required by manufacturing occupations for the same pay level.

These statistics suggest that the bad-jobs theory is not as strong as the fact that the opportunity to increase pay relates more to education and gender than to whether the person works in a service or manufacturing job. The demand for not-so-well-educated labor has fallen dramatically. At the same time, the supply of college-educated persons has increased more quickly than has the supply of people with only a high school education. But the number of jobs requiring college-educated persons has outstripped even the increase in supply.[15] This suggests that the United States has many "good" jobs but is likely to have difficulty filling them. It further suggests that the less-educated younger workers are having a tragic time in the job market. Higher-paid, lower-skilled manufacturing jobs are disappearing and are being replaced by lower-paid, higher-skilled service jobs or high-paid, high-skill jobs, and people at the bottom of the earnings distribution are unprepared to compete for the available higher-paid jobs.

Productivity growth in the United States has fallen. In the private business sector, output per hour of labor increased 3.3 percent per year between the mid-1940s and mid-1960s, but the rate of increase declined to 1.4 percent per year between the mid-1960s and mid-1980s. Had productivity growth continued at the pre-1965 rate, U.S. output in the 1980s would have been 45 percent higher than it was, with no additional labor utilized to gain the higher productivity.[16] Higher productivity relates to a growth in real income. Unless productivity grows, workers will suffer stagnant or falling living standards. This suggests that in the next decade, America must focus on improving educational levels and more effectively utilizing technology to increase productivity. That includes human resource programs that make employees more productive.

Service Sector Requires Technology and Increased Productivity

The *Economist* defines services as "anything sold in trade that could not be dropped on your foot." *Scientific American*[17] defines services as output that is not a physical product or construction, is consumed at the time it is produced, and gives added value in nontangible forms that are expressed in terms such as communications, transportation, finance, health care, and education. The service sector accounts for over 68 percent of the GNP and over 75 percent of all jobs. Many of the industries in the service sector are as large and well grounded in technology as manufacturing. Technology can increase productivity, quality, and economic output in the service sector. This makes it possible that a service-dominated United States can support increases in real earnings for the long term. However, because of the technology required, job requirements are stringent and talent is scarce.

Is productivity as important to services as it is to manufacturing? Service industries must have the scale, capital intensity, and sophistication to apply technology. Services are stereotyped as small-scale, unsophisticated undertakings that make few equipment and technology investments; this does not match the communications, transportation, health care, pipeline, and electric utility industries that comprise much of the service sector. Others, such as banking, entertainment, retailing, financial services, car rental, and package or message delivery are also moving toward technology. Investment in technology per "information worker" has grown quickly since the 1960s and exceeds that for workers in basic industry. In a Bureau of Labor Statistics study, almost half of the thirty most capital-intensive industries were service industries. *Fortune 500* data suggest that large service organizations compare favorably in relative profitability and size to large manufacturers. Service organizations can afford to buy technology and are important to the development and utilization of new technology for services and products. Citicorp developed the first automated teller machines, and Federal Express made significant package-sorting innovations. Other examples of technology include hand-held computers for inventory control, pen computers, voice mail, and imaging technology for electronic scanning of paper documents.

In service industries, productivity is hard to measure. Compared to manufacturing, it is more difficult to identify a unit of output, because there are no physical goods to count or weigh and the quality of the output has to be considered. However, when customers can select between services or between the service and a product that serves the same purpose, the resulting revenue—or its "sales value"—gives the organization an indication of the quantity and quality of output. A comparison of sales value and labor or capital input can frequently provide a credible measure of service industry productivity.[18] The Bureau of Labor Statistics indicates that for the last thirty-five years, some service industries (such as the communications industry) could sustain a productivity growth rate comparable to those in manufacturing over long periods of time. Although rates of productivity gain vary among service industries as greatly as they do in manufacturing, productivity gains have been less for the service sector than the manufacturing sector since 1980; service sector productivity has hardly increased at all.[19] Service organizations will need to focus on improving productivity to strengthen the economy.

How fast technology can improve service sector productivity affects the relationship between pay levels in service and manufacturing. The more productive the service sector becomes, the more it will be able to pay higher wages. Productivity increases the demand for higher skills and sustains higher wages in specific service industries, such as transportation and communications, compared to manufacturing. While employees in manufacturing industries must accept poorer wages and working conditions to keep organizations from moving their manufacturing overseas, many service sector workers can earn good wages if they are able to acquire the skills to perform the service sector's technology-generated jobs.

While much of the service sector was able to be less productive than the manufacturing sector in the 1980s because of lack of competition, increasing competition from deregulation and foreign investment makes the service sector the productivity challenge of the 1990s.[20] As an initial reaction, service organizations have increased technology and reduced staff to streamline operations, reduce costs, and improve productivity. However, after that initial action they find that they have to change the way they manage themselves, including how they manage their employees, to improve productivity. Otherwise, service sector jobs may see the same thing happen to them as what happened to manufacturing in the 1980s—jobs moving overseas. Already, some U.S. service organizations are moving "back-office" clerical and technical jobs (e.g., data entry, claims processing, accounting, telemarketing, and technical product support) overseas to countries where wages are lower, people speak English, the government is more favorable to business, and telecommunications instantaneously provide linkage with the organization's computer in the United States.[21] The message is clear to the service sector— improve productivity through better application of technology and improved management practices.

Services are important to manufacturing. They are not merely outside support elements to the manufacturing process, added to facilitate production or goods distribution; they have become key elements of manufactured products. Service activities in the manufacturing sector generate approximately 75–85 percent of all the value the average manufacturer adds to produce the product. Product pricing reflects the product's quality, characteristics, and availability (which are created by research, product design, quality control, and marketing) more than the product's raw materials and direct labor. This indicates that the focus of improved productivity will not just be on the manufacturing floor, as it has been in the past, but will focus on professionals and managers in the manufacturing sector in addition to all types of workers in the service sector—and this is where new pay plays a role.

Help Wanted in America

In the United States, a 5 to 6 percent unemployment rate is above the 4 percent full-employment level that economic theory traditionally states should start labor shortages. While absolute percentages of unemployed may change during different economic periods, the ranking of the percentages among different types of workers is similar. When unemployment is in double digits for minorities and teenagers, the rate is 4.9 percent for white men, 2.4 percent for managers and professionals, and 2.6 percent for executives and administrators. Slow population growth will create a labor shortage that could remain until 2000.[22] In the 1990s, annual growth of labor supply will average 1.2 percent, down from 1.9 percent in the 1980s and at half the growth rate of the 1970s.[23] The growth will also come from different populations than in the past. Women, minorities, and immigrants will comprise the majority of the twenty million new workers between now and the year 2000, so organizations will have to learn how to manage a diverse work force.[24]

The labor-shortage problem is exacerbated by a growing mismatch between workers' skills and the skills organizations need. Organizations that are unable to find qualified workers are increasing training budgets and offering additional basic and remedial education. This skill gap is a difficult challenge, especially in the dominant service sector. *Workforce 2000* says that if employees are not better trained to do the jobs that are available, organizations will need either to send jobs overseas or to buy new technology. In contrast, Mishel and Teixeira conclude that there may not be a labor shortage and that job skills will not increase as fast as *Workforce 2000* suggests. However, they also conclude that employee educational/skill preparation and the composition of available jobs are problems, and that work-force skills should be focused on developing a solid foundation of work-force quality that will enable work reorganization to improve performance. They see this challenge as being particularly critical for non-college-educated workers.[25] Regardless, it will take time to upgrade the skill level of the work force even if this mismatch receives immediate attention. The lack of skilled employees is also affecting the supply of qualified managers. In the early 1980s many organizations eliminated middle-management jobs. However, even the remaining jobs were becoming more and more difficult to fill with able people.

The Skill Gap

According to the Hudson Institute, 25 million workers will have to upgrade their job skills by the end of the century as the United States shifts to a postindustrial economy.[26] By 2000, service and high-technology jobs requiring higher job skills will replace lower-skilled jobs across the nation.

While the current average skill level of the American worker as determined by the Labor Department is reading safety rules and equipment instructions and writing simple reports, the average required skill level by the end of the century will be reading journals and manuals and writing business letters and reports. By 2000, 40 percent of employees will be required to read scientific/technical journals and financial reports and be able to write journal articles and speeches.

By 2000, 40 percent of the net increase in jobs will be in professional or technical positions, and most of the others will be in marketing and sales, administrative, supervisory, and other high-skill jobs. In 2000, only about 2 percent of the available jobs will require a lower level of skills than the average skills of American youths today.[27] To compete, the average worker must employ skills at a ninth- to twelfth-grade level, compared to a fourth-grade level after World War II. In the past an expanding labor pool allowed organizations to satisfy demands for skills by skimming off the top. Since the late 1970s, the number of sixteen- to twenty-four-year-olds had dropped from 22.4 million to 20.2 million.[28] Because of this, organizations must play a much larger role in training and retraining employees.

Organizations will also provide training and apprenticeship programs, because the education gap is not just in skills but in applying the skills in the workplace.[29] Compared to school tasks, work tasks are more difficult because they involve greater personal responsibility in gathering, assimilating, and integrating complex information from a wide range of sources (both people and data) in a more difficult environment—one of shifting priorities, multiple tasks, and a low tolerance for error.[30] The U.S. Labor Department Commission on Achieving Necessary Skills reports that the foundations learned in school of the basics (reading, writing, mathematics, speaking and listening), thinking (solving problems, creativity), and personal qualities (responsibility, self-management) need to be supplemented by the following job skills: resources (allocating money, material, time, staff), interpersonal (working on teams, leading, serving customers), information (acquiring and evaluating information, using computers), systems (understanding, designing, and improving social, organizational, and technological systems) and technology (applying technology to specific jobs) for all workers.[31] Organizations need to train employees in these job skills.

Organizations that intend to be competitive will be prepared to integrate technology into the workplace. This will require that vast sums be spent to train employees to interrelate with these technologies. The test will be to match the available work force with the technology that is essential to future organizational productivity. Without this training, the U.S. work force cannot be effectively utilized, skilled labor shortages will increase, productivity will not keep pace with other countries, and the U.S. economy and real worker income will stagnate. Organizations will be more proactive in retraining workers and increasing the training investment to achieve the growing returns from education. However, this is not all that organizations are beginning to do—they are also improving management practices, including the way they manage people.

Conclusions

U.S. organizations need all the help they can get to compete effectively in a changing world business environment. The United States is in a productivity crisis in both the manufacturing and service sectors. At the same time, people need to be better prepared to perform the higher-skilled jobs that will result from organizations' attempts to improve performance through increased technology and employee involvement. Increases in productivity are required to provide real income growth for workers. The future will place new demands on organizations. Our objective is to show that new pay, which focuses on improving performance, is the only practical way to help organizations deal with the challenges to come. We see no way for traditional pay to accommodate the changes foreseen in nations, economies, organizations, and employees. However, by changing pay so that employees and organizations are linked in a constructive manner, the opportunity to introduce a positive force toward improved productivity and performance exists.

2

Organizational Strategies and New Pay

New Strategic Directions

In response to the dramatic economic and competitive changes in the workplace discussed in the previous chapter, management has begun to explore new strategies and tactics that are better able to meet the challenges of the future and to enhance performance. For example, practice prior to and continuing into the 1980s was characterized as follows:[1]

- *Functional structure.* Because the external environment was more stable, people remained in their jobs for a long time. The organization was structured functionally, with jobs unchanging for long periods of time, and was organized along functional lines such as human resources, marketing, manufacturing, sales, and finance. This caused employees not to know each other's jobs and to perform their own jobs very efficiently with a strong emphasis on making as few errors as possible.
- *Vertical communication.* Organizations had single decision makers, with problems flowing up and solutions flowing down. People became highly specialized, and the relationships among functional areas could only be resolved high in the organization.
- *Loyalty equals security.* Employees were expected to be loyal to the organization and do whatever it was the organization told them to do. In exchange for loyalty, organizations provided security to employees as their primary reward. Employees spent their complete careers with the organization because they were loyal.

- *Prefer no-go errors.* Organizational style was to perform in order to avoid making a mistake. This meant that given a "gray" risk opportunity area, the best solution was not to take the risk. This strategy prevented errors, but also lost many valuable and profitable business opportunities that could have been exploited.
- *Little continuing innovation.* Organizations were functionally organized so that certain departments were "responsible" for innovation and others were responsible for operational and administrative issues. Because employees did not know very many jobs, continuing innovation needed to be institutionalized, with someone "in charge" of innovation.
- *Undifferentiated business strategy.* Organizations were in the "go out there and be all things to all people" phase, where all business opportunities seemed to be equally exciting and to offer equal promise for the future. Organizations avoided finding out what they did best and only doing that. Rather, computer companies tried to compete in all possible applications areas, oil companies tried to cover both service and gasoline business, and health care organizations tried to care for everyone's total health care needs.
- *Operational efficiency.* Organizations "cut expenses" whenever problems of performance and organizational success arose. Organizations believed that the easiest way they could attain organizational effectiveness was to reduce staff by laying off employees. Staff cuts and hiring freezes were viewed as major ways to improve operational efficiency. The goal was to become the lowest-cost provider of products and services.
- *React to business cycle.* Changes in the environment were viewed as uncontrollable; therefore, nothing organizations could do could change the impact the external environment had on organizational performance. Once the business cycle was "upon" them, organizations responded to minimize the negative impact or maximize the positive impact the economic environment had on their performance.
- *Create customer interest.* The strong focus was on selling others on the products or services the organization was producing. Organizations tried to create customer interest in what they wanted to sell.

In the 1990s, management is facing the drastic changes in the economy by instituting major changes in how business is performed. In large part, these changes are making organizations more responsive to dynamic changes, better able to communicate, and more flexible in approaches and solutions. Some of these changes to new strategic directions in response to aggressive competition include the following:

- *Market structure.* Rather than by function, organizations are becoming organized based on the customers they serve. Often, this means organizing so that research, manufacturing, marketing, sales, finance, and other areas become a single business unit to deliver the product or service for which they are responsible as a team to their customers.
- *Horizontal communications.* Flexible organizational structure requires that decisions and accountability are shared horizontally and vertically across the organization. Information moves up, down, and sideways throughout the organization in order that it is available where it is needed the most.
- *Entrepreneurial spirit.* Employees are encouraged and rewarded for creating their own job security by making a significant impact on operational success. Organizations no longer are able or willing to retain less than satisfactorily performing employees. Job security is based on results achieved rather than on loyalty to the organization.
- *Permit go errors.* Rather than studying things to death, organizations are making educated "ready, fire, aim" decisions that make good business sense based on the available information. However, this approach requires that organizations permit—and even reward—employees who take reasonable risks. When in doubt, rather than not going, organizations proceed and undertake the prudent business and financial risks that accompany the opportunity to contribute. We are talking about reasonable risks, and not those that caused savings and loans and banks to gamble on junk bonds and risky real estate ventures.
- *Experiment and adjust.* To "learn from where the pebbles are dropping," organizations are encouraging employees to try new approaches and tactics and to address issues and adjust tactics and behavior based on what they have learned. This is counter to

an "only one way—the old way" approach to managing an organization.

- *Niche hit.* Organizations are not able to be all things to all customers. Rather, as Peters and Waterman[2] suggest, organizations do a better job if they stick to things they do best. The best results can be obtained by seeking out what the organization does best, innovating in this area, and being the very best in the niche. The organization focuses on its best area and gets the results it needs in this manner.
- *Organizational effectiveness.* Rather than only reducing cost and expenses, organizations are learning how to do things better and why they got the results they did the last time around. Doing things well—focusing on quality—is the solution once organizations find that cost containment is not the only way to improve organizational performance. Once all is said and done, organizations must perform to win.
- *Exploit business opportunities.* The best business and financial strategy is to go for the jugular when the opportunity presents itself. The characteristic of winners is that they take advantage of opportunities and aggressively exploit them wherever possible and practical.
- *Demonstrate value added to the customer.* Rather than selling what they have, organizations are finding out what customers want and offering this to them. The best organizations demonstrate to their customers that they can meet their own goals and the customer's goals at the same time.

With all the important changes that are under way, many organizations are still hesitant to change traditional pay programs to correspond with new practices and principles. Unless organizations are willing to explore their pay programs critically, as well as other policies and practices, it is unlikely that they will have reward systems that are compatible with the challenges the future portends.

Pay Is Important

Someone said, "Pay is not the most important thing that makes organizations attractive or unattractive places to work. However, it is much more important than whatever comes third or fourth." Many things in addition to pay make an organization successful or unsuccessful, make it an attractive or unattractive place to work, or cause it to be emulated by other organizations as a place that "does it right." However, this does not detract from the importance of pay. Strategies that combine both extrinsic rewards (pay and promotion) and intrinsic rewards (sense of responsibility and accomplishment, and personal growth and development) appear to result in the highest degree of institutionalization.[3] A practical conclusion that the research supports is that pay is important to people as a reward, and to organizations as a motivator of people's behaviors and performance.[4] When designed properly, pay plans can be one tool management uses to facilitate organizational effectiveness.[5]

People are the principal variable in organizational success. In labor-intensive organizations this is true because employee costs are the largest cost, and therefore employees are best focused on performance results. In capital-intensive organizations this is also true: although human resource costs are secondary, people leverage performance greatly, since their behaviors have a strong impact on how capital resources are employed and deployed to benefit the organization. Given similar circumstances and challenges, the organizations with the best-prepared and best-focused employees will outperform competitors. This is why most organizations acknowledge the value of doing whatever they can to encourage employees to perform consistent with organizational goals and expectations. Pay can facilitate the linkage between employees and organizational success.

Considerable research on pay has been conducted over the years.[6] Most suggests that organizations that are able to design their pay programs to pay the best performers better than other performers are able to accomplish several important organizational imperatives:

- *Make excellent performance financially worthwhile.* This creates a climate in which excellent performers are encouraged to sustain their performance.
- *Communicate to satisfactory performers the importance of acceptable and better performance.* This creates a climate in which employees understand that satisfactory and better performance is financially worthwhile and provides encouragement for them to improve their performance where possible in order to earn the rewards.
- *Communicate to less than satisfactory performers that their*

performance must improve or they will be encouraged to find employment where their abilities more closely match the performance expectations of the organization. This creates a culture where employees who are not performing to organizational standards either improve their performance or leave the organization to find gainful employment elsewhere.

All of this sounds exceedingly simple. However, U.S. organizations have not been successful in operationalizing pay-for-performance cultures in very many instances. Several key impediments to paying for performance exist that are important to any discussion of pay and organizational performance. These are as follows:

- *Individual performance is difficult to evaluate.* In the United States, the individualistic pioneering spirit focuses primarily on "toughing it out" as an individual. As a result, organizations have focused on measuring and rewarding individual performance. They have found this very difficult to do because, in many instances, success in complex organizations depends on interdependency and teamwork. The need for people to collaborate and support each other's efforts has made measuring an individual's performance difficult and even counterproductive. If an organization needs people to work together to survive, paying only for individual performance may create more of an internally competitive climate than that which is essential for overall success and performance.

- *Managers and supervisors are hesitant to evaluate employee performance.* Many American managers and supervisors are more closely allied with the employees under their direction than they are with the goals and expectations of their organization. Because of this, they find it very difficult to make performance distinctions for pay purposes if this process results in one employee receiving a larger pay increase than another. Thus, performance management in the United States has become a shambles, with heavy focus on "proper appraisal forms design." Little attention is being given to the constructive dialogue that is necessary between supervisors and employees and is at the seat of performance management. This has resulted in making "merit pay" plans nothing more than cost-of-living plans.

- *Measurement of employee performance is a continuing challenge.* American organizations and managers look for the ability to measure individual performance objectively to provide "fair and equitable" feedback to employees about their performance as compared to expectations. Because human behavior and performance are not easily quantified, organizations and managers avoid differentiating between levels of performance. Few understand that performance management is a crude art form at best, and that organizations and managers must learn to differentiate based on the available measurement tools.
- *America's traditional pay systems hinder performance recognition.* As the result of many factors that occurred from 1900 to 1970, the union movement primary among them, U.S. pay programs tend to be based on factors unrelated to the performance of organizations or employees. These factors include how long the employee has been with the organization, what the cost-of-living increase is over the last year, what other employees in the organization are paid, what other organizations are doing under similar circumstances, or what the value of the job is in terms of how many people the job supervises or how "clean" or "dirty" the job is to perform.

Effective Human Resource Management Innovation Exists

While many organizations continue to behave as though human resource practices from the 1960s will continue to permit them to compete effectively, some key organizations are implementing radical changes in how they do things. The changes are designed to recognize the importance of positive employee treatment and involvement, to permit room for employees in the decision process, and to change how human resources are led and managed. Often the goal is to focus on improving performance, productivity, and the quality of products, services, and work life. Recent literature that supports the willingness to experiment with enlightened perspectives concerning how employees are viewed includes the following:

- Xerox, Tenneco, and Westinghouse improved productivity and organizational performance by implementing changes in management practices that facilitated employee performance and productivity, according to Belcher in *Productivity Plus*.[7]

- American Telephone and Telegraph, Bell Laboratories, Bank of America, Ford Motor Company, General Electric, General Foods, and General Motors report positive results from changes in management programs including the use of quality circles, employee feedback, union–management quality-of-work-life programs, and gainsharing, according to Lawler in *High-Involvement Management*.[8]

- As the result of employee participation and gainsharing, employees are encouraged to improve productivity by scheduling more efficiently, finding better methods, avoiding scrap and rework, improving quality, reducing downtime, reducing inventories, and providing excellent customer service, according to Doyle in *Gainsharing and Productivity*.[9]

- High-technology organizations are innovating in the area of human resource management as a result of internal and external factors that are making traditional practices obsolete, according to Kleingartner and others in *Human Resource Management in High Technology Firms*.[10]

- IBM, Intel Corporation, and others are tailoring their performance appraisal systems to meet specific strategic and business needs and integrating these systems into other human resource programs, according to Mohrman and others in *Designing Performance Appraisal Systems*.[11]

- ARCO, Boeing, Dana Corporation, Domino's Pizza, Federal Express, Hewlett-Packard, Pacific Gas & Electric, Standard Oil of California, and others are finding that positive results are available when management stays in direct contact with its organization and employees, becomes more concerned about employee involvement, focuses employees on forming constructive customer relationships, rewards risk taking that is necessary to innovation, assumes leadership, and forms a partnership with employees at all levels, according to Peters and Austin in *A Passion for Excellence*.[12]

- New pay approaches to compensating employees are more likely to exist in top-performing organizations (as judged by financial results) than they are in organizations that perform less well through good economic times and bad, as reported in *Management Compensation in High Technology Companies.*[13]

Important organizations are finding that traditional human resource management methods have a negative impact on employee and organizational performance. These organizations are changing employee-relations practices to permit the sharing of information, decision making, and rewards, and report that these changes have a positive impact on the organization's ability to compete effectively.

New Pay and New Strategic Directions

New pay acknowledges that the role of the United States as an effective business competitor is not guaranteed. Consistent with this perspective is an understanding that changing times have created the need to evaluate the appropriateness of how organizations are led. Organizations with a new pay view believe the following principles are essential to differentiating themselves from others in competitive times:

- The organization remains open to customer information and bases decisions concerning products, services, techniques, and organizational directions on its best evaluation of this information. The organization views the customer as its CEO, and behaves accordingly.
- Employees are the primary reason the organization is able to remain competitive and the reason the organization becomes unable to compete effectively. Because of this, the organization views the management process as the facilitator of employee performance, productivity, and innovation. Management means leadership rather than hierarchy and bureaucracy.
- Employee communications are viewed as critical to future organizational success. Although the organization believes that employees work for many reasons in addition to the pay they receive, it views pay as one key element of communication with employees that can be managed to ensure that it carries the proper message.
- Because of the need for flexibility to respond to environmental changes, the organization aggressively seeks to change management principles that in the past served to inhibit flexibility.

When it finds that pay programs inhibit flexibility, it aggressively changes them to become more effective facilitators and communicators of change.

Often organizations with a new pay view have experienced a trauma initiated from outside the organization. This series of events created the need to rethink and change management principles that had historically been viewed as consistent with organizational needs. Prior to these negative experiences, these organizations managed themselves consistent with the more traditional methodologies. Other organizations with a new pay view are successful and believe they can gain more mileage from new pay than from traditional pay because it communicates the importance of organizational success, teamwork, quality, and innovation better than does traditional pay.

The "environment" of new pay is the same as the business environment of the organization. It is the sum of all the external elements that make it difficult to view the organization as an independent country, isolated from its surroundings. The organization with a new pay view is concerned about any management practice that serves to make it difficult for the organization to anticipate and understand customer needs and to respond appropriately.

New Pay Provides Positive Rewards

New pay rewards a high level of customer focus, recognizes sustained financial results, rewards innovation and creativity, recognizes performance and productivity, encourages the development of needed skills, discourages bureaucracy, rewards product and service quality, and helps create a win–win work environment. New pay does this as follows:

- It encourages the development of a total compensation strategy that is an extension of the organization's business and financial strategy and culture. New pay contends that traditional pay solutions, such as internally focused point-factor job evaluation systems and merit plans, are seldom functional to any organization in any situation where the organization must compete to survive. New pay differs from total compensation strategies that focus only on issues of competitiveness, internal equity, and the like.
- It applies some methods that are not new, such as gainsharing, in

new ways and to new situations and to organizations where these methods have not been used before. These newly applied solutions are more supportive of strategies that focus on high levels of performance results than are other "old" methods.

- It provides mix-and-match remedies. "Old" solutions such as gainsharing and flexible benefits are combined with new solutions such as skill-based pay and winsharing to reflect strategy and communicate direction. In new pay, the use and design of pay programs depend on the organization's business strategy and goals, rather than on copying the practices of others.
- It provides that the only situation in which some "old" solutions—such as internal equity-driven point-factor plans, cost-of-living increases disguised as merit plans, and goals such as being a 75th-percentile payer of base pay (paying at the point where one quarter of competing organizations pay higher and three quarters pay lower) without concern for the ability to pay—are appropriate is in organizations that need not compete for business and are not interested in encouraging employee excellence.

New pay is not value free. New pay means continually seeking solutions to changing challenges to organizational and employee success.

Addressing Impediments to New Pay

If new pay is such a good idea, why don't most organizations use it? Besides being locked into copying the practices of others, the two most frequently used arguments are that "we can't measure performance" and "we can't afford new pay."

Whether or not organizations believe the performance of employees can be measured, the performance of both the employees and the organization as a whole is constantly being measured by the organization's customers. The belief that employee performance and its relationship to organizational performance cannot be measured keeps an organization from learning and understanding the measures customers use in making buying decisions. Emphasizing measurement improves measurement quality; attempting to measure performance results in learning how to measure it. Saying "we can't measure it, so we won't" results in measurement only by customers.

The "we can't afford it" argument does not take a total compensation perspective. Organizations need to examine their total pay expenditure, including the way it is allocated, to determine the value received for the pay dollars spent. Those exploring new pay want to maximize performance leverage from pay dollars. Organizations examine the current mix of pay (the proportions allocated to base pay, variable pay, and indirect pay), possible changes in the mix, and the relationship between pay and organizational performance to determine if pay is linked to organizational results. Modeling different what-if scenarios determines the amount of dollars that should be spent on the various pay elements. Variable pay plans are modeled under various performance contingencies so that both the organization and its employees believe the sharing from the variable pay plan is acceptable for the results achieved. The relationship between pay cost and performance results is especially important in labor-intensive organizations where labor costs are a larger portion of costs than in capital-intensive organizations, but where improvements in employee performance can result in significant gains to the organization.

Conclusions

Effective pay planning is an important element in making an organization both a desirable place to work and an effective performer. Organizations have proven that they are not able to recognize differences in employee performance through traditional pay practices. This means it is possible that traditional pay has outlived its usefulness to organizations that must compete for business and are not able to pass on to their customers labor costs that are not related to quality or performance. New strategic directions are evolving that show value for improved performance and productivity; a role for new pay is included in these strategies.

PART TWO

Moving to New Pay

Designing New Pay Strategies

Strategic Total Compensation

A rigid, management-centered organization, with or without a contemporary business and financial strategy as a guide, has become anachronistic in the United States. Organizations that are willing to evaluate directions and programs critically on a continuing basis and experiment with alternatives will be more likely to survive and succeed. Strategies are the natural catalyst for experimentation. Strategies can link pay programs to the need for flexible responsiveness to new challenges and opportunities. Human resource strategies define how people will be deployed to support the tactical and strategic goals the organization determines are essential to sustaining financial survival and continued reasonable growth. Strategies measure the need, ability, and willingness to change.[1] Total compensation strategies are components of human resource strategies.

Organizations need a starting point to evaluate objectively the "health" of present pay plans. Without the means to combine objective analysis of organizational needs with total compensation planning, it is possible that an organization's move to new pay approaches could become a "fad" that is followed without proper critical evaluation of available alternatives. It is important to understand why an organization should use new pay and what its effect might be in order to prevent new pay from becoming a short-term trend.

A total compensation strategy addresses the following questions:

- Should pay design play a leading or supporting role in the organization's direction? If the answer is a leading role, what should that role be? If a supporting role, how can this role be defined?

- Should pay plans contribute to or participate in any organizational changes that are under way? If yes, should they play a leading role or a supporting role?
- What short- and long-term goals does the organization have that can be reinforced by pay programs? Which goals are more critical? Less critical?
- How can pay plans best be designed to ensure a strong customer focus? How can this focus be sustained? Can it be intensified?
- What shortcomings exist with current pay programs that make it difficult to continue to use existing approaches to gain the desired ends? What can the organization learn from an evaluation of present practices?
- Are the organization and its employees ready for new pay, which will require increased levels of employee participation, involvement in decisions, and empowerment to affect the work environment?
- What role, if any, should employees play in the development of pay programs? How will this involvement be organized, focused, and administered?
- Which element of total compensation is most important to effective communication of business goals and objectives? Base pay? Variable pay? Indirect pay? Why?

Total compensation strategy development is central to both the new and traditional pay planning processes. The strategy will determine whether or not the organization is ready for new pay, or what must be done to get the organization ready. Strategies can also provide guidance on how to get the most from traditional pay if new pay does not fit. Strategies provide a road map from where the organization is presently to where it wants to be in the future. Equally important, the process determines the match between current practice and strategy, clarifies what must be done to make practice correspond to strategy, defines why and how any change will be implemented, and subsequently evaluates the quality of the change process relative to the strategy.[2]

New pay requires more than merely aligning pay plans with business, financial, and human resource goals. New pay requires that organizations answer strategy-building questions consistent with the basic principles of new pay. These principles are summarized as follows:

- "World-class" organizations actualize business, financial, and human resource goals that are customer driven.

- Customer driven organizations form partnerships with customers and suppliers—they are externally rather than internally driven.
- To form partnerships with customers and suppliers, partnerships must be formed with employees.
- Employee–organization partnerships require that employees have a positive vested interest in the success of the organization. Teamwork is required to form this bond between the organization and employees.
- Employee pay is one reward that is valued. Employee pay must vary with the fortunes of the organization. Only new pay is sufficiently flexible to support employee–organization partnerships.
- New pay provides that direct pay is more flexible than indirect pay and should be emphasized. Also, variable pay is more flexible than base pay and should be an organizational priority.

This means world-class total compensation strategies will be patterned after new pay. Just answering the questions about total compensation is not enough. Answers ought also to relate to new pay principles.

For example, Schonberger discusses what may have resulted in aligning a Ford Motor Company business and human resource strategy in the 1920s. The business strategy was productivity driven, and the human resource result was making many small jobs from larger jobs. Jobs became trivialized, and unskilled employees with minimal wages were hired who were supposed to quickly learn the simple jobs ("Man number one puts the bolt in the hole, but does not put a nut on it. Man number two puts a nut on, . . ." etc.). Ford found that this formula for low-cost productivity did not work. However, the trivialized jobs remained. To quote Schonberger,

> The company gave job titles to each one (bolt putter? nut turner?) and hired costly staffers to maintain the system: wage and classification experts studied the jobs and set different wage rates on each; time study analysts timed them; production controllers counted output so the paymaster could pay efficiency incentives. If there was a union, it put its stamp of approval on all of it: a contract grounded in work rules.[3]

This is a good example of traditional pay and a "bad" human resource response to a business strategy. Although this human resource solution may have responded to the business strategy, it was not consistent with world-class strategy-building or new pay principles.

Developing Total Compensation Strategies

Much of what has been written and said about the value of strategies and planning processes to the success of organizations appears to be very sound. However, experience suggests that no one can predict some of the most important events that affect organizations, divisions, departments, or work units. No matter how much analysis and planning are undertaken, no organization can plan for all things that may occur. Organizations need a business and financial strategy and a supportive total compensation strategy that is simple, straightforward, and flexible.

New pay total compensation strategy has a built-in review that allows for automatic evaluation of the extent to which the strategy continues to match future needs and to make necessary adjustments. When basic elements in the life of the organization (such as fundamental business directions) change in any way, the total compensation strategy can respond accordingly.

Total compensation strategy "aims" pay programs at what the organization wants to accomplish. A simple strategy is preferred because strategy is only equally as important as the action the organization takes from it. Action and experimentation are more important than the volume or complexity of the strategy. Simple and flexible strategies are most likely to encourage action; complex and rigid strategies are more likely to create confusion and inaction.

Traditional Total Compensation Strategy

Traditional pay practice was not unplanned or poorly directed. Most traditional discussions of direct and indirect pay practice include a statement about pay management that suggests the objective is to help the organization "attract, motivate, and retain" employees. Subsequently, the statement often continues to address issues related to the individual elements of direct and indirect pay and defines where, in very general terms, these fit in the "attract, motivate, and retain" equation. This is probably how traditional total compensation practice began in the 1940s.

Human resource management was not historically viewed as a key element of the basic business process. Because of this isolation from the key operations, human resource planning was separated from the general business planning process. This isolation included the pay planning process. Organizations generally had, and many still have, a "strategy" to pay equal to or better than the competition, or to be at the 60th percentile of competitive practice, or to try to outreach other organizations relative to the pay level paid on any particular job. This is because without a link to what else is going on in the organization, the focus of the total compensation strategy can only be on the programmatic and competitive attributes rather than on the more important strategic or tactical issues.

It is not always possible or practical to attain a desired target of competitiveness compared to other organizations. Organizations determine competitiveness as a result of sharing direct and indirect pay practice information annually. Based on the statistical information exchanged, organizations often adjust how they pay to try to hit, in effect, a moving target. However, the organization may not be able to afford this competitive level or may not need to pay at the level of competitiveness it has set as its desired competitive position. In the studies discussed in chapter 17, employers that pay the highest are not necessarily the best financially performing organizations. Organizations with moderately competitive base pay levels and variable pay opportunities financially outperformed organizations with highly competitive base pay levels by some margin.

Wise leaders understand the importance of pay plan design and set direct and indirect pay policy to gain some business and financial advantage from the dollars spent on direct and indirect pay. The new pay strategic view of competitive practice suggests that achieving competitive pay should be contingent upon providing a level of work quality, productivity, or performance results that permits the organization to be competitive from a business standpoint. This links competitive pay directly with competitive performance results. In order to generate competitive pay, performance results must justify pay levels that reflect expected reasonable goal performance. The approach contrasts importantly with the entitlement view, wherein total compensation is uniformly competitive for excellently, satisfactorily, and less than satisfactorily performing employees. This approach fails to link competitive pay with competitive performance results.

In truth, organizations that do not want to adopt new pay do not need to develop total compensation strategies to manage their direct and indirect pay; instead, information gathered from other organizations can be used as the basis for pay practices. Only when top management is interested in change, in the belief that new pay will provide some performance advantage, is a strategy beyond "follow the leader" necessary. Specific goals and objectives concerning financial results, products or services, customers, market share, sales and marketing, and quality are the basis for establishing pay programs and communicating performance expectations. Under this scenario, forming performance objectives or a strategy is important to the entire pay management process.

Habit as the Adversary of Change

Unless strategies instill a perspective of flexibility and experimentation, they can be the source of habits that prevent an organization from adopting more contemporary management techniques when and where they are needed. Habits create the dominant norms, systems, procedures, and written and unwritten rules that define "how things are done here."

This is why new pay systems often work well in start-up organizations. In a start-up, the organization has no standard ways of doing things. Mark Twain said, "Habits cannot be flung out the window; they have to be coaxed downstairs, a step at a time." Decision makers sometimes fear change because, deprived of the protection they get from habits, they might be accused of doing something that either is or looks foolish. However, an organization, even one with a long history of good performance, needs to introduce fresh management energy to stave off the forces of decay.

The wave of restructuring, spinoffs, mergers, and acquisitions is not accidental. This disruption indicates that atrophy in U.S. organizations is at a high level. Restructuring is a powerful force for change, despite the pain and high human cost. Restructuring is an indictment of management's past inability to manage organizational renewal effectively, according to Waterman in *The Renewal Factor*.[4] Waterman suggests that there are three kinds of managers. The first are the custodians, who make sure that nothing happens on their watch. Because the world is changing fast, something does happen on their watch and the organization atrophies. Second are the manipulators of wealth, busy doing financial deals. Although these individuals may get rich, no added value is created since they contribute little to growth in the gross national product. Under this type of leadership, the best the United States can hope for is transfer of wealth from one set of hands to another; at worst, as in the late 1980s, wealth is destroyed. The third type is Waterman's "new American folk heroes" who find ways to "renew and refresh" their units, departments, and organizations. These are the sponsors of needed innovation and constructive change. It is with this last group that the opportunity for experimentation with rewards for organizational success exists. The "new American heroes" must subscribe to this philosophy if the United States is to remain competitive in the world economy.

Alignment with Key Goals

A new pay strategic view of total compensation that focuses on the organization's business is a strong communicator of values, performance expectations, and standards. Effective communication about reinforcement of present directions or changes in organizational directions and priorities is one reason for developing a total compensation strategy. This is accomplished by differentiating between the groups and individuals that perform consistent with standards of performance and those that do not in terms of meaningful rewards. This approach communicates fairness and equity in terms of the chance to differentiate pay based on performance rather than in terms of similar pay without regard for results achieved.

Total compensation programs are obviously best designed to reward results and behaviors that are consistent with the key goals of the organization. Where an organization has an objective of customer focus, financial performance, market share, new products or services, quality, or restructuring or redirection, these objectives become the foundation of the communication and performance recognition strategies. Although effective total compensation strategies focus on what the organization wants to attain, they are also flexible and responsive to changes the organization must implement to overcome unforeseen obstacles or to emphasize new priorities.

Proper goal alignment is often a problem in larger organizations where the pay system takes on a "life of its own." When the pay program becomes isolated from a reasonable business and total compensation strategy and goals, any threat to the status quo is viewed as a breach of policy and practice. Much of traditional total compensation practice may at one time have been developed to respond to some long-forgotten strategy or objective that was important at the time. However, over time, the underpinnings of the reasons for the programs erode, leaving only the direct and indirect pay plans with the corresponding slogans that go with them. The absence of reasons or justification for current pay practices results in follow-the-leader pay plan development and implementation. Seldom does an external pay survey identify why an organization does what it does or what advantages are gained, so practice expands as a result of copying what others do.

Communicating with Total Compensation Strategy

Executives often reject new pay because it differs from traditional practice. Giving top executives an active role in the planning process permits the organization to communicate the relationship between business goals and new pay. Once executives jointly deal with difficult organizational and important pay issues and develop a strategy that establishes how people will be paid, these leaders often champion the resulting new pay strategy.

The process of developing and implementing the total compensation strategy is as important as the written strategy itself. Planning involves communication, and involvement in planning most often resolves the mysteries of understanding why organizations take particular actions in the pay area.

The strategy-setting process can be facilitated by addressing a series of important issues in the form of questions that relate to total compensation management. Involvement in setting and approving strategy results in a higher level of executive understanding and acceptance of the strategy. Often an executive is asked to approve an already developed strategy without involvement. In this case, the executive does not understand the issues and questions that went into its development. Participation in strategy setting involves addressing the issues, evaluating the alternatives, and subsequently setting policy from a position of understanding the basis for the strategy.

Questions such as the following (which includes a few of the possible responses) help define the strategic role of total compensation:

- What role should total compensation play in helping the organization attain its business and financial goals?
  - Business and financial considerations are of primary importance and should drive the design of total compensation. Total

compensation plans should link employees to the organization's business and financial strategies.
- Total compensation offers little strategic opportunity but should be managed in a cost-effective manner.
- Employees are important, and total compensation should keep people satisfied at all costs.
- The focus should be on financially rewarding only the fully satisfactory and excellent performers and making it attractive for less than adequate performers to leave the organization.
- Some combination of the above should comprise the role of total compensation.

A number of questions in the area of variable pay also need to be addressed during the strategy-building process. For instance:

- What should be the role of variable pay in the organization (individual variable pay, group variable pay, gainsharing, winsharing, lump-sum awards, long-term variable pay, etc.)?
  - Variable pay should not be used
  - Variable pay should only be used for executives
  - Provide the performance element to supplement base pay
  - Permit pay costs to vary based on changes in the business and financial fortunes of the organization
  - Put pay "at risk," or put potential base pay increases at risk, to attract more people who will risk pay based on results expected
  - Supplement base pay to make total cash compensation (base pay plus variable pay) more competitive
  - Accommodate manager/supervisor inability or unwillingness to evaluate performance by making mistakes easily repairable in future years because fixed base pay is not increased
  - Provide executive/management/employee rewards for organizational performance, individual performance, or group performance
  - Reward group performance for circumstances where business and financial goal attainment requires teamwork and collaboration
  - Permit the organization to control fixed base pay costs more effectively and make performance management more practical and meaningful

These types of questions help define the total compensation strategy of the organization. Once the questions are answered, a written strategy statement is developed to guide the process of pay program review and design. This statement can either be traditional or consistent with new pay principles. The appendix provides additional sample questions that are essential to preparing a statement of total compensation strategy.

Strategies from the Employee Perspective

With all the concern about the business and organizational implications of pay, it is important to remember that pay is above all an employee-relations issue and that how employees view pay is important to the success of a total compensation strategy. The foundation of justifying a total compensation strategy is the belief that employees have a need and right to understand what their organization expects from them in terms of behavior and performance. New pay treats employees as important partners in the operation and success of the organization. Employees have the right to determine whether the values, culture, and reward systems of their organization match their own. The total compensation strategy is a management responsibility, but management has the obligation to communicate this strategy to employees. Without communication, the strategy has no value.

Obviously, employee perspectives should be considered in determining the total compensation strategy of the organization. Further, employees with some means to increase continually their involvement in the organization have the best chance of helping it succeed. However, it is clear that not all executives agree with this perspective. If an organization is to be managed without much employee involvement, employees should understand this so that they can decide whether or not they are comfortable with this situation.

An ideal new pay total compensation strategy communicates the values, mission, strategy, plans, and future of the organization to employees and defines the role employees will play in each of these elements. The organization implements base pay, variable pay, and indirect pay plans that are direct extensions of the total compensation strategy. When the organization does well, employees should do well. Employees share rewards based on demonstrated results rather than upon tenure or other factors unrelated to the success of the organization. Employees who are not able to contribute as the organization expects are given every opportunity to contribute to the extent of their ability and are compensated accordingly. Those that cannot contribute are humanely managed out of the organization to find an organization where they can contribute.

Conclusions

Organizations differ in terms of goals, form, and structure. This means that even though most total compensation strategies say pay must attract, retain, and motivate, few of these strategies are direct extensions of the business, financial, and human resource strategies of the organization. Rather, they are copies of what others do either successfully or unsuccessfully. Strategic planning has been applied to nearly all elements of business except total compensation. Wisely prepared total compensation strategies will seldom result in the application of traditional direct and indirect pay practices. Instead, forms of new pay will better suit organizations interested in high levels of performance. New pay is also consistent with becoming a world-class organization by forming a partnership with employees. Organizations cannot form partnerships with customers and suppliers unless employee interests are considered.

Total Compensation Strategy Statements

Examples of Total Compensation Strategies

Good strategy statements are by definition those that reflect how an organization views total compensation as an element of its own total management process. Examples of new pay total compensation strategies developed by means of the process described in chapter 3 suggest how total compensation strategy may be aligned with the priorities of the organization.

Exhibit 4.1 shows the total compensation strategy for NewCorp. NewCorp believes in new pay and in the concept of the employee–organization partnership. The total compensation strategy is aligned with the business and financial strategy of the organization. The result of the NewCorp total compensation strategy is moderately competitive base pay and benefits that are designed so that variable pay forms the basis for the partnership. NewCorp uses many variable pay plans in the form of business plan gainsharing, winsharing, group incentives, and other rewards that vary with organizational success and ability to pay.

Other total compensation strategies are possible based on the organization's view about the role pay should play in the overall organizational strategy. Exhibit 4.2 shows the total compensation strategy for ProCorp. ProCorp is a new pay organization interested in making employees important to the success of the organization. The goal is to have employee pay and the success of the organization linked. Employee involvement is key.

Not all total compensation strategies involve new pay. Some are traditional in scope and character. Exhibit 4.3 shows the total compensation strategy for UsualCorp. UsualCorp illustrates that even traditional

Exhibit 4.1
Total Compensation Strategy for NewCorp

- NewCorp intends to become a world-class organization, forming partnerships with customers, suppliers, and employees.
- The business, financial, and human resource strategy of NewCorp will be communicated with the aid of employee pay programs. As strategies change, the communications value of specific pay programs will be evaluated and changed when necessary.
- NewCorp employees at all levels are a key element in our success. Only employees and customers can make NewCorp a success. Because of this, it is important that employees be partners with NewCorp.
- NewCorp employees will be rewarded for gaining a differential advantage over our competitors at all levels of the organization. Our differential advantage will be through listening to, understanding the needs of, and responding to our customers.
- Cash compensation is the key element of total compensation because it is flexible and can be changed to respond to new goals, priorities, and contingencies. Cash compensation is more important than benefits as a communicator of goals and objectives.
- Variable pay is more important than base pay because it is the most flexible reward NewCorp has and can significantly recognize teamwork and collaboration and achievement of results.
- Base pay will be positioned at market so that NewCorp can vary total compensation costs with financial results by means of variable pay. Through variable pay, employees will be able to earn additional compensation based on achievement of results that make NewCorp successful.

- Group performance will be the primary focus of rewards because we value sharing information and teamwork to accomplish varied and challenging tasks. Financial performance will be the primary measure of employee contribution to NewCorp. Quality and customer value measures will be defined, refined, and used to measure employee contribution.

- Variable pay plans will be used throughout the organization wherever employees as a group have the opportunity to share in the financial success of NewCorp.

- Employee benefits will provide a basic level of protection from unexpected health, life, and disability risks. NewCorp assumes that employees will contribute to their own future security and will share in the cost of employee benefits.

- Employee-benefit costs will be permitted to fall below competitive levels. When this occurs, flexible benefits will be implemented to provide employees a choice. However, benefit costs incurred by NewCorp will not exceed those of direct business competitors.

- NewCorp will aggressively manage health care costs and will enlist employee assistance in cost management. Employees will have the opportunity to share in health care cost reductions.

- The defined benefit retirement plan will be phased out and replaced by a 401(k) plan. Also, an employee savings plan will be instituted, with a portion matched by NewCorp to encourage employee saving.

- Total compensation programs will be evaluated annually, and when the need for change is identified, these changes will be implemented and communicated.

Exhibit 4.2
Total Compensation Strategy for ProCorp

- ProCorp intends to become a leader in a global business environment where customers are scarce and competition is very strong.
- ProCorp intends that employees will directly share in the success of the corporation in order that they are able to help ProCorp succeed.
- Wherever practical, employees will participate in variable pay plans based on measures that contribute to the financial success of ProCorp. These measures include customer satisfaction and value, profitability, quality, new product/service development, and cost management.
- Employees will participate in the development of pay programs and play a role in these programs' administration, evaluation, and improvement.
- Variable pay in terms of gainsharing, winsharing, lump-sum awards, and other group or individual incentive plans will be used wherever such plans give ProCorp the chance to outperform its competitors.
- Base pay will involve paying for the acquisition of skills that are valued by ProCorp. The acquisition of skills will result in moderately competitive base pay. Employees who participate in skill-based pay can participate in variable pay plans.
- Employee benefits will be moderate and provide the opportunity for cost sharing between employees and ProCorp.
- ProCorp will aggressively manage health care costs and tie financial rewards to employee wellness programs; good health habits are worth extra financial recognition.
- Employees will participate in the evaluation of benefit plans and help management actively work to provide reasonable benefits at the lowest cost.
- The current profit-sharing plan will be retained so that retirement is based on profit performance. The focus will be on providing benefits employees value, such as vacations and time off, rather than traditional benefits offered by business competitors.

Exhibit 4.3
Total Compensation Strategy for UsualCorp

- The objective of pay is to attract, motivate, and retain excellently performing employees throughout UsualCorp.
- UsualCorp will pay base pay and benefits that are equal to or better than the 75th percentile of competitive practice. Competitive practice will be defined based on UsualCorp's direct business and labor market competitors.
- Base pay will be internally equitable and fair. All jobs of equal internal value will be paid similarly.
- A merit system will be used to grant base pay increases based on individual employee performance.
- Employee benefits will ensure that employees have an attractive retirement after a full career with UsualCorp.
- UsualCorp will provide very competitive benefits to ensure that employees are well protected. A defined benefit retirement plan will provide income replacement at 50 percent of the average of the final three years' base pay prior to retirement.
- Executives will be paid at the 75th percentile of competitive practice, and all executives will be eligible for incentives and stock options.

---

total compensation strategies exist and can be operationalized. The problem with many of these strategies is that it is difficult to tie them to the organization's business direction and goals.

Taking three business strategies and tying total compensation strategies to them helps demonstrate the link between the total compensation strategy and what the organization is trying to accomplish. The first of the following examples is an organization that is experiencing financial performance difficulties and needs to institute a better focus on results. The second example is a very large and excellently performing organization that has decided to try to get better results from its pay programs. The last example is an organization that wishes to experiment with pay programs that are different from the plans they have had in place for years, to determine whether these programs provide any advantages over current practice.

RehabCorp Total Compensation Strategy

RehabCorp is an organization that experienced many years of excellent financial performance. Because of this performance, it was able to have a combination of liberal base pay and benefits. The organizational structure had many levels of management that were well paid and had many perquisites and benefits. Professional, support, and hourly employees were paid on a merit-increase plan that granted similar increases to both average and excellent individual performers.

Over the last five years, RehabCorp has been faced with intense competition from the standpoint of better quality, pricing, and customer value. Profits dwindled at some of the fairly autonomous operating companies, and operating companies laid off several levels of middle management and many professional, support, and hourly employees. Labor costs were very high; earnings, innovation, quality, and long-term focus dwindled. Employees became internally focused on their own survival, and communication and teamwork waned. A new corporate president was appointed and developed a new business and financial strategy and a corresponding total compensation strategy.

BUSINESS SITUATION PRIOR TO TOTAL COMPENSATION STRATEGY. RehabCorp was in great pain because traditional responses such as layoffs had not improved the organization's overall performance results, nor results at specific operating companies. Labor costs continued to increase, and quality, productivity, and customer satisfaction continued to lag measurably. This is an organization that moved to new pay because it was no longer in a position to retain reward systems that were not closely focused on improved performance results.

PAY PROGRAMS PRIOR TO TOTAL COMPENSATION STRATEGY. Rehab-Corp had installed a corporatewide point-factor job evaluation plan years ago and was strongly focused on internal equity and "fair pay" based on job content rather than results achieved or ability of operating companies to pay. Employees were encouraged to rise to supervisory or management levels within the organization, because that was where the points were. The corporatewide merit-increase plan was keeping pay competitive with direct business competitors, but many operating companies were unable to pass on labor costs to their customers. Pay programs were developed during different times when the performance of the organization was very sound and when labor costs were less of a problem.

NEW TOTAL COMPENSATION STRATEGY. A total compensation strategy was developed in order that RehabCorp could gain whatever advantage would be available from the dollars expended on pay. This strategy consisted of the following components:

- Business Considerations
  - All RehabCorp employees should be encouraged to get involved to improve quality, customer service and value, productivity, teamwork, cost management, and financial results wherever possible. Employees should understand that RehabCorp and its operating companies must perform better to survive.
  - Operating-company differences will be considered in developing total compensation programs. The corporate direct pay and benefit strategy will be designed so that operating companies are able to compete effectively for business.
  - RehabCorp wants to form a partnership between the employees and their operating company where the financial success of the operating company impacts the pay of all employees. This is based on the design of pay plans that share financial success as well as costs with employees based on the operating company's ability to pay.
  - Employees should be encouraged to work more collaboratively to accomplish the complex objectives the operating company needs to meet. Because of this, teamwork will be as important as individual performance in earning financial rewards.

- Summary of Total Compensation Strategy
  - Employees make a performance difference in forming a customer-focused organization, and this must be better encouraged in the future. Results are more important than tenure. Employees who perform at a less than satisfactory level will be identified, given every opportunity to improve, and, if the improvement is not there, asked to leave the organization.
  - Because variable pay is more flexible than are base pay and

employee benefits, variable pay will be used wherever advantageous to tie the performance of an operating company to that of its employees. Profitability of an operating company will determine the existence of any variable pay funding.

– Base pay will be moderately competitive compared to an operating company's competitive labor market. A combination of group variable pay and moderately competitive base pay will permit RehabCorp to pay high levels of cash compensation when a specific operating company excels financially, and no more than competitive cash compensation when performance is less than adequate.

– Base pay will be focused on the need to grow in terms of skills and abilities. Base pay will not encourage the development of a bureaucratic organizational structure.

– Benefits will be moderately competitive and permit costs to vary with the ability to pay. Employees will share in paying for benefits to help defray costs and to help employees understand the value of benefits.

– Retirement funding will be based on the profitability of RehabCorp. The present defined benefit plan will be replaced by a profit-sharing plan and phased in within the next twelve-month period.

– In the future, as employees share in more of the costs, flexible benefits will be offered, but total benefit costs must not rise above the costs incurred by direct competitors.

This strategy has had an impact on the programs RehabCorp has utilized. It has taken several years to change how the programs relate to the business, financial, and human resource strategy.

BASE PAY CHANGES. Using a management–employee task force at the operating-company level, the principles of base pay were changed. Base pay ranges were modified in order that base pay could not increase to be higher than the average of competitive practice for comparable jobs in other organizations that competed with a specific operating company for business or labor. To accomplish this, market rates replaced the former base pay range midpoints, and base pay is no higher than the market rate. Market rates are base pay maximum levels that represent the operating company's maximum willingness to pay base pay. RehabCorp set market rates at the median of competitive base pay practice for each operating company. Operating companies throughout RehabCorp were asked to develop variable pay plans to supplement the new base pay program.

The organization installed skill-based pay in several manufacturing facilities. Career ladders were established in specific technical and scientific areas. The focus of these programs is on improved skills and career growth based on the flexibility to perform a series of important tasks and assignments. The point-factor job evaluation plan was replaced by job evaluation and skill-based pay at the operating-company level with a market, rather than internal, focus to reduce the focus on internal comparisons.

VARIABLE PAY CHANGES. Operating companies were given the opportunity to develop variable pay programs that best matched their goals and needs. Variable pay plans are formally evaluated each year and improved frequently. The main provision of all variable pay plans is that they are funded by some overall measure of operating-company profitability or cost savings that is selected annually so that when variable pay awards are made, they are funded by improved financial performance results. A direct relationship exists between increased operating-company profitability and increased variable pay awards.

INDIRECT PAY CHANGES. Any increases in the cost of benefits are shared by employees and RehabCorp. The retirement plan was changed to a profit-sharing plan from a defined benefit plan. RehabCorp is considering changing to retirement plans at the operating-company level based on the financial success of the operating company rather than a single corporatewide plan. Indirect pay costs were permitted to fall to moderately competitive levels. Flexible benefits were added over several years. RehabCorp heavily communicated the partnership concept, where fixed pay costs are being shifted to costs based on variation in the organization's financial success and ability to pay.

VISION FOR THE FUTURE. The objective is to have pay plans communicate to employees the need to improve the financial performance of RehabCorp and all operating companies. The focus is on involvement, quality, the customer, and teamwork. Differences between operating companies are recognized. Base pay and indirect pay are controlled, and variable pay plans are expanded. Variable pay is based on a combination of operating-company, group, and individual performance and relates to operating-company profitability. Indirect pay programs and costs are curtailed.

ExcelCorp Total Compensation Strategy

ExcelCorp is a potential world-class organization that enjoys a consistent financial advantage over competitors and has had a combination of both liberal direct pay and benefits of a highly traditional nature. ExcelCorp has become concerned because little difference exists among the financial rewards granted to employees below the executive level based on actual employee performance. The organization believes it can extend its advantage over competitors if it encourages employees throughout the organization to perform at an excellent level.

ExcelCorp has revised its business, financial, and human resource strategy to create a need for more focus on employee performance results. Because of this, a total compensation strategy is being developed to acknowledge a change in focus.

BUSINESS SITUATION. This is an excellently performing organization that has good profitability, excellent future planning processes, and satisfactory market share. The human resource strategy views employees as important, but the organization has made no comment (until now) about the importance of employee performance to its success. The business strategy is to gain more mileage from all possible sources, which is a change from former practice. The new business priority is to get employees more involved in improving quality and customer value, gaining an advantage, innovating, and generally participating in the future of the organization.

CURRENT PAY PROGRAMS. Present pay plans are competitively very liberal and lack a performance focus. High labor costs can be passed on to customers because the organization is a very strong performer. Only executives participate in incentive plans, and executive incentives have a short-range focus. Total compensation focuses primarily on staying competitive and on internal equity issues.

NEW TOTAL COMPENSATION STRATEGY. The total compensation strategy focuses on communicating to employees that they are important and that even though the organization is a good performer, employees must help the organization continue to achieve. Employees at all levels will be rewarded for gaining a differential advantage over external competitors; everyone counts in satisfying customers. The organization wants to make sure that employees don't take the high level of organizational performance for granted. Also, it wants to encourage involvement and the partnership concept to demonstrate and acknowledge the employees' role in making the organization a success.

- Business Considerations
  - Employees are important to the future of ExcelCorp, and everyone should do what they can to make the organization innovate, produce, and improve customer value, service and product quality to become world class.
  - It is important that ExcelCorp be financially successful to pay high levels of pay. ExcelCorp wants only the very best employees and will reward them well for strong performance. Less than strong performers should improve their performance or leave the organization.
  - In the future, competition will intensify, and ExcelCorp must be better prepared to compete effectively. ExcelCorp intends to stay "lean and mean" before it is in pain, and will undertake changes now to avoid pain at the last minute.

- Summary of Total Compensation Strategy
  - Organizational, group, and individual performance will be measured based on contribution to the success of ExcelCorp. Where results are excellent, monetary rewards will be excellent. Where results are below expectations, pay will directly reflect the performance problem. The performance focus will be on the smallest employee group that can be measured accurately and credibly, with the desirable level being team or individual. Employee involvement and understanding will be a management strategy.
  - Variable pay plans will be used wherever they can provide an advantage over base pay programs in terms of tying the performance of employees to the pay they receive. Operating-company presidents will be responsible for implementing variable pay plans wherever possible.
  - Base pay will become moderately competitive in the future in

order to control fixed labor costs and to make variable pay more workable and affordable. Significant upside variable pay opportunity and moderately competitive base pay will allow ExcelCorp to pay better for results achieved.

–The competitiveness of benefits will be permitted to fall in order that ExcelCorp will be a competitive, but not high, payer of benefits compared to direct business competitors. This is because pay in the form of variable pay is a stronger communicator of performance. Where possible, employees will share in benefit cost increases, and any changes in the retirement area will result in having a portion of retirement funded by profit sharing.

–A core carve-out flexible benefit plan will be used to provide choices without adding indirect pay costs.

This strategy suggests a change in the posture from believing that high pay without concern for results will ensure that employees will perform at an excellent level to using pay to communicate the concept of the employee–organization partnership.

BASE PAY CHANGES. ExcelCorp was a 75th-percentile payer of base pay in all portions of the organization. To introduce variable pay, base pay ranges will increase more slowly than competitive practice for a few years so base pay ranges have a midpoint at no more than the 50th percentile or median of competitive practice. Over the next three to five years, the organization intends to control base pay progression and to redirect dollars that are now paid in the form of base pay toward being paid in the form of variable pay. Although the merit base pay increase program rarely strongly differentiates individual performance, the organization is retaining the program for now and is encouraging managers to use it more differentially for the outstanding performers.

VARIABLE PAY CHANGES. Variable pay plans are being expanded below the executive level to include all managers and supervisors. These plans are funded by a combination of total organizational and sub-organizational financial results and subsequently reward individual performance. Managers and supervisors are trained to become accustomed to having their performance measured and rewarded in the form of variable pay. Operating-company presidents are forming a series of management–employee task forces to implement business-focused group variable pay plans in a wide range of operating units. Employees must meet individual job or skill standards to receive a reward under a group-oriented variable pay plan, and awards may be differentiated based on individual performance.

INDIRECT PAY CHANGES. Indirect pay plans are frozen at their current provision levels, and no additional benefits will be added. As benefit costs increase, these are shared with employees. A core carve-out flexible benefit plan will be installed that reduces the baseline protection offered to all employees on a uniform basis by a certain percentage of cost and allows employees to choose additional benefits to replace the percentage of cost reduction. The flexible plan will not be permitted to add benefit costs to current costs adjusted for inflation. Flexible benefits will be used only to redistribute fixed benefit costs to choice making rather than to add to total benefit costs.

VISION FOR THE FUTURE. ExcelCorp will incrementally move more toward variable pay rather than higher base pay costs. Since the organization is a strong financial performer, it is willing to spend more in variable pay dollars than what it would have spent in base pay costs under its old total compensation strategy to facilitate its slow transition from high fixed pay costs to variable pay costs. Employee involvement opportunities will increase dramatically. Group variable pay, winsharing, business plan gainsharing, individual incentives, and lump-sum award programs will be expanded in order to move to reusable pay costs and to communicate the concept of partnerships between the organization and employees. ExcelCorp wants to reward both group and individual performance and wants to use variable pay awards and base pay increases to do so.

TestCorp Total Compensation Strategy

TestCorp is an organization that is an average financial and quality performer in a highly competitive industry where providing value to the customer matters. The organization has tried to manage traditional direct and indirect pay programs effectively to get the maximum mileage from these programs. While financial performance, quality, and productivity are viewed as adequate, the opportunity for improvement exists.

The organization has decided to experiment with new pay to see whether it can provide an opportunity to gain an advantage over business competitors. The total compensation strategy has been revised to account for this necessity.

BUSINESS SITUATION PRIOR TO TOTAL COMPENSATION STRATEGY.
TestCorp is an adequate performer with a traditional management structure. Management has not had much experience with employee involvement and wants to see if new pay would have any impact on the success of the organization. The view of new pay is mixed with many unanswered questions; however, the focus is on testing new pay programs selectively to see if they improve the organization's performance.

PAY PROGRAMS PRIOR TO TOTAL COMPENSATION STRATEGY.
Traditional direct and indirect pay programs were used in this organization. Although its employee benefit program is centralized, operating companies had several approaches to base pay. TestCorp had point-factor plans of various designs, and incentives were limited to sales professionals and executives. Employees had not had a role in the design of direct and indirect pay programs.

NEW TOTAL COMPENSATION STRATEGY.

- Business Considerations
  - TestCorp believes employees are important and views pay as important. In the future, current human resource programs and attitudes may not meet TestCorp's needs. It is time to experiment with higher levels of employee involvement in reaching decisions.
  - While performance is adequate, TestCorp wants to experiment with new human resource strategies that may be more helpful than current, nonparticipative approaches.
  - Employee excellence at all levels throughout the organization is important. Whatever it takes to improve results achieved is worth consideration and experimentation.

- Summary of Total Compensation Strategy
  - Performance is important, and employee performance can be objectively measured in terms of financial performance, quality, productivity, cost management, customer value, and other

measures. Performance measurement should be more extensively used in the future.

- TestCorp will experiment with variable pay in the form of winsharing, business plan gainsharing, group incentives, and lump-sum awards. Presidents of operating companies should undertake experiments and document results over a three-year period. These programs should not add cost to current levels of financial performance.

- Base pay programs are getting expensive, and some of the experimentation should be in the area of skill-based pay and career ladders that are based on demonstrated performance, not years of experience. Experiments should not increase the total cost of getting the current level of financial results. Experiments should be in the area of redistributing current levels of total compensation or placing potential base pay increases at risk if other programs are to be tested. Total cash compensation costs should only increase as financial performance improves.

- Base pay plans tested will involve simplification by reducing the number of jobs and focusing on the market value of jobs.

- Total employee benefit costs to TestCorp will be frozen at their current levels. TestCorp will use future dollars available to fund variable pay experiments primarily but will also experiment in a limited way with using benefits as a reward. Several locations will be encouraged to experiment with indirect pay plans that reward wellness and offer additional time off as a reward for performance.

- Operating companies may utilize any retirement plan other than a defined benefit plan to match their needs. This includes individual retirement plans, profit sharing, 401(k) plans, savings plans, or other methodologies that do not create a fixed future financial obligation for TestCorp.

Experimentation in involvement in human resource program design is the focus of this organization. TestCorp will try several programs to see what works best. Financial results and pay costs will be monitored to ensure that pay costs increase only when financial results improve.

BASE PAY CHANGES. Skill-based pay is being tested in specific circumstances. The point-factor plan has been changed in several of the operating companies to involve a more market-based emphasis. Career ladders have been developed for certain types of employees, instead of each employee having his or her own job description, to enable more flexibility in job responsibility. All experimentation is focused on programs that take the organization away from a strong focus on internal equity.

VARIABLE PAY CHANGES. Business plan gainsharing, winsharing, lump-sum awards, and group incentives are being tried where they seem better suited to how employees work and to organizational performance. Criteria have been developed to evaluate the success of programs from the employees' and organization's viewpoints to help decide whether programs should be continued, modified, or discontinued. Variable pay at the executive level is being focused on a three- to five-year period. This introduces a longer-term emphasis on sustained financial and quality results for executive performance.

INDIRECT PAY CHANGES. Indirect pay plans have not been expanded. Any new dollars that are available are focused primarily on experimenting with new pay in the form of base pay and variable pay. Employees pay more of employee benefits when costs increase. Some new dollars are to be used to experiment with benefits that reward what makes the organization successful, such as performance and wellness. Later experimentation may be with limited choice making.

VISION FOR THE FUTURE. TestCorp is willing to see if a better way exists. If one solution does not work, the organization will try other solutions. Involvement opportunities are expanding. The programs that work best will be kept, and others will be changed. The organization keeps testing solutions to find a better way to pay and reward employees.

Readiness for New Pay

Unless the strategy-setting process indicates a willingness, readiness, and culture that are conducive to new pay, proceeding with new pay is not viable until the organization is ready to change. Some of the clues to readiness to move to new pay that can be found in a total compensation strategy include the following:

- an acknowledgement that traditional pay systems are not getting the job done and must be changed
- the willingness to endure considerable pain to move from a culture of tenure and entitlement to one of performance, empowerment, employee involvement, teamwork, and employee–organization partnership
- a readiness to focus on the group, instead of the individual, as the unit of measurement and on variable pay as the primary focus of the total compensation strategy
- the willingness to determine base pay as a result of skills and the external market, rather than only based on internal equity
- an acceptance that indirect pay cannot be used to reward desired results and therefore is of secondary value to the total compensation strategy that involves new pay
- viewing pay as an opportunity cost, and a willingness to tie pay to organizational success so that employees and the organization have a vested interest in each other's success
- a willingness to permit active involvement by employees in organizational issues that affect them

New pay is not consistent with a total compensation strategy with the following elements:

- a strategy to "recruit, attract, and retain," which is a giveaway that the focus is on what percentile of competitiveness a pay plan should achieve or how competitive and internally equitable pay should be
- a focus on base pay, variable pay, and indirect pay as independent issues, rather than as elements of a total compensation strategy, and an unwillingness to determine which is best suited to an organization's need to perform well
- the willingness to rely only on layoffs, rather than pay design, to vary labor costs based on an organization's ability to pay
- the unwillingness to reduce indirect pay levels and expenditures over time to focus on variable pay
- the belief that only management top-down decisions are best for the organization and its employees

Organizations with such elements as these in their total compensation strategy are better served with traditional pay, but may be even better served with a commitment to change to a point where a new pay total compensation strategy is possible.

Conclusions

Although the process for effective development of total compensation strategies is consistent, results may vary. Although traditional total compensation strategies are consistent from organization to organization, new pay strategies vary based on how the organization views its future and that of its employees.

New pay requires an alignment between what the organization wants done and the role total compensation plays in helping the organization and employees win together. Good strategy requires a process for implementation and communication in order that the organization can benefit from new pay.

From Strategy to Practice by Involvement

Strategy Needs Implementation

Sometimes well-intentioned and potentially effective pay strategies end up on the shelf because of inappropriate implementation methodologies. In chapter 3, the development of a total compensation strategy was described. Because of direct executive involvement in the development of strategy, the key decision makers have an important stake in the result, understand the implications of the strategy, and support implementation by championing the new pay programs that result from the strategy. In traditional pay circumstances, once the organization obtains approval from top management, implementation is rapidly undertaken. The thought is that once the senior executives have "bought on," the rest of the process is relatively easy. Perhaps this is one reason why so many traditional pay programs have failed to remain attuned to changes in organizational and employee circumstances.

Employee involvement in the development, implementation, and monitoring of total compensation programs is clearly a new pay tactic. Employee desire for added empowerment opportunities and the need to have employees involved in performance improvement will cause the best-managed organizations to provide room for employees who want and are constructively able to participate to become directly involved in the decisions that impact their work life. However, employee involvement in issues related to pay matters offers both opportunities and challenges. The concept of getting employees involved in new pay issues sounds very good at first blush. However, making a high-involvement culture a practical reality is a major challenge.

Implications of High Involvement

Someone said that employee participation is much like dancing with a bear. You ask the bear to dance, but the bear lets you know when he is done dancing. Moving from strategy to practice is seemingly much easier without employee involvement. However, the success of the effort is greatly enhanced as a result of high-quality employee involvement that matches the readiness of the organization to make employee involvement work (or the organization's willingness to change to a high-involvement culture). The extent of involvement varies greatly among organizations from a little to a lot, based on culture and management attitudes toward involvement or toward the necessity to change to a culture that is based on a higher level of employee involvement.

Most experts agree that employees will help the organization make a new pay program work when they have had a role in its development, even though it may be a less effective plan from a technical standpoint than could have been developed without involvement.[1] The management task is to ensure the technical quality of decisions reached while permitting an appropriate level of involvement in the selection, design, and implementation of solutions. The technical quality of decisions involves such issues as selecting employee groups for plan participation, picking performance measures for variable pay plans that ensure that both the organization and the employee share appropriately based on results, defining cost parameters for skill-based pay, selecting sites for new pay programs (such as skill-based pay and group variable pay) that take advantage of the pluses of the methodologies while being able to tolerate the possible negatives, and ensuring that pay plans are critically reviewed annually to make sure they continue to match organizational goals and needs.

Leading or Supporting Change

Should employee involvement and new pay programs match the organization's readiness for change, or lead an organizational change? If the organization wishes to change to a culture with greater focus on employee performance results and more employee involvement, is new pay a good way to lead this change? Should the organization first change its culture and management style, then align pay programs and employee involvement in pay issues to support the change in progress? These issues are critical to defining the way the organization will start with an effective strategy and subsequently modify existing pay plans or develop new pay plans to correspond with this new strategy. Involvement and new pay can be used either as the leading element in a move toward organizational change or to support needed change that is being facilitated by some other form of intervention. In either role involvement and new pay can be effective.

Many factors contribute to organizational effectiveness. The most important is the quality of decisions as judged by the goals and objectives of the enterprise. High-quality results have been achieved based on moderate levels of involvement, and poor-quality results have been the outcome of high-involvement efforts. Uncontrolled and unmanaged involvement can result in the development and implementation of programs and strategies that enjoy a high level of commitment but are designed in a less than effective manner. Successful involvement defines when the "bear" is asked to dance, the music that provides the dance rhythm, and also when the bear should stop dancing in order that employee and organizational expectations can be mutually satisfied. This means the parameters of involvement are best established and communicated before the involvement is undertaken.

Management needs to define the level of employee involvement up front and to communicate this so that employees feel their involvement expectations were met. If the organization decides to implement a new pay plan of some type, management needs to be clear as to the goals and expectations of the program and then enlist employee involvement at the defined level. Typically, before involving employees, management has conducted its own feasibility study (ranging from extensive to very limited) about developing a new pay program and has decided that it is worth pursuing. If employees invest energy in developing a plan that management later decides is not worthwhile, employees will resist involvement in future projects because management lacks credibility.

Organizations vary dramatically in their comfort level concerning the extent of employee involvement in the design of a pay program. Typically, this comfort level relates to the extent to which employees have been involved in other decision-making processes in the past and the quality of the results derived from those processes.

Assessing Employee Climate

Is the organization ready for new pay? What is the organization's level of readiness for employee involvement? If the organization is not ready for involvement and new pay and these are called for in the total compensation strategy, what can be done to prepare the organization for change? Three factors are assessed in determining the move to new pay: (1) the appropriateness of new pay to the business direction and goals of the organization, (2) the degree of top management support for new pay, and (3) employee readiness for new pay and employee involvement. If the total compensation strategy supports the move to new pay, new pay has satisfied the first two factors. New pay has been determined to support the business strategy because the total compensation strategy was developed taking into consideration the goals and objectives of the organization. New pay also has the support of top management because they developed the total compensation strategy. The third factor—the attitudes of employees, supervisors, and other managers toward (and their understanding of) the organization and its goals, performance, and pay—can be assessed by a climate survey.

Climate Surveys

Many new pay feasibility studies involve normative climate surveys or "attitude surveys" that are intended to explore the state of various human resource programs and plans from the perspective of the employees. Climate surveys can be very helpful to new pay when they are specific enough to gather actionable information. Care is necessary to ensure that employees' expectations are not raised by exploring new pay areas that the organization has no plans to respond to with new or modified policies, programs, or procedures. It is also important to know what employee attitudes must be changed to gain their support of a higher level of involvement and a move to new pay.

Some guidelines are important to the design of a climate survey:

- Avoid questions that can be misunderstood from the standpoint of the employee or from the standpoint of the interpreter of the findings. Make sure the terminology of the survey is the terminology of the organization.

- Investigate only areas the organization would be willing to change should the need for change be proven and the direction of the change be clearly defined.
- Be prepared to tell climate survey participants what the organization plans to do as a result of the survey. Be careful about employees' expectations and the organization's willingness and ability to address the issues.

Many paper-and-pencil questionnaires designed to evaluate an organization's human resource climate are deficient in their ability to evaluate employee perceptions and attitudes toward total compensation programs. For example, questions that explore the following can create potential problems:

- How does your pay compare to that of others in similar jobs in other organizations?
- How does your pay compare to that of others in similar jobs in your own organization?
- How well do you understand the pay program in your organization?

In many cases, the first two questions are answered in the situational negative. The problem is that the organization does not know what the employees are using as comparative standards—for example, who the employees are comparing themselves to and whether they are comparing based on job content or performance. Nearly everyone would like more pay and thinks they are worth more pay than they are now receiving. Studies show that most people view themselves as better than average performers, so they believe their pay should be better than average.[2] This results in people reporting dissatisfaction with their pay, especially if the organization says it pays for performance.

Because absolute scores on such questions are meaningless, wise organizations compare scores to normative standards. The issue is whether employees give a more negative response to the questions than were provided by employees in the organizations that constituted the norms. In many instances, these surveys provide organizations with information that suggests people are not satisfied with their direct pay unless absolute values are ignored and only comparison to norms is considered. Often, employee benefits come out better than direct pay.

A problem with many questionnaire climate surveys is that the organization is left to figure out what actions need to be taken to improve the organization's "score" in the area of direct pay. Often the information gathered is of a general nature, so the organization's response is general. Some organizations interpret the displeasure expressed in a paper-and-pencil climate survey as a major communications problem. These organizations believe the survey exposes a need to expend major effort in developing ways to help employees better understand direct and indirect pay programs. Communications pamphlets and booklets are produced; employee group meetings with executives, human resource representatives, supervisors, and managers are scheduled; video presentations are developed; and a major flurry of communications effort is undertaken. Major communications efforts of a general nature normally miss the mark, however, because they are not lasting. Other organizations interpret paper-and-pencil climate survey results by taking specific actions they believe are suggested by the survey results, when a more thorough investigation and understanding that can be gained from focus groups involving discussion of the issues may or may not support such action.

FOCUS GROUPS. Rather than attempting to gather a complete understanding and interpretation of how people view their direct and indirect pay by using a paper-and-pencil questionnaire as the information-gathering tool, selective employee focus groups may provide better, more reliable, and more usable information. Using focus groups offers the following advantages to an organization exploring the climate of understanding and acceptance of pay programs:

- The opportunity to probe specific areas of interest exists, so investigators can more thoroughly seek specific answers. This is critical to determining readiness for new pay.
- Investigators and employees can discuss issues in detail, and suggestions can be solicited in each area of opportunity. Again, this is critical to new pay.
- If desired, gathering information can be expanded into employee involvement in the decision-making process. Employees who will be of the most help in any further steps the organization takes in developing solutions to the problems defined by the climate study can be identified. This can be very valuable to new pay where involvement is increased.

The advantages of focus groups, which involve face-to-face contact, over paper-and-pencil questionnaires as information-gathering tools is that group interviews give the organization the chance to explore issues and opportunities in great detail. Focus groups give employees the chance to talk directly to those who will later apply the information. This chance for the exchange of thoughts and ideas avoids the problem of gathering only general information of limited use. For example, some of the most confusing issues to explore involve the following:

- When employees say they want the organization to "pay for performance," do they understand that this may mean less money for less than satisfactory performers? Do they believe that "pay for performance" means giving everyone more money?
- When employees say they are not "competitively paid" or not "fairly paid," what comparisons are they making? Do they have an accurate or inaccurate perception of what the comparison group is paid?
- When people discuss the relative importance of pay compared to other aspects about their job, with what aspects are they comparing their pay?

Specific answers will prepare the organization to decide on the best solutions. Gathering specifics prevents general solutions from being implemented that may not be related to the issues that require direct attention.

Gathering opinions and gaining insight are critical to understanding the organization's human resource climate. However, wise organizations review and critique the information-gathering process carefully. Unless the organization's culture has accustomed employees to providing information by paper-and-pencil questionnaires, focus groups involving face-to-face contact are the best investigative method to employ when attitudes toward pay are explored. Focus groups permit participation and let investigators seek the reasons for specific attitudes and beliefs. Involvement is often very important to the successful change from total compensation programs that hinder effective human resource management to those that accommodate it. This involvement can start with the use of focus groups to explore perceptions and concerns about pay.

If the organization's total compensation strategy is more aligned with new pay, the following issues can be addressed to determine the readiness for new pay or what must be done to facilitate new pay:

- extent of communication in all directions (upward, downward, and horizontal)
- level of understanding and support of the mission, goals, and objectives of the organization
- ideas about what the employees themselves can do to improve productivity, quality, and results
- level of teamwork and collaboration
- level of trust in management
- level of understanding of how the organization's products or services fit into the market and are perceived and used by the customer

These issues show the extent to which the employees identify with the organization. The greater the understanding, support, and identification, the more easily a partnership can be formed and employees can help the organization be successful. If the level of trust is very low, the organization may need to work on raising this before proceeding with new pay. As discussed earlier, new pay can either lead or support organizational change. New pay often is used to lead organizational change because pay is a strong communicator and other methods of communicating have not changed behavior or produced results.

Developing New Pay Programs

Regardless of the degree of employee involvement, experience suggests that several important steps are needed to move from a new pay strategy to implementation of a new pay program by means of a high-quality involvement effort. These include the following:

- *Step 1*—defining project and expected results
- *Step 2*—involvement process
- *Step 3*—design
- *Step 4*—communications and training
- *Step 5*—monitoring and evaluation

Although the specific steps can be modified to match the situation, the elements of each of these five steps are critical to a satisfactory high-involvement process.

Step 1—Defining Project and Expected Results

The project definition could be a feasibility study to determine whether a new pay variable pay plan is appropriate for a specific group, a study to investigate the possibility of developing a skill-based pay plan, or a study to design and implement a pay program that has already been determined to be appropriate for a specific situation. The expectation is that the quality of acceptance will be substantially improved if employees are involved in the developmental process. Additionally, the organization will have some technical requirements that are essential to satisfactory completion of the undertaking; these may include quantitative and qualitative expectations that will guide the process. Also, time expectations should be established so involvement does not become protracted and fail to generate a timely result.

Defining what is to be done seems obvious, but it is essential to determine how and when the organization expects to benefit from the project. The involvement ground rules are clear from the start and involvement works best if it has some parameters. Some of these include the following:

- What can be gained from involving people that cannot otherwise be accomplished?
- What is the organization's tolerance for high involvement? How will it be managed?
- How will involvement be focused so that the quality solutions will be forthcoming?
- Who will be involved in what specific decisions? Top management? Managers? Supervisors? Employees?

The organization also defines the technical expectations it has from the project. Technical expectations can be changed as the undertaking evolves, but it is critical to have an understanding concerning what the results should be at the end of the project. Some of these are as follows:

- How will the merits of solutions presented be evaluated for workability?
- How long will involvement continue before a decision must be made?

- How can course corrections be implemented to ensure that the solutions derived from involvement actually address the key issues?

The objective is to define expectations effectively so that high involvement does not result in less than satisfactory outcomes from a technical and quality perspective.

If the organization has little or no tolerance for involvement, is the use of new pay questionable? While elements of new pay can be successful without extensive involvement, some employee involvement is essential to form an effective employee–organization partnership. It is possible that the organization can implement a job evaluation plan based on the market rather than on internal equity or reduce indirect pay levels without significant employee involvement. This is because management generally has the information needed to make design decisions in these areas and may not need employees to change their work methodologies for the program to be successful. However, organizations need employee involvement in such undertakings as the implementation of a skill-based pay plan or the development of group variable pay, since employees need to change the way they work to be successful in these pay programs and their involvement in the early stages of the program increases understanding and buy-in.

While no rules of involvement exist (except that effectively managed involvement that generates usable results is key to new pay), testing the water for involvement opportunities is wise. Some believe it is best to try involvement for the first time in areas other than pay because of the opportunity for negative cost implications of a poorly managed involvement process. However, new pay is one of the major opportunities an organization has to increase levels of employee involvement and to implement programs that strongly affect the organization's ability to compete effectively. An ideal opportunity to institute organizational change is by means of a new pay strategy and the programs that result from this strategy.

Step 2—Involvement Process

For organizations deciding in favor of involvement, the process is defined in some detail below. Involvement has little chance of helping unless the involvement process begins early in the new pay project. Involvement is best structured to be consistent with the organization's comfort with employee involvement. For example, a high level of involvement in the development of a new pay plan in an organization with high tolerance for involvement can be defined as follows:

- A task force of eight to twelve employees, supervisors, and managers helps top management determine whether a new pay plan of some sort is feasible for a specific group. People are selected for involvement because they have an understanding of all aspects of the organization's operations and are well respected by others.
- At the beginning, top management defines expectations concerning what must be in the final result for both the organization and the employees involved. For example, if the goal is productivity improvement, how will the benefits of productivity improvement be shared between the organization and the employees? What is the relationship between financial performance and variable pay funding? Will new variable pay be in addition to current base pay, or will it place some of the current or potential base pay increase budget at risk in order to share more of any "high-end" productivity improvement?
- The task force explores possible alternatives, including the possible available solutions to achieve the objectives of the pay program. For example, if the project is a feasibility study for variable pay, the following could be considered: performance and productivity measurement options, suggestion and employee involvement opportunities, and degree of fit with other parallel programs (such as a quality program). Issues such as employees' readiness to accept new pay at this time are also considered. The goal is to improve effectiveness, which is defined and used to measure the value of the solutions available.
- Management, human resources, finance, information systems, and engineering support the effort by providing measurement information that is required during the feasibility study. Training is provided in the economics of the operation under study in order that solutions make technical sense.
- Management is involved throughout the process so that its approval is not deferred until the last moment. This means the

task force receives continuing feedback from management as the process evolves, which avoids the possibility of negative impact if part or all of the proposal is eventually revised or rejected. The goal of the task force is to produce an approved result; continuing management involvement is critical.

- The new pay proposal is presented to management and is subjected to specific predefined requirements. For example: (1) the proposal cannot increase labor cost without accompanying productivity improvement that can be measured in bottom-line financial terms; (2) employees involved must share based on overall financial performance of the operation; (3) during time periods in which productivity performance does not meet preset standards or goals, no variable pay award will be paid.
- Recommendations are presented to top management. Management has the opportunity to accept or reject any or all of the proposal. Management can also modify the proposal with the help of the task force that participated in the developmental effort. The final decision is management's, but they work with the task force during the process of acceptance or rejection.
- If the project is a feasibility study and the result is a decision to proceed, the task force helps in design and implementation. New requirements are defined, and the project continues.

Involvement opportunities vary from organization to organization. In some instances, organizations involve only supervisors and managers in the development of new pay programs and find this to be valuable and successful. In others, a very high degree of involvement at all levels in the organization is encouraged and viewed as essential and practical. If a level is not involved in the developmental phase (e.g., first-line supervisors), that level may not support the program during implementation.

Involvement in determining the funding of a new pay program also varies among organizations. In some cases, top management determines the funding and reward/cost relationship, and a broader group of employees designs the other features of the plan. In other organizations, top management provides objectives concerning funding and the reward/cost relationship, and a broader group of employees designs the funding consistent with the objectives.

Employees, supervisors, managers, and executives who are involved in reaching new pay decisions have a vested interest in the results of the decisions. This is why involvement works well if effectively managed. However, sometimes involvement provides a result that is viewed as practical only by those involved and does not meet the critical tests of management, technical, and financial representatives of the organization. Wise organizations define accountability for reaching decisions at the start of the process. Accountability can be shared by employees and management, be retained by the employees, or rest with management with only the obligation to communicate the logic of the decision to employees.

It is best to share decisions between employees and management, because this makes it critical to set down requirements for success at the start. Subsequently, employees and management evaluate the accountability to proceed against the same measurement criteria. Accountability retained by management can also provide good results, depending on the organization's style of management and employees' level of trust in management. Although possible, it does not seem likely that employee accountability alone works. If it were to work, it is most likely to work in an organization that has had a long history of involvement and resulting trust and knows how to manage employee involvement very effectively.

Step 3—Design

High-involvement design efforts offer many opportunities to lose focus on the fact that the objective is to develop and implement a program that meets specific organizational requirements. Guidelines to help keep the design process on track include the following:

- Hold involved employees accountable for results achieved in both qualitative and quantitative terms. The effective process does not become excessively linear and without measurable or observable results. High-involvement efforts need measurable results to be valuable.
- Periodically evaluate progress critically to determine whether the process has gotten off track. Make it natural for the process to be evaluated at least monthly by those involved in the effort, as well as by whatever evaluation process outside the involved group is established.

- Discuss results with affected parties so that new information is brought into the involved design group. Keep a constructive eye out for new opportunities to improve based on learning from others.
- Build in monitoring and evaluation processes so that continuing evaluation is an expected and accepted part of the effort. This will prepare involved employees to accept feedback on their work without being hurt by change or constructive comment.

The well-conceived design effort accounts for the organization's readiness for new pay and employee involvement. Simpler solutions are more easily communicated and implemented. Because new pay plans are reviewed at least annually, it is always possible to add complexity when necessary. The goal is success during the first performance period in which the program is in operation. Involvement in the initial stages needs good results. This means the results of the design effort are practical, workable, and likely to produce positive results in order that involvement is a rewarding experience.

In designing features, the shorter- and longer-term pay strategy should be considered. For example, if a skill-based pay program is being designed, the task force considers the organization's longer-term goal, which may be to pay for results through variable pay. The shorter-term strategy is to have employees better understand how what they do relates to what others do, and to achieve greater work-force flexibility. In this example, lump-sum awards may be paid for skill acquisition, or employees may receive less base pay than they might otherwise receive for the acquisition of skills because in two years they will receive variable pay awards for achieving results that were facilitated by skill-based pay.

The task force also considers the new pay program being designed in the context of the rest of the organization that is not participating in the program. Continuing the example above, the task force considers how other portions of the organization will view the skill-based pay plan. Will pay be higher for employees under the skill-based pay plan than for supervisors or other support employees, and why is this acceptable? Will costs be higher than other similar organizations without skill-based pay, and can the costs be justified based on expected results?

For each design element, the task force works through the advantages and disadvantages of various alternatives and determines which alternative is most consistent with program objectives. Sometimes task force members develop a consensus on each of the design elements; other task forces have members vote on each element so that all voices are counted. The resulting program design needs to have an acceptable relationship between pay costs and results. The task force models out the relationship between costs and expected results on spreadsheets to ensure that the relationship is sound. Modeling a variable pay plan is generally a straightforward matter because the funding measure is usually financial. Modeling a skill-based pay plan is usually more difficult because assumptions need to be made about what financial gain will result from greater work-force flexibility. This does not inhibit the modeling; assumptions can be made of the best guess of expected results, the best-case scenario, and the worst-case scenario. A new pay plan with a sound financial analysis of costs and results will gain more acceptance from top management because it demonstrates that the task force is thinking of the organization's potential return on investment.

Step 4—Communications and Training

If the decision has been reached to implement a new pay program, the change needs extensive communication to facilitate employee understanding and acceptance. At least three vehicles are used in successful communication—top management, members of the task force, and supervisors. Top management's role is to clarify how the change fits into the organization's mission, strategies, and goals and to demonstrate support for the change. The task force's role is to communicate the design of the new program, to answer questions, and to support the change. The supervisor's role is to ensure that employees understand the change and to provide the leadership for employees to accept the program and be motivated to achieve the goals of the program. Often a "champion" is identified in the organization who serves as the leader of (and cheerleader for) the change and facilitates program understanding, acceptance, and implementation.

As with any communications about pay, wise organizations spend significantly more time and effort communicating a new pay program than they do communicating other issues. However, usually the organization is interested in communicating new pay because new pay programs are more than just a pay delivery system—they serve as a communications vehicle about what the organization is trying to accomplish.

Communication involves the reasons for the change, the plan design, and how the program relates to other programs that the organization may be implementing or has already implemented (quality or employee involvement programs, just-in-time techniques, etc.). In addition, communication includes the process for employees to be successful in achieving the goal of the program.

Employee communication is more important to new pay because new pay most often represents significant change. If the organization wishes to communicate new pay to its employees in a lasting manner, the supervisor is the most effective channel to use, and the communications effort must not be limited to a flurry of broad-based activity. Effective communication is a planned and sustained effort that places the supervisor at its center. Communications materials that can be used by the supervisor in direct personal contact with employees on a continuing basis work best with new pay. Communications materials supplement supervisor–employee discussions that set the communications effort in the context of defining how the programs impact employees in both general and specific ways. New pay communication programs having the following characteristics most often prove successful:

- The communications message is clear, truthful, balanced and specific to the employee. It does not try to sell the pay program to employees.
- The supervisor is "on board" concerning the communications message and accepts the message as one he or she believes in. Communication requires that the information be communicated to employees directly and personally by their own supervisor, and this communication can be supplemented but not replaced by other people, including task force members, other involved employees, and management.
- Flashy video presentations that intend to communicate the need for organizations to manage pay effectively create credibility problems among employees. Expensive "one-way" presentations create communications problems and are not as effective as are supervision-centered communications efforts that are continuing in nature.

Communication is important because pay is a powerful medium for carrying the message concerning organizational values and objectives and how direct and indirect pay programs relate to those values and objectives. The most important relationship to reinforce is the one between the employee and the organization. This can best be accomplished if the supervisor is well prepared to discuss pay with the employee face-to-face and to answer questions and resolve concerns with each individual employee.

In high-involvement organizations, employees assume more of the responsibility for communicating new pay programs. The supervisor serves as a facilitator, coach, and trainer, and team leaders and natural employee leaders serve key roles in communicating and supporting the program. The task force ensures that all of these communicators are trained in the objectives of the program, the way the program works, and how to respond to the common questions that employees will ask. The program is communicated consistently by the communicators to reduce the potential for misunderstanding and confusion.

Communication requires repetition. Often, at least two phases of communications should be planned. The first phase of communications involves explaining the new pay program to employees and answering any initial questions employees have; the second phase a few days later gives employees the opportunity to ask additional questions after they have had the opportunity to think about the program. After initial communications, a sustained supervisor/employee-centered communications plan is implemented. If the new pay program being communicated provides that some employees are excluded from participation, a special communications effort to excluded employees is often essential to the process. Communications is also where the opportunity for fun exists; using T-shirts and kickoff events to bring attention to the new program is helpful in making the program a success.

When a new pay plan is installed that is very different from current programs, employees sometimes become concerned and often spend time discussing and debating the merits of the change. Clear communication about the changes and their implications from supervisors and task force members is important—both the upsides and the downsides. Once employees understand the changes, communication moves the focus from the plan design to the ways the organization and employees will achieve the goals of the change. Often when employees are worried about change, they are concerned about the difficulty of achieving the goals or receiving the rewards. The sooner employees are focused on what needs to be done and involved in figuring out how to get it done, the more likely the change will gain acceptance.

Negative reception sometimes tempts management to change the plan as soon as it is instituted. If the new pay plan has a sound design and a participative design process, the wise organization sticks with the change until the plan has had a chance to work or not work. Otherwise the organization never knows the impact of the change, task force members who believed they were doing a good job will be discouraged from future involvement, and management will lose credibility. Often the design changes suggested by those concerned would satisfy one group's needs but not another's, and they are often inconsistent with the organization's total compensation strategy.

Step 5—Monitoring and Evaluation

Programs of any type need monitoring, review, and evaluation. When a new pay program is installed based on an involvement effort, evaluation provides the opportunity for the organization to remain flexible and change the solutions that no longer meet its goals and objectives. It is possible to become locked into a result derived through an involvement effort as easily as it is to become locked into one that lacked involvement. Issues of employee commitment and ownership can cause a solution to be extremely rigid because it is an outcome of a participative effort. When people are involved, they like the result and are likely to defend it rather than permit the flexibility and change essential to a quality final product.

Effective review follows the same process as the developmental effort. That is, an involvement review process permits the evaluation to be undertaken the same way as the developmental effort was conducted. If the review and evaluation are scheduled at the start of the design process, it is most likely to be conducted in a constructive and positive manner.

In the review process, a variety of issues are assessed, including the following:

- Was the plan implemented and administered as designed? If not, why not?
- Was there sufficient communication about the plan? Was it timely? Did employees understand the program?
- Were the objectives of the program met? For example, if the goal

of the program was to increase productivity and improve quality, did both of these occur? If one of the objectives is to shift to more variable pay from fixed pay over the longer term in order to provide more stable employment, is this process under way? How is this measured?

- Did performance improve? For example, did performance on the measures in a variable pay plan improve?
- Did other performance measures—both quantitative and qualitative—that were assumed to relate to the goal of the program improve? For example, with a skill-based pay program, in addition to the question of whether the needed skills were developed, did employee satisfaction increase? Did productivity improve because of greater work-force flexibility? Did absenteeism decrease? Did overall labor costs decrease for a particular level of volume, even though labor cost per employee may have increased?

New pay programs are frequently evaluated after the first ninety days to ensure that the program is on track with the objectives. The annual review feature of new pay programs allows for a planned evaluation on a scheduled basis. This typically occurs before the end of each plan year in order to make any necessary changes or improvements for the following year. It is important to remember the longer-term objectives of the program at this time to determine if any modifications are needed to be consistent with the objectives. For example, a variable pay plan may have been designed using a customer value measure that would be refined over time as the organization and employees gained more experience with the measure (and more understanding of the customers' changing expectations and the components leading to customer value). A provision would be made to evaluate the measure and determine if it should be refined, broadened, or modified. Additionally, the task force may decide that one performance measure is strongly correlated with another and that since the employees understand the relationship between the measures, they do not need to continue to measure both. Or the organization's business strategy may have changed, and the measures need to change correspondingly to have the pay plan be consistent with the new business plan. Also, if the objective is to shift from fixed pay to variable pay, the task force determines how variable pay opportunities would increase while containing or slowing the movement of fixed pay costs. Evaluation allows a new pay plan to evolve as the organization evolves so that the plan remains current and relevant as a communications vehicle and a reward system and does not become viewed as an entitlement.

Example of Employee Involvement in the Design of a New Variable Pay Program

The following high-involvement process was used by a high-tech organization to develop a new pay variable pay program.

STEP 1—DEFINING PROJECT AND EXPECTED RESULTS. The organization's objective was to develop a stronger link between pay and performance. It needed to contain base pay costs and wanted to reward employees well for results that made the organization more financially successful. The organization wanted to implement the plan at the beginning of the next fiscal year, which meant that the plan needed to be approved three months before the beginning of the fiscal year in order to allow sufficient time to develop plan communications, communicate the plan and the corresponding involvement process, and have employees begin to participate in the involvement process so they could achieve the needed performance results. The technical requirements included the following:

- Fixed pay costs could not continue to increase at the current pace.
- The organization was willing to pay variable pay awards at a specific minimum threshold level of quantitative and qualitative performance.
- The organization was willing to share significant gains with the employees for very strong performance results.
- The greater the containment of base pay costs as a result of the plan, the greater the sharing of rewards would be.
- Performance measures need to be consistent with the organization's business plan and strategy.

STEP 2—INVOLVEMENT PROCESS. The task force that was formed included representatives from all levels in the organization and all major job functions. The task force was jointly led by a senior line manager and human resources manager, who kept the process moving. Progress on the design was periodically reported to top management. Top management retained decision accountability for the funding of the plan and the relationship of funding to both base pay increases and performance results; however, the task force recommended the design. The task force retained decision accountability for other performance measures (e.g., quality), eligibility issues, methodology for distribution of awards, methodology for allocating base pay increases, and creating the linkage between the employee involvement process and the pay program.

STEP 3 — DESIGN. The task force first reviewed and ensured understanding of its objectives and then educated itself on new pay. The design process took several months of periodically scheduled meetings that involved debating design features and modeling the relationship between cost and results. The task force designed the plan using information provided by finance (e.g., historical financial performance, business plan goals, relationships among financial measures, financial reporting systems), information systems (what was needed to ensure timely receipt of information used to report results and pay out awards) and human resources (e.g., current competitiveness of pay, historical performance on and goals for human resource measures indicating employee satisfaction). The resulting plan design was presented to top management. However, the plan was not a surprise to top management because they had been kept informed on the debating of the issues and the thought processes that led to the plan design.

STEP 4 — COMMUNICATIONS AND TRAINING. The task force called in the assistance of the communications department to help develop a communications strategy. Even before the plan design was completed, the task force began to think about communications and had named the plan. The task force was instrumental in the communication of the new pay plan. Supervisors were enrolled in a "train the trainer" program so they would support the new pay program and be able to answer questions.

STEP 5 — MONITORING AND EVALUATION. The task force met monthly during the first few months after implementation to develop the material that was used to report performance results and comments on successes and needed improvements to employees. Annually, the task force evaluates the plan and reviews the risk/reward relationship. The task force still has many of its original members but also has changed members so that it remains responsive, is open to new ideas, and does not become rigid in its own solutions.

Conclusions

Involvement is important to new pay. It is one thing for management to develop a new pay strategy and another to gain employee acceptance. Once the total compensation strategy is completed (and sometimes before), wise organizations use a climate study to measure employee readiness for change and/or determine the actions that are necessary to prepare for change. Throughout the process of moving to new pay, communication is important. New pay cannot be sold into existence; it needs honest communication in the short and long term, especially at the critical point of contact—the supervisor and the employee.

Although new pay works best if associated with high involvement, organizations differ in their readiness and willingness to involve employees in total compensation decisions. Organizations use new pay to lead organizational change or to support organizational changes led by other management practices. New pay is well suited for either role. Involvement alone is not enough; new pay plans must be technically and qualitatively sound in order to get the job done for which they are intended. New pay requires involvement and plan designs that are practical and workable.

PART THREE

New Base Pay

Principles of New Base Pay

Base Pay Challenges

Base pay is traditionally viewed as fundamental to all aspects of employee total compensation. Organizations use base pay to reflect the relative importance of jobs, to compete economically for talent in the external marketplace, and to acknowledge differences in performance among people. Both indirect pay and variable pay are most often represented in terms of a percentage of base pay. New pay intends to limit base pay to doing what it does best; this is essential because base pay increases are not only permanent but expensive. Base pay changes cause increases in benefit costs that are substantial. Of the 37.6 percent equivalent of base pay that the U.S. Chamber of Commerce reports as representing total benefit costs, 27.4 percent varies as a result of base pay changes, while only 10.2 percent is unrelated to changes in base pay.[1]

The "attract, motivate, and retain" objectives are focused principally on the base pay program. The lore about effective pay management is also directed toward base pay. This makes changing to an alternative pay strategy, however attractive it may be, a major management challenge. Base pay programs outlive top management teams, human resource executives, and even business and financial strategies. Base pay is seldom changed to support a vision of success and high performance. New pay requires that the role of base pay change.

Too many requirements have been placed on base pay. This is why traditional base pay detracts from organizational success. Rather than trying to force base pay to serve purposes for which it is ill suited, new pay provides that base pay will be limited to functions it performs better than variable pay and indirect pay.

Attitudes Toward Change

Many organizations using traditional pay have had their existing pay programs for so long that they fear change. The pay programs have taken on a life of their own and seem to be driving the organization, rather than the goals of the organization determining the proper pay plan to be used. Too often organizations agonize through the annual ritual of determining the merit-increase budget and deciding how competitive base pay should be. They spend hours debating whether their competitive pay line should be at the 60th or 75th percentile of competitive practice, or trying to decide whether the "merit budget" should be 5.0 or 5.3 percent. Once these annual rituals are concluded, executives and pay administrators heave a sigh of relief because "this is handled for another year." Many subsequently spend the rest of the year worrying about whether a job should have 400 or 420 points on the job evaluation plan. New pay intends that these executives and professionals spend their time on issues that are more important to their organization's performance.

For example, when a major bank named a new CEO, he found an organization driven by how many job evaluation points a job had. The job evaluation methodology greatly inhibited his ability to get people to accept new jobs when the job to which employees were to be moved for developmental purposes had fewer points, even though the bank's new directions had nothing to do with how many points jobs were worth. When the CEO took charge and terminated the point plan because it was operating counter to bank objectives, the organization could accept how he wanted to lead it. Organizations that consider new pay are driven primarily by the need to encourage employee performance and gain a competitive advantage through their pay systems.

Traditional base pay focuses only on the individual employee, the job to which the individual is currently assigned, and the next higher job hierarchically. Because of this, employees may become concerned only with themselves and the internal relationships around them. Traditional base pay may cause employees to focus only on vertical career growth and internal job and pay relationships, rather than on horizontal job and skill opportunities and helping the organization outperform external business competitors. This often encourages attempts to rise to supervision and management even when additional levels and layers are the last things the organization needs. Traditional base pay can cause employees to compete with each other for control of people and assets because this makes their jobs "bigger."

New pay requires employees to be concerned about what goes on around them and to focus on making the organization a success in terms of results achieved. Also, because new pay encourages the acquisition of skills and knowledge, horizontal growth is important, and employees are rewarded for preparing themselves to perform a wider range of duties and responsibilities that add value to the organization.

Rewards for Performance

With traditional pay, base pay increases according to merit-increase systems that theoretically grant the best performers larger increases than average performers and the average performers larger increases than marginal performers. However, statistical analyses of base pay increases and individual employee performance in nearly every organization show that little difference exists between the size of base pay increases granted to "average" performers versus the "best" performers.[2] Although a 2 percent difference in the size of pay increases for meets-expectations and excellent performers has major impact on employee total compensation and cost to the organization over time, as will be shown in chapter 9, this size difference is often viewed by employees as too little to make excellent performance financially worthwhile. New pay assumes that good performers tend to seek organizations where performance is recognized and rewarded. Mediocre employees are likely to prefer organizations where performance is less important.

New pay is geared toward employees who range from satisfactory through excellent in results achieved and who are willing to place some portion of their current or future pay at risk to share in the future financial fortunes of the organization. New pay is also for less than satisfactory performers by communicating the importance of performance improvements and by withholding rewards, encouraging either better performance, or—if better performance is not possible—the desire to seek employment where results are less important.

Attitudes Toward Organizational Performance

Traditional pay follows industry practice without concern for its impact on organizational results. Only when organizations are in financial trouble and unable to have competitive "merit budgets" does the performance of the organization receive consideration. New pay permits the organization to experiment with different approaches to pay management in search of a better way to reward demonstrated results that affect financial performance. If one possible solution does not generate expected results, others are tried until one does.

Traditional approaches permit direct and indirect pay costs to increase without concern for improvements in performance, quality, and productivity. Instead, only competitive practice and internal equity drive direct and indirect pay levels. New pay is concerned with the organization's ability to pay and with sharing success, and it associates increases in direct and indirect pay costs with organizational performance and productivity.

The New Pay Role of Base Pay

Where organizations are genuinely interested in improving human resource performance, base pay programs best accomplish the following goals:

- reflect changes in the economics of the labor markets in which the organization elects to compete for talent
- serve as the foundation for variable pay
- reflect either the economic, market, or strategic value of jobs (or the skills required to perform jobs)

These objectives reflect how new pay defines the role of base pay by limiting base pay to what it does better than variable pay and indirect pay.

Reflect Economics of the Labor Market

Base pay effectively represents the market value of jobs or skills and is well suited to be the center of job evaluation plans or skill-based pay plans. New pay provides that jobs or individuals with skills having a greater external market value receive higher base pay. The focus of new pay is on the external labor market more than internal equity. For organizations that are concerned with issues of internal equity, which cause job or skill value to differ from market value, managing base pay is critical because base pay leverages indirect pay costs. Organizations that are willing to pay two jobs or skills of different market values the same level of base pay must understand that all elements of total compensation are generally leveraged by this decision. The leveraging is always up rather than down, increasing the cost of doing business.

In the 1990s, the only organizations that can afford to focus on internal equity will be those that do not have to compete for business and hence can pass on to customers labor costs that are unrelated to improved quality, products or services, or productivity. Utilities and the government are two such examples. Recently, Southern California Gas Company completed a job evaluation study in which the telephone customer service representative job was determined to have equal internal value to the appliance service representative job that provided service at customer locations.[3] As would be predicted, the base pay for the telephone customer service representative increased to the level of the appliance service representative, thereby increasing labor costs. Southern California Gas's internal equity was not substantiated by the labor market, but since it does not compete for business or customers, it could pass along the additional labor cost of the customer service representatives. An example of the public's reaction: "date-rape of the rate-paying public by a regulated monopoly."[4]

Base pay appropriately provides employees with a standard of living based on the organization's interpretation of competitive practice and represents what the organization will pay to fill jobs or hire people with the proper skills. As certain jobs or skills become more or less expensive in the external market, base pay can respond to these changes and communicate this change to managers and employees. This is especially true if pay is not encumbered by strategies of internal equity that prevent organizations from responding to the realities of the external competitive market for jobs and skills.

Foundation for Variable Pay

Successful new pay programs gain employee acceptance. This entails base pay that is moderately competitive compared with the external market, taking into account total compensation opportunity in terms of both variable pay and indirect pay. In some cases, new pay designs set base pay below competitive practice but provide significant variable pay opportunities. It also means that the recognition of performance is left to variable pay. If base pay levels rise no higher than the average or median of competitive practice, the organization is well positioned to add variable pay for results achieved. Moderately competitive base pay, plus variable pay tied to the group's and/or organization's success and financial ability to pay, equals new pay. New pay costs and messages to employees vary as a result of changes in organizational achievement in economic terms.

Employees are paid base pay according to the labor market or the strategic value that their jobs and skills have to the organization. Variable pay is used to measure individual, team, business unit, and/or organizational performance results that change from performance period to performance period. This is because variable pay is "reusable" pay. Variable pay does not become an annuity to the employee based on a single year's performance.

Reflect Economic Value of Jobs or Skills

Base pay does a good job of reflecting the relationship between paying for the job and paying for the skills the person possesses. Traditional base pay focuses only on the value of the job. New pay can focus on either the value of the job or the worth of the individual in terms of skills demonstrated. One of the first things a new compensation professional learns, and subsequently spends a career trying to convince management of, is that it is important to separate the individual employee from the specific job when determining the value of a job. Tradition says differences among individuals will cause the organization to view jobs differently. For example, a high-performing employee may influence the value of a job, as might a poor-performing employee. Managers often respond that this is acceptable because employees influence job design, and these changes should be considered in the job evaluation process. However, under traditional pay, the need for uniformity generally prevails, and the manager is left with some other solution to get around the system and gain the recognition the employee needs in the evaluation process by placing the employee in some other job or describing the current job "creatively" to escalate its value. New pay permits the organization to value the skills the employee applies to perform the job.

Traditional pay uses base pay ranges that surround some combination of the internal and external value of a job. Employees performing the duties of the job are assigned to this base pay range. Individual differences such as variations in experience, ability to negotiate base pay during the hiring process, ability to perform the job, length of service, or other factors influence whether the employee is paid near the top, middle, or bottom of the base pay range. However, employees are always paid at least the minimum of the range.

New base pay intends to control the fixed cost of base pay so that the organization is not placed in a disadvantageous competitive position by having excessive fixed labor costs. It does this by causing the price of jobs and/or skills to increase only as a result of changes in the economics of the external labor market. New base pay is set at the market price for programmers, secretaries, and accountants (or the skills associated with these occupations). It does not try to establish a relationship between programmers and accountants, because they are not worth the same in the external market. Secondarily to the labor market, the organization may want to consider the strategic value of jobs or skills to the organization. Some jobs or skills may have more strategic value than other jobs or skills based on their impact on something that is critical to the organization. Strategic valuing may, for example, result in higher base pay (or lump-sum awards) for employees in jobs or having skills essential to the organization's focus on quality, market share, customer service, or some other priority. Subsequently, when some other strategic values such as profit margin, cost containment, or new product/service development become more important, other jobs or skills may be paid at a premium and return to pay at the market value when strategic directions again change.

Strategic value is driven by organizational priorities to succeed. This is in contrast to internal equity, which attempts to value jobs and/or skills based on some comparable element such as how complex the knowledge required to perform the job or skill is, how much effort must be expended to perform the job or skill, or the scope of responsibility associated with the job or skill. New pay leaves it to the external market to test the economic worth of these factors and uses the market as the base pay foundation.

Conclusions

New pay suggests that base pay should be reserved for the things it does best and not try to perform functions better performed by variable pay. Base pay does a good job of providing the economic foundation for new pay. In this role, base pay can accurately communicate the worth of jobs and skills.

Paying the Individual

The Role of Paying the Individual

Although most organizations have job evaluation systems, many find it difficult to separate the value of a job from the value of the employee in the job. These pressures cause organizations to focus either on the job and the employee or on the employee alone. Three pay strategies are influenced by the individual, although the impact differs:

- job families
- career ladders
- skill-based pay

The first of these is clearly in the traditional school of pay management. The second is a less traditional approach and may be a new pay solution, depending on its design. The third is a new pay approach.

Job Families

Jobs in one family are described in terms of several "sizes" of the same job. For example, an organization may have three levels of programming jobs, defined as programmer 1, 2 and 3, respectively. This is often established originally because the organization has three job levels, which can also be identified and surveyed in the external market. The job levels often describe several sizes of job responsibility within the family and include experience and educational requirements. Other job families exist throughout the professional, technical, clerical, and other nonexempt areas.

As organizations mature or as employees spend considerable time in a specific job family, more job family levels are often created to accommodate the experience and skills of employees. This may cause the organization to move, for example, from three up to five levels of programmers. This occurs either because the organization actually has five levels of computer programmers or because it needs more levels above its "real" programmer jobs to provide artificial career growth for employees who have many years of programming experience and no further career or base pay opportunities available to them within the organization. Although this practice is costly to the organization if the additional job family levels are not needed, it does begin to acknowledge the impact individual employees have on a job. However, unnecessary levels create hierarchical job families that do not provide added value to the organization.

Job.families are a characteristic of job-based evaluation systems and focus on the content of the job. However, transition from one job level to another is most often described in terms of years of experience, without concern for the type or nature of the experience. The difficulty with using only years of experience is that one employee may have more valuable experience than another employee. For example, one employee may have ten years of varied and increasingly pertinent experience, while another has ten years of duplicated experience. Semantics used to define differences in job accountability from one level to another commonly lack clarity. For example, the words *limited, considerable* and *major* are frequently used to describe differences in responsibility between job levels in a specific family. Job families often do not have true job performance or skill "hurdles" to cross before the employee is placed in a higher job level. In fact, often the placement in the job family is dictated more by the employee's current pay than by the employee's ability to provide skills and results of value to the organization.

Career Ladders

Career ladders are a series of defined steps within a specific area (e.g., programming, clerical, managerial, engineering) that define organizational requirements at each level, starting with the employee's entry into the career ladder. Well-prepared career ladders are combinations of individual-based and job-based pay systems that define routes of legitimate career growth for employees. However, progress is based on growth in responsibilities and demonstrated performance results. They are often used to define the route to success.

For example, a major commercial bank wanted to define career opportunities that communicated to professional employees a number of important objectives:

- Three parallel career ladders exist within the bank—credit management, business development, and supervision. All are of equal strategic and therefore financial value in terms of reward opportunities.
- Career growth is both a horizontal and vertical matter, and success in the organization does not require employees who were not suited for management to become managers to succeed.
- A career in credit management—a key to the success and economic health of a financial institution—is of equal value from the standpoint of base pay and status as business development and supervision, which were traditionally perceived as the preferred route to success.
- The requirements to move from one step to another are in terms of job responsibilities and results achieved. Tenure alone will not result in career growth.

The bank's career ladders included results that were expected at each level, such as the type and quality of sales calls and new clients generated (with consideration for the level of participation in making the sale), new business net profit growth, ability to improve or maintain the credit quality of the portfolio, ability to develop a quality action plan to address problem loans, level of retention of desired current client business, and the size and complexity of the portfolio managed. The result of the introduction of this career ladder into this bank was the following:

- Professionals understood what it took to progress in the organization. They understood the relationship among jobs, the skills needed to perform the jobs, and the performance results required.
- Credit management, a banking priority, was able to attract high-talent professionals. High credit quality was communicated as a strategic priority.
- The organization became "flatter" because supervision was not something professionals were forced into after performing a series of nonmanagement jobs. Those who were the best managers and

wanted to be managers became managers, and those who were best at managing credit and developing business and wanted to perform these functions were attracted to career ladders that placed them where they were most valuable to the organization.

Career ladders allow the organization to reduce the number of individualized, specific jobs that have basically the same types of duties. Fewer jobs and levels simplify pay programs and make them more understandable and easier to administer.

Career ladders have an advantage over job families because they do more than merely provide more jobs in which to place employees. Rather, they define how the organization can form a partnership with employees, so employees clearly understand what the organization expects and what is in it for them when they provide the expected results. Career ladders reward skill acquisition. Career ladders are most useful if the following principles are followed:

- Career ladders should define the route employees follow to become more valuable to the organization in terms of skills, abilities, and expected results, and should communicate the economic rewards and career satisfaction opportunities available.
- Successful career ladders are reviewed annually so that they can change to match the needs of the organization. As in the bank example, they have a goal. The bank's goal was to make credit management as important as business development and to make management one of three possible career tracks, not the sole end result of excellent professional performance.
- Career ladder growth is based on the successful performance of defined requirements and demonstrated results. It is not based only on tenure or experience. For example, in nursing, career ladders are called "clinical ladders." These are often based only on the acquisition of additional experience and tenure with the hospital rather than on the demonstration of added skills. New pay career ladders have specific, measurable, and observable performance hurdles to cross to demonstrate growth and are not the result of merely taking additional educational courses or gaining added years of experience.

If the career ladder is administered loosely or does not have sufficiently well-defined performance hurdles, the organization may need to set a requirement of organizational need for a level to be filled before an employee can be promoted to that level in the career ladder. For example, a utility implemented an engineering career ladder program. Although the criteria involved a combination of skills, demonstrated performance, and years of experience, the organization had a long history of promoting based primarily on years of experience. As a safeguard, promotion in the career ladder to the project-engineering level, for example, required that the organization have a business need for an additional project engineer.

Career ladders differ from skill-based pay in that the focus is on the value of the job, the skills of the employee, and the performance results generated by the employee, rather than only upon the employee's skills (although skills are clearly introduced and used to define growth requirements). Career ladders tend to focus on an increasing depth of skills in one area, while skill-based pay may focus on any combination of depth of skills, horizontal skills, and upward and downward vertical skills. While attempts are made to control access to higher levels, career ladders seldom involve testing to demonstrate skills and have no periodic refresher courses or periodic retesting of employees on a specific career step to ensure that they are still performing at the same level of ability. Career ladders do not verify that all employees at the same level are similarly skilled; skill-based pay programs ensure that comparably paid employees have comparable skill levels. In addition, career ladders require the use of job grades or bands, which are not a feature of skill-based pay.

Skill-Based Pay

Skill-based pay recognizes employees for the depth, breadth, and types of skills they obtain and apply in their work. Pay is determined by the skills of the employee rather than the job to which the employee is assigned.[1]

The foundation of skill-based pay (or "pay for knowledge") is paying more as employees demonstrate that they are obtaining and using more and more skills that are valuable to the organization. Most skill-based pay organizations are organized into work teams or self-managing work groups.

The centerpiece of skill-based pay is flexibility to allow the performance of a wider range of tasks and demonstrate a wider range of skills than is possible in a pay program that focuses only on the duties and responsibilities of the job. Organizations that are experimenting with and using skill-based pay believe these programs encourage employees to grow in value by providing the motivation to become more flexible, highly skilled workers. While job-based pay assumes the employee is qualified when assigned to the job, skill-based pay does not pay unless the skill is obtained and sometimes only when it is specifically utilized by the organization and performed by the employee.

Who Uses Skill-Based Pay?

Skill-based pay seems to work best where the blocks of skills needed to accomplish the goals and objectives of a specific organization can be readily identified, defined, and communicated. Skill-based pay has been used in new manufacturing operations contained within a single physical facility. This is most likely because the organization has no habits to overcome that are negative to skill-based pay. Similarly, new employees are more receptive to new approaches because they also are not used to another system. A single facility is important because communication is easier when the entire operation is visible to the people involved in the skill-based experience.

However, organizations such as General Motors, General Mills, and Northern Telecom have installed skill-based pay programs in existing organizations with success. The existence of unions appears not to hinder the success of skill-based pay. Skill-based pay is frequently found in continuous-process manufacturing settings where employee performance is highly interrelated. It is also being implemented in service organizations—for example, insurance companies, retailers, and banks.

Most skill-based pay systems are used in facilities organized around egalitarian principles, such as an all-salaried work force and the absence of class-oriented symbols such as time clocks. Skill-based pay programs are products of a high-involvement working environment because they require more employee participation in the pay system than is possible in job-focused base pay programs. The team leader, rather than the first-line supervisor, is often associated with the team concept and skill-based pay. Leaders are often chosen by team members and may be paid at a higher rate than their earned skill-based pay level while filling this role.[2] Skill-based pay programs are also found with gainsharing plans, a variable pay plan based on group performance and discussed in chapter 11. The skill-based pay program rewards individuals for skill acquisition; the gainsharing plan rewards groups of employees for performance results.

Organizations use skill-based pay to organize and manage work better. This often involves addressing such factors as the importance of meaningful work, control over the work process, performance feedback, and the use of a broad range of skills.[3] Also, skill-based pay enables work to be organized around products rather than by the traditional methodology of functions.

Ledford[4] indicates that satisfaction with pay and a preference for skill-based pay are possible outcomes of a proper skill-based pay installation. Among the factors that seem to contribute to a successful installation are (1) employee involvement in the design, administration, and monitoring of skill-based pay; (2) employee perceptions that skill-based pay is fair compared to what others outside and inside the organization receive for comparably skilled performance; (3) fair and understandable management of the skill-based pay program; and (4) adequate opportunities for training and rotation. Involvement reduces employee skepticism concerning a move to skill-based pay and combats employees viewing "speed-up" (working faster) as the reason for the change. Skill-based pay argues that management concepts should be based on a combination of both human and economic success where both are pursued. This is the concept of the employee–organization partnership. Organizations consider skill-based pay systems to improve effectiveness not only by paying for skills but also because employees prefer these systems to job-based pay systems.

The Service Sector as a Frontier

With job growth focused in the service sector and with the need for higher-tech jobs in the service sector, skill-based pay will play an important role in service organizations that may surpass its role in manufacturing organizations. The service sector needs to provide opportunities to hire unskilled or semiskilled people and turn them into highly skilled employees. Skill-based pay systems are the only approaches to base pay that can be combined with training to ensure that skills are learned and applied in the interests of both the organization and the employee.

Service sector organizations often tend to follow the army model of organization—someone is the general, and others follow along as corporals and privates. Many have seen service organizations with legions of paper processors and a supervisor sitting at the "lead desk" running the show. Skill-based pay offers the opportunity for employees to learn a wide range of skills and permits them variation in what they do from day to day. Also, skill-based pay can be arranged such that many career paths in addition to supervision are financially attractive as alternatives to the formation of a bureaucratic structure.

Skill Identification, Training, and Acquisition

Skills are generally selected through employee involvement in skills identification and a skills audit by a team of individuals who are experts in identifying required skills. The challenge is to select from the skills the employees have those skills that are needed to perform the required work. This means that not all existing employee skills may be necessary. It also means that skills the employees do not have may be needed to get the work done. Not only must specific skills be described, but if a skill exists in varying levels of complexity and application, these levels must be clearly differentiated.

The result is a list of all needed skills in the area in which skill-based pay will be utilized, regardless of where these skills are currently employed among the employees in the organization. The area in which skill-based pay is used depends on the business goals of the organization and how the work is organized. For example, if the area to use skill-based pay is an assembly line, all assembly skills are identified. If the area is a manufacturing unit, maintenance, machining, and materials-handling skills, as well as assembly skills, are identified. For an insurance customer service area, status changes, program explanation and interpretation, and claims-processing skills for the variety of different types of claims are identified.

Like career ladders, skill-based pay may involve depth of skills in one area of specialization. It may also involve breadth of skills that are upstream, downstream, or parallel in relation to the employee's original job. In addition, skill-based pay may involve self-management in terms of scheduling, leading, problem solving, or coordination with other areas.

The skills are arranged in skill blocks based on how they will be performed by employees. Skills may be combined based on technical depth—as, for example, with telecommunications field technicians and field engineers. Alternatively, skills may be combined logically based on the work performed, with each skill block being of equal or varying complexity. The skill blocks may have levels within them. Although only limited research concerning skill designs has been conducted, Gupta[5] found that the perceived effectiveness of skill-based pay programs was related only to the number of skill blocks. The larger the number of skill blocks, the less the perceived effectiveness of the program. This might be due to a large number of skill blocks either making a program more difficult for employees to understand or lessening the worth of each skill block.

It is important to decide how employees will acquire skills. Organizations moving to skill-based pay often fail to understand that they are making an implied promise to provide the means for employees to acquire the skills needed to increase their value to the organization. Because of this, most organizations appropriately determine the extent to which they will assume responsibility for providing skill-acquisition opportunities.

The wise organization does not make promises about training or how quickly employees will reach the top skill level. This does not mean that the organization will not provide training—skills acquisition is the basis of skill-based pay. However, the organization may find it cannot provide the training as rapidly as originally thought. During training, productivity is reduced because of training time and also because employees are less proficient and less productive while learning skills on-the-job. Some organizations tell employees that training opportunities will depend on the organization maintaining a certain level of productivity or performance. Also, employees may not move as quickly through the skill blocks as originally thought because, for example, rotational blockages (due to one skill block requiring performance by only a few employees) take a long time to provide the opportunity for all interested employees to train at that skill block.

Other design issues include whether skill blocks are sequenced—that is, whether one skill block needs to be learned and performed before the next skill block. Sequencing depends on the nature of the work and how it is performed. The length of time employees stay in any one skill block is based on how long it takes to learn the skill and how long the organization requires proficient performance to receive a return on the training investment while ensuring that employees feel they have had the opportunity to learn all the skill blocks they want during a reasonable time period (and thereby have reasonable pay opportunities). Skills change over time, so skill-based pay programs are designed to be flexible in order to stay current and relevant. Employees who need to acquire new skills to replace skills that are obsolete or no longer relevant are typically given a period of time during which their pay is "red circled" (i.e., their base pay is maintained at its current level even though they no longer meet the criteria to deserve that level of base pay).

Employees are assessed or certified to ensure that they have a skill before being paid for that skill. The assessment involves actual work performance and may involve an oral or written examination of knowledge in such areas as emergency safety. Most programs provide that supervisors assess whether employees have acquired and retained the needed skills. In a few high-involvement organizations, peers determine whether fellow employees possess skills. As a safeguard, some of these organizations have a policy that if an employee assesses and certifies another employee who does not truly possess the certified skill block, the base pay of both employees is adversely affected.

Retention of skills is ensured either by periodically reassessing employees or by having employees rotate through previously mastered skills. This is necessary so that the organization is certain it is getting the skills and knowledge for which it is paying.

The assessment process reflects the actual skills performed. Often, organizations have little technology geared toward assessing employees to determine levels of skill acquisition or whether skills are being retained at a high level of capability. This means the technology must be developed or acquired to ensure assessments are credibly performed.

Pricing the Skills

Most skill-based pay programs pay for the ability to demonstrate performance of skills. An employee's base pay is determined by the number and complexity of skill blocks that he or she is able to perform, and does not vary based on actual usage of the skills. Sometimes level of skill performance is combined with number of skill blocks demonstrated to determine an employee's base pay.

Organizations are skilled at pricing jobs. In contrast, pricing skills is a challenge because it is not yet possible to exchange pricing information on individual skills or blocks of skills. However, it is essential that an organization establish a viable relationship between a skill-based pay program and the external market. This is true for the same reasons that pricing jobs is important.

There are several ways to establish the market value of skills in a skill-based pay program: (1) arbitrary skill pricing; (2) assembling skill blocks into "jobs" and comparing these to job pricing systems; (3) pricing skill blocks and adding "economic value"; and (4) internal valuing at the expense of market value. All result in determining the monetary value of a skill-based pay system, and none are as direct as the traditional job pricing system.

Sometimes skills are arbitrarily assigned a dollar value without concern for the external market. This often occurs during experimentation when a design task force is strongly focused on developing the skill-based pay program and views the external market as an afterthought. Not only is it likely that these programs will prove not to be good tests of skill-based pay because of market disorientation, but when the arbitrary values are added up, the sum of the skills is often more expensive to the organization than a market-priced job structure would have been. This approach may make skill-based pay impractical and economically vulnerable in some circumstances.

Skill blocks may be assembled to form "jobs" that can subsequently be priced in the external market. Skill blocks can be assembled to compare these combinations of skills or skill blocks with jobs with like skills that represent the entire spectrum of the pricing range. For example, "jobs" made of skill blocks may be formed at the entry, middle, and highest levels of skill block combinations. The highest and lowest combinations of skills can be priced externally and the skill levels in between estimated, or several points from low to high can be selected and priced accordingly. Until organizations are better able to price individual skills and skill blocks, the preferred way to proceed is by translating skill-based pay systems into job-based pay systems for pricing purposes.

Although skills cannot be individually priced in the external competitive labor market, they can be valued in the market to the extent that skill blocks are combined to form simulated jobs and compared with similar jobs in other organizations. This means that rather than being compared in terms of duties and responsibilities required, jobs are defined in terms of the skills necessary to perform the job. The skill-level definitions can be combined to describe a job that can be priced by means of an external survey. This process changes how survey data are exchanged but provides a technology that organizations can use to determine the external market value of skills.

Organizations concerned about paying for value received consider both the external market and the economic value of skills in determining how skill-based pay programs are priced. For example, some skill combinations are of high economic value to a continuous manufacturing process because a single employee with these skills is able to restart the process in the event of a malfunction. Three skills of moderate market value that can get a line restarted may be more economically valuable than three skills of high market value that cannot do this. When designed properly, organizations are able to receive an adequate return from skill-based pay and are also able to communicate to employees the economic value of the skills.

The organization can elect to value skills internally, just as it can in the internal valuing of jobs. For example, a skill with high market worth may be valued as highly as a skill with a lower external market value. The problem with this is similar to the problem of an internally focused job evaluation plan—going counter to the market tends to pay too little for skills with a high market value and too much for skills with low market value. Clearly, the preferred strategy is to value skills based on the market in order to pay what other organizations pay for the skills needed to make the organization run, unless the organization can demonstrate the financial gain from altering the skill-based pay program from actual market value.

As skill-based pay is combined with a market-based view of job valuing, pricing skills will become more important. Certain skills have higher market value alone or in combination with other skills than do others. Specific sets of skills can be combined into jobs and assigned a market value. Progress between jobs, based on the acquisition of skills, can be related to market value.

When skill-based pay is implemented in an existing organization, often some employees are receiving higher base pay than their skills warrant. Typically these employees have their base pay frozen until they demonstrate more skills. The labor market tends to increase so that skill-block pay levels will increase over time, and eventually the skill level of these employees will catch up to their base pay regardless of their skills acquisition. Alternatively, the base pay of these employees may be reduced over time if they do not demonstrate more skills.

Some organizations are concerned that base pay will become too high in a skill-based pay program relative to return in terms of organizational performance. Modeling the cost and the expected results of skill-based pay is advised. Modeling involves determining what the employees' current skill levels are, how long it will take for all employees to reach the top pay level (assuming they all want to acquire the skills necessary to be paid at this level), and what the expected gain to the organization is. What greater productivity can the organization expect because the work force is more flexible? Will staffing levels decrease for the same level of product produced or service provided? Will staffing levels be the same for a higher level of production or service? Modeling increases understanding of the pay–gain relationship and may also contribute to setting the top pay level. Although there may be variability based on the type of employee population, generally not all employees want to progress to the top skills-acquisition level. The same modeling can be done on expected skills acquisition and at different times after program introduction (e.g., after six months, one year, two years, or three years). From this modeling, program expectations and milestones can be set to help evaluate the success of the program.

In most skill-based pay programs, an employee's pay level is based on being able to demonstrate skills and does not depend on actual skill usage. In contrast, some programs pay only when additional skills are performed. For example, a multiskill pay program pays craftspeople additional money on the days when they perform skills outside their primary craft. On days when an air-conditioning mechanic performs an air-conditioning repair job at a location and also does the additional electrical work, avoiding the cost of a second craftsperson traveling to and coordinating work at the location, the air-conditioning mechanic receives extra pay for crossing craft lines. In this multiskill example, the organization can easily calculate the labor hours and cost saved by having a multiskilled craftsperson perform both jobs and can share this cost savings with the employee. Here, financial gain or economic value can be demonstrated, and the organization can determine its return from the investment in skill-based pay. As an aside, this approach is the opposite of a master-craft approach that pays additionally for craft specialization. The way work is performed in the organization determines which type of base pay program is most appropriate.

Other approaches are also possible. For example, a lump-sum award can be granted for learning and retaining a skill; the level of performance in applying the skill—producing results and performing well—brings the employee additional base pay.

Another approach is to develop pay rates based on the labor market, with an entry base pay rate and a second rate that employees receive after acquiring the skills in a key skill block or for demonstrating satisfactory performance in core skills. Each additional certification and recertification on a skill block provides a lump-sum award, and some form of group variable pay rewards group performance. This latter approach can be used with jobs with a very narrow range of base pay rates in the labor market—for example, registered nurses. There is flexibility in design, and the organization needs to think through at least its direct pay strategy for an employee group before embarking on skill-based pay.

Variable pay can be used in the event the program provides for pay when employees are prepared to perform the skills and no opening is available. For example, a lump-sum award can be given for skill acquisition when the chance to employ the skills does not exist, and additional lump-sum awards can be granted for keeping skills current while this situation persists. Also, opportunities in other portions of the organization can be explored to determine whether lateral transfers are possible to keep employee attention and skill usage fresh.

Professional Applications

Professional employees require a pay program that provides rewards not only for learning and using necessary skill blocks but also for keeping skills current. Programmers, scientists, engineers, accountants, and others have professions that require skill acquisition and are compatible with skill-based pay. Job-based pay systems for professionals fail to provide a mechanism for encouraging professionals to remain contemporary in their specific area and to learn skills that will make them more valuable to the organization. Skill-based pay for professionals permits the organization to accomplish the following:

- Identify the skills the professional must learn and provide financial rewards for learning them.
- Clearly define a career path for the professional, based on skills and the demonstration of skills, that is independent of tenure. This will ensure that highly-paid professionals do not become technologically or professionally obsolete.
- Permit the organization to change directions and encourage new learning based on the organization's focus in a research area, product development area, financial analysis methodology, or other change that is worth the organization's money to encourage.

Skill-based pay in the professional area includes the requirements that the professional employs the skill successfully during job performance and that the skill is needed by the organization. Because of the nonrepetitive nature of professional jobs and the latitude given to professionals, skill-based pay might best be a lump-sum award, with results and productivity additionally measured and rewarded through another pay program. A lump-sum award ensures that skill performance is rewarded by means of variable pay and does not become a skill-based annuity to the employee.

Managerial Applications

Under job-based pay systems, on a given day professional, technical, or hourly employees are performing nonsupervisory tasks at a satisfactory level, and the next day they are supervisors. Once they are made supervisors, they are paid as such, without concern as to whether or not they have the basic supervisory skills to perform the job. After the fact, supervisory training programs are expected to train employees very quickly to perform their supervisory jobs. Often, after employees have been made supervisors, the organization finds they lack the aptitude for the job. This causes the organization either to keep people in supervisory jobs for which they lack skills or to demote them back to the job that they were performing at an excellent level before the promotion. This is a "lose–lose" situation for the employee and the organization.

Many basic skill blocks for supervisory and managerial jobs exist that can be organized into a skill-based pay program. Before promoting an excellent nonsupervisory employee to a supervisory or management job, it is advisable to evaluate whether the employee can actually learn and apply the skills necessary to be a supervisor or manager. Employees that can demonstrate and constructively apply supervisory skills will be more likely to perform as supervisors to the satisfaction of the organization, themselves, and the employees they are expected to supervise.

Much has been written about the rigid, bureaucratic, me-first, cover-your-tail management style and practices that exist in many organizations and how these must change in order for the United States to return to a role of productivity leadership. Changing culture, values, and practices is viewed as a difficult task. A transition to a more constructive management style can be accomplished if skill blocks are built around the principles and practices the organization wants to have as a norm and are introduced by means of management and supervisory skill-based pay. Managers and supervisors are paid for learning and applying the new skills and are not paid for continuing the practices and procedures the organization wishes to discourage.

Organizations have much to communicate to supervisors and managers. Experience proves that conventional training methods cannot ensure that the results of change are learned, implemented, and practiced at a high level. This is because change is not rewarded. Merit base pay increase systems lack the leverage and ability to cause supervisors and managers to adopt new ways of managing, and individual variable pay plans may not be a good foundation for moving supervisors and managers to accept the accountability for facilitating the formation of partnerships within the organization, encouraging shared values, or requiring subordinates to work as a team to earn rewards. However, paying for learning and applying these skills by means of skill-based pay is a way for the organization to ensure that the message is heard and accepted.

Skill-based pay in the managerial area permits organizations to define the skill blocks required for growth to a leadership position in the organization and to identify both vertical and horizontal career paths to organizational growth. It also places the organization's emphasis on paying for management skills that are needed to keep the organization on the right track. Also, skill-based pay ensures that supervisors and managers remain current on skills, because employees must continue to demonstrate the ability to perform and actually employ a skill to get paid for it.

Advantages of Skill-Based Pay

The value of skill-based pay is that organizations learn they can expend pay dollars consistent with the demonstrated ability of employees to enlarge their range of skills and to expand their opportunity to be of more value to the organization in exchange for base pay or variable pay dollars received. Skill-based pay offers employees the opportunity to earn financial rewards for demonstrating skills within their specific career field without being forced to compete internally for assets and people to add value. Encouraging learning is extremely important to organizational success and employee work satisfaction. Organizations that are unable to recognize growth in employee skills will have difficulty filling or creating high-skill jobs that will need to exist at all organizational levels in the future if U.S. organizations are to remain effective. Organizations that have made learning skills a part of their culture may have an easier time in the future, given the projected labor shortage and increased demand for workers with skills.

Skill-based pay is consistent with new pay because it is driven by the motivation of employees to grow and prosper. The onus is on the employee to take advantage of the organization's training and development opportunities. The organization provides the opportunity and training; if the employee does not learn the skills, tenure and complaining will not make up for the deficiency. Once the employee learns and employs the skills, rewards are available because the employee is more valuable to the organization and demonstrates the flexibility necessary to help the organization prosper.[6]

Skill-based pay encourages the proper values in organizations that are focused on performance improvement, better collaboration, and expenditure of dollars on human resource activities that are in the best interests of organizational success. Many employees are strongly attracted to a pay system that encourages learning new skills and provides the opportunity for variety in their work experiences. Although skill-based pay should not be oversold, it does offer organizations capabilities and features that are not otherwise available.[7]

INCREASES FLEXIBILITY. While job-focused base pay administration is constrained by the specific jobs that can be designed, this is not the case with skill-based pay. Jobs are necessarily driven by the structure of the organization, which can limit an organization's ability to move employees from job to job and also to recognize new skills when they become important. Skills are not dependent on organizational structure for their economic value.

Flexibility is important. Skill-based pay permits the organization to move employees from assignment to assignment with the understanding that employees can perform a wide range of tasks. Flexibility means the ability of the employee to perform a wide range of tasks of differing value without the influence of a tightly written job description that limits the opportunity to perform the tasks. Today's organizations need to be able to deploy people to accomplish whatever needs to be done. With labor costs a major business expense, organizations want to be able to use employees on several assignments when necessary. This means encourag ing employees to be prepared to perform a wide range of necessary activities.

ENCOURAGES SKILL ACQUISITION. When organizations are struggling to obtain people with above-minimal work skills, pay systems that reward learning are most likely to result in a work force that is dedicated to self-improvement. Job-focused systems do not always provide a clear learning track from one group of important skills to the acquisition of a set of more important skills.

As technology changes quickly and challenges become more complex, organizations will need to make it worthwhile for employees to learn and apply skills that they may not have had in less challenging work opportunities. This is more likely to occur with pay systems that reward learning than with pay systems that encourage performance of restrictive and inflexible job duties and responsibilities.

Change in direction is also difficult to operationalize with a job-based system, because job-based systems create jobs and then require employees to figure out how to get them. Skill-based systems can define learning paths for employees to follow. Employees learn the skills, earn the rewards, and perform the skills consistent with the realigned priorities of the organization.

When an organization is planning changes to how work is performed, a skill-based pay system that can be modified to reward the acquisition of more useful and needed skills can be important to a smooth transition. Change is difficult in a system where jobs are threatened and where the future may be less secure than the past. Rewarding a response to change by acquiring new skills can make change and the future more acceptable and the transition easier.

IMPROVES CUSTOMER SERVICE. Often service organizations such as insurance companies or financial institutions develop specialists who are only able to deal with customers on one issue, not the variety of issues that a customer may have. Skill-based pay prepares employees to handle a wider range of customer issues without switching the customer from place to place. This is more efficient for the organization and the customer.

ADDRESSES MORE COMPLEX PROBLEM SOLVING. Employees who are focused only on the performance of single tasks and jobs are often unprepared to solve problems that are beyond the direct relationship between what they are doing and what the few other workers they know in their specific area are doing. Employees having the ability to perform several skills are in a position to see the complete operation and to make suggestions concerning improvement and changes that are beyond the narrow job duties common to most organizations.

Is the Value Worth the Cost?

The downside of skill-based pay is primarily the cost of the program—pay costs, administrative costs, and training costs. Formal research demonstrating that organizations get direct financial gain from skill-based pay does not exist. However, if the organization can manage the costs wisely and can demonstrate measurable organizational gain for the cost expended, the program is worthwhile. Organizations can calculate the increase in labor, administrative, and training costs due to skill-based pay and compare that total cost with performance measures such as staffing levels, productivity, employee turnover, and absenteeism to determine if skill-based pay is paying for itself. The return on investment may not occur for a period of time, but the organization concerned about value received can decide when a return is expected.

New pay is dominated by the need for an organizational return on investment in new pay alternatives. This means focusing the program on avenues that lead to economic gain and providing a calendar of expectations that will show how and when the benefits of the changes will be enjoyed.

INCREASED PAY COSTS. Because the objective of skill-based pay is to pay more to individuals as skills are acquired, as skill-based pay works, labor costs per employee increase. Unless the acquisition of the encouraged skills is related to the productivity and financial performance of the organization, it is probable that skill-based pay will result in increased pay costs and the development of at least some employee skills that are unnecessary to organizational success. Because the requirement is on employees to gain added skills, it is likely that in the future organizations with mature skill-based pay programs will attract employees who are willing to put a portion of their current and future pay at risk contingent upon their demonstrated ability to learn new skills. Skill-based pay places a premium on the willingness to be flexible, and as flexibility is demonstrated, pay costs per person increase. Employee benefit costs may also increase under skill-based pay due to lower turnover and more long-service employees. These labor cost increases need to be defrayed through increased productivity (e.g., increased volume of products created or service provided or fewer employees for the same volume).

While job-related pay is controlled by changes in competitive practice or changes in the cost of living or is affected by some sort of merit evaluation, skill-based pay can operate independently of these variables. If an organization uses skill-based pay in a specific manufacturing or service operation and pays more for skill acquisition, this pay needs to be reconciled with issues of economic change, labor market changes, and individual merit. With all these forces operating on the pay of one group of employees, without regard for organizational effectiveness, costs can climb.

The prime question of concern is, what are the goals of skill-based pay? Organizations that move to skill-based pay are well advised to do so for strategic reasons that have to do with organizational and employee effectiveness. Acknowledging that the organization will incur added labor costs per employee is a first strategic step. Understanding this, the potential user organization is concerned with structuring skill-based pay to focus employees on learning skills that result in improved productivity and effectiveness. Financial results are to be expected from skill-based pay in exchange for increased labor costs; skill-based pay requires an investment that should return financial and quality value to the organization. This is consistent with the employee–organization partnership initiative.

ADMINISTRATIVE COSTS. Keeping track of skill development of individual plan participants in a large organization can be costly. Employees obtain skills at different rates, and assessment and the administrative rules and regulations involved in skill-based pay add to administrative complexity. Skill-based pay programs that are installed without corresponding computer-based administrative systems cannot be sustained in an economical manner. Because skill-based pay programs change and evolve, it is necessary to have computer support that can help administer these as efficiently as possible.

Organizations find that some costs may increase (e.g., meeting time, skill assessment time, or pay administration time) while other costs may decrease (e.g., the cost of hiring, due to lower turnover and better hiring practices; or costs related to absenteeism). As in the case of labor costs, administrative costs are necessarily recovered as part of installing skill-based pay.

LARGE INVESTMENT IN TRAINING, RETRAINING, AND KEEPING CURRENT. Much has been written about the importance of training and development in organizations. The pending need for added education and training was emphasized in chapter 1. If organizations are to fill their needs for quality people in times when the tasks and skills to be learned are becoming more complex and the capabilities of people to perform them are not keeping up, training is essential. Assume that an organization is unable to find enough employees with the minimal skills at the entry level and has an objective to pay for learning and demonstrating additional skills and abilities in a skill-based pay program. The organization needs to be willing to invest in major training and retraining programs to prepare people for the program and subsequently to keep them productive and current.

The training expense involves getting employees to a reasonable level of skill performance initially and then implementing a workable program that provides the opportunity to keep skills current and to add skills when they are needed to operate effectively. Organizations implementing skill-based pay programs must implement parallel training programs. Without incurring the cost of training and development, it is not possible to sustain skill-based pay. However, if predictions of pending labor shortages are realized, organizations will need to implement major training programs whether or not they elect to adopt pay programs that are geared to skills acquisition.

Already, major organizations such as IBM, Kodak, and Xerox allocate large portions of their human resource expenditures to training and development. It is probable that while training may be needed for specific skill-based pay programs, organizations may eventually need to allocate major expenditures just to keep jobs filled at the needed level of technology.

RESISTANCE TO CHANGE. Skill-based pay is a change from tradition. For example, some managers and supervisors may not be needed as subordinates' skills are developed. Also, some staff functions become less important (and some jobs may not be needed) as the way work is performed changes. These cost reductions can help offset some of the added skill-based pay costs. Employees in high-skill jobs are threatened by skill-based pay and may resist the general learning of skills. Union prerogatives are threatened in the event that the union does not play an active role in the program. Skill-based pay is a major change in how people are paid and deserves careful attention; addressing resistance to change is costly and time-consuming. Employee involvement is essential to gaining acceptance of change.

Perhaps change to employee involvement can start by first using work-unit teams where the managers and supervisors provide the team with the information it needs, lead team conferences and meetings, and coach the problem-solving process. Later, as trust is established, self-managed teams may evolve where employees elect a team leader rather than use supervisors or managers in this role. It is likely that a transition from a supervisor-dominated workplace to one where employees are responsible for results achieved is a lengthy, incremental learning process.[8]

What the Future May Hold for Skill-Based Pay

Organizations that use skill-based pay are generally satisfied. They focus on factors such as greater employee satisfaction, increased work-force flexibility, reduced turnover rates, reduced absenteeism, improved product quality and quantity, and leaner staffing as the reasons for their satisfaction. They also warn that locations should have the proper work processes, attitudes, cultures, and strategies for implementation, administration, and communication.[9] Several important issues may interact to make skill-based pay more important in the future. First, organizations may eventually tire of the bureaucracy and hierarchy created by internally focused, job-based evaluation methodologies. Second, market-based, computer-assisted job evaluation programs are beginning to provide the basis for pricing the components, including skills, that comprise jobs of low and high complexity. Third, skills development is necessary for U.S. organizations to compete effectively. Making the attainment of these skills worthwhile from a financial perspective makes practical sense and may also make addressing the problems that skill-based pay may present worth the time and effort.

The future may show a movement of skill-based pay into service organizations and high-value skill areas. For example, hospitals are experiencing a great shortage of nursing professionals. Nursing skills are a natural for skill-based pay since this type of pay system can pay most for skills in the shortest supply and reward the acquisition of additional skills. This concept applies to many high-value skills that are difficult to attain. For instance, scarce engineering skills can be made financially attractive by means of skill-based pay. The organization can focus strongly on what it needs the most by paying most for the acquisition of skills that are in shortest supply and that are the most difficult to attain.

The challenge in skill-based pay for professional jobs is defining the many skills involved in complex jobs—such as engineers, scientists, analysts, attorneys, and accountants—and determining when they are being performed. Skill requirements vary from day to day and involve a wide range of complex and less than complex skills. It is likely that experimentation will move into more complex service areas, especially those involving professional careers where keeping current in the field is critical.

It is more difficult to consider skill-based pay for supervisors and managers. However, skill-based pay may be even more valuable here than it is for professional and manufacturing employees. This is because organizations can identify needed management skills and pay for them only when they are learned and applied. It is difficult to provide training on some managerial skills—judgment, wisdom, decisiveness, and avoiding major errors; however, many can be learned through training (e.g., planning, organizing, and human resource development). Skill-based pay may go a long way toward providing organizations with a means to ensure that employees have the skills to manage and supervise before they are assigned this responsibility.

If organizations can combine both skill- and job-based pay in one system for determining base pay levels, the concept will become credible for wider applications. This is because skill-based systems can be used where appropriate and job-based systems can be used elsewhere.

The future of skill-based pay will be secured when organizations can demonstrate a return on the pay, administrative, and training investment required. When organizations are able to determine in financial terms the value they are receiving for the added cost, it is more likely that skill-based pay will be accepted widely.

Conclusions

Paying the individual rather than the job offers organizations the opportunity to focus more closely on the skill development that will be required to improve organizational effectiveness during times of short supply of high-skill employees and increased need for employee flexibility. It is likely that the future includes a strong role for alternatives that are better aligned with the need to make employees and organizations partners in the organization's success.

Programs such as skill-based pay are not without their challenges. Organizations need to introduce measurable change in their relationships with employees to gain acceptance of new programs. Additionally, the role of supervision, management, and training needs to be revised significantly to make skill-based pay workable. Also, there must be something in it for the organization to change the basis of paying people. This means organizations must focus strongly on economic considerations when evaluating skill-based pay programs.

Evaluating Jobs

The Role of Job Valuing

Organizations evaluate jobs, whether or not they have a formal job evaluation methodology. Even an approach that states "we pay what it takes" is a job evaluation (or individual employee evaluation) approach. The question is not whether jobs will be evaluated; they will. The only issue is whether a formal job evaluation methodology will be employed. Job evaluation provides a process for determining the level or range of base pay that an organization should pay for a job. It is necessary for an organization of any size to have a formal or informal approach to evaluating jobs, unless they are able to evolve to an approach that evaluates people as individuals (as discussed in the last chapter).

Unless organizations have some way to monitor and manage human resource expenditures in the form of base pay, they often cannot compete effectively. Base pay costs, which leverage benefit costs, will become excessive and make organizations financially noncompetitive. Because of this, some formal way to manage base pay in moderate- to large-sized organizations is generally required.

Overview of Traditional Job Evaluation

The concept of evaluating jobs, starting with preparing detailed job descriptions, performing job analysis to determine the elements that comprise each job and job family, identifying the compensable job elements, establishing the internal relationship between jobs, and attempting to relate all of this to the external market, is well established in base pay administration lore. Communicating this to employees as a rational process and subsequently managing it practically are challenges facing all compensation professionals and managers in organizations committed to conventional job evaluation techniques.

Although many approaches exist, traditional job evaluation, typified by the point-factor methodologies in use since the 1940s, compares jobs on an internal basis. This internal result is subsequently interpreted in the external labor market. Internal equity of all jobs across the organization is primary; the labor market is secondary. Traditional job evaluation factors used to compare jobs involve skill, effort, responsibility, and working conditions and communicate the values of hierarchy and bureaucracy. They award more points for becoming managers of people or assets and stress vertical rather than horizontal growth. The focus of the organization with a traditional point-factor approach is internal.[1] Employees compete with each other for more points rather than think about how to position the organization to compete externally more effectively with fewer people and less assets.

Overview of New Pay Approach to Job Evaluation

The new pay approach starts with the external labor market and does not try to create total internal equity across the organization. Rather, it establishes internal equity within broad job functions (e.g., information systems, human resources, marketing, manufacturing, finance). It pays the labor market for these job functions and then develops internal equity for jobs within a job function. It does not try to compare or create internal equity across job functions such as comparing accounting jobs and engineering jobs. The elements that create job value are the market value of the functional area of the job and the key skills required. The focus of a new pay approach to job evaluation is external rather than internal; the organization determines a competitive labor market rate for all jobs and may modify this subsequently if a job has significant strategic impact on the organization. The organization pays moderately competitive base pay and spends any additional dollars on variable pay to reward performance rather than wasting valuable pay dollars on internal equity that is not founded in the marketplace or based on the organization's business strategy.

Job-Based Evaluation Plans

Formal job evaluation plans provide the opportunity to apply a uniform approach to the management of base pay. This means jobs of the same value in all portions of the organization will be treated similarly. This makes transfer and promotion manageable and lets base pay be administered from a centralized location with uniform judgments applied no matter how complex or widespread the organization may be.

If the organization is composed of large, diversified, or complex businesses, it can use the same job evaluation plan but modify the competitive labor market by business line. For example, if a financial institution adds an investment banking organization, the labor market for the investment banking organization is different and higher than that of the rest of the bank. A wise allocation of base pay dollars will pay support staff (e.g., secretaries) in the investment banking organization at a comparable level with the rest of the institution and pay only the investment bankers according the investment banking labor market.

If the organization has a core business but has diversified into different types of industries where higher base pay levels of the core business cannot be supported, the division itself may suggest that the centralized base pay structure is unaffordable and no longer meets the division's purpose. Large organizations need to be flexible in allowing pay in suborganizations to be at a similar competitive position (e.g., 50th percentile) but reflect the labor market of the industry in which they compete for business and talent.

Job evaluation plans are powerful communicators of rules and regulations concerning how the organization will be governed and the role employees will play in making the organization a success. Pay causes the organization to communicate concerning what sort of behaviors and results will cause pay to be distributed and what will cause pay to be withheld. For example, if the organization wants employees to seek management jobs, management jobs will be evaluated higher than will professional jobs that could be viewed as being equally important. Or, if length of job experience is more highly valued than the ability to create new ideas, the job evaluation program can communicate this value.

In the last few years, job evaluation has been computerized for internal use by organizations. Computerization has not changed the principles of traditional point-factor plans; it has only automated them. Computerization is useful, however, in that it enables the organization to estimate the costs of different pay models before implementation. It also provides managers with data on the pay of employees in their organizational unit so that they can more effectively manage a significant cost of doing business. Since base pay is the largest pay cost, it is critical for managers to have base pay information such as actual pay compared to base pay structure, base pay increases compared to budget, and promotional increases, as well as position control information, to manage their human resource assets effectively.[2]

Traditional Point-Factor Job Evaluation

Point-factor job evaluation is the most popular method of job valuing in large organizations. It involves developing a rating scale for each factor and applying these factors to evaluate jobs. The sum of the scores on each factor for a job results in the job's total score. This score is used to place the job in a hierarchy with the other jobs in the organization. Point systems provide the stability of point scales, and accuracy and consistency in rating increase with rater familiarity and job knowledge.

The traditional point-factor method most often involves first selecting the compensable factors to be used to determine the value of the jobs. This generally includes factors that define the skill, effort, responsibility, and working conditions the organization is willing to pay for where they exist throughout the organization. Subsequently, various levels of each compensable factor are defined to attempt to include the complete range of possible jobs that will be evaluated by the factor. Jobs are then evaluated, and the point value of each job is determined. Jobs with the most points are determined to be the most valuable, and those with the least points are of less value.

Points are converted into the market value of jobs by fitting the results of the internal evaluation of jobs to the market value of jobs. This is accomplished by placing all jobs in a given range of points into a specific base pay range. For example, jobs with 400 to 499 points are placed in one base pay range, and jobs with between 500 and 599 points are placed in another range. The major challenge arises when jobs of both high and low point value have the same market value, or when jobs of high and low market value have the same point value. The most likely result is to pay some jobs less than their market value and others more than their market value. This makes little sense in times when labor costs are major challenges to organizational success.

Job Evaluation Factors

The compensable factors used to determine the internal value of jobs communicate to executives, managers, and employees what characteristics of jobs within the organization place a job at a higher level in the organizational hierarchy. In this sense, job evaluation factors communicate the values of the organization concerning what makes jobs more or less important. For example, job evaluation factors can communicate that the degree of cleanliness or dirt in the workplace is important to setting job values. Job evaluation factors can also communicate that customer relations accountability is more important than accountability for internal relationships with fellow employees.

Most large organizations use different job evaluation factors and plans for broad groups of jobs (e.g., hourly jobs, nonexempt jobs, exempt jobs) to permit these major groupings to move more closely with changes in competitive practice. However, few organizations attempt to match the job evaluation factors with the message they intend to present to their employees about what determines job value. Instead, organizations communicate the values that are made available to them in whatever job evaluation plan they have in effect. This is probably because of the use of many "ready-made" plans with standard factors that offer little or no opportunity to match the specific needs of the organization.

The use of compensable factors such as the number of people supervised encourages people who are interested in managing assets and people rather than those who are interested in managing ideas and concepts. Point-factor plans based on internal equity encourage the accumulation of larger organizations in terms of people and assets, as well as competition with others within the organization for command of organizational units. Because most point-factor plans focus strongly on internal job relationships, employees see the route to success as building a large organization under their control, rather than working to gain the maximum results desired with the minimum possible people and effective deployment of assets. This does not seem appropriate during times of increased competition for business.[3]

Although lists of factors used in traditional point-factor plans are extensive, they generally can be reduced to skill, effort, responsibility, and willingness to work under certain conditions. The ready-made plans differ only in the weight granted the factors and not in the factors themselves. For example, in 1948, Otis and Leukart provided a list of compensable factors that remain intact today:[4]

Skill Required to Perform Job

education	mental development
trade knowledge	schooling
experience	training
accuracy	ingenuity
initiative	judgment
mental capability	intelligence
resourcefulness	versatility
manual	dexterity
job knowledge	mentality
physical	details
aptitude	difficulty of operation
social	complexity
decisions	management
leadership	

Effort Expended to Perform Job

mental	application
mental or visual	concentration
application	physical
physical application	fatigue
strain	monotony
comfort	routine
dexterity	

Responsibility Assumed in the Job

safety	material
product	equipment
process	machinery
work of others	supervision
cost of errors	effect on other operations
necessary accuracy	spoilage
protection	physical property
plant	services
cooperation	personality
dependability	adjustability
coordination	details

quality	cash
records	methods
contact	goodwill

Conditions Under Which Job Is Performed

hazards	exposure
danger	surroundings
dirtiness	environment
job conditions	attendance
disagreeableness	monotony
travel	

As early a work as that by Lawshe at Purdue in the 1940s suggests that the choice and number of factors used have little impact on differences in the internal relationships between jobs.[5] Since then the internal factors used by traditional point-factor plans have not changed.

If job evaluation factors have not changed since the 1940s, it is unlikely that many of these plans remain responsive to the changes that have occurred in organizations since that time. Organizations and how they perform have changed measurably since the 1940s. New industries and jobs have evolved since then, making it unlikely that a system that could evaluate jobs during World War II could still match the needs of contemporary organizations.

Organizations cling religiously to outmoded job evaluation and base pay administration programs. If they were so grounded in other business systems that were accepted in the 1940s, it is likely they would still be using manual typewriters with carbon paper and pocket slide rules and viewing them as contemporary business equipment.

Primary Focus on Internal Equity and Secondary Focus on Market

The primary focus in traditional point-factor plans is internal equity across all the jobs in the organization. It is difficult to determine what is internal equity beyond functional areas with consistent agreement among employees and managers. The "line of sight" for internal equity among employees, who need to believe the program is credible, is within functional areas (e.g., within marketing, within manufacturing, within human resources, within engineering), rather than between them. Trying to create internal equity across functions is subject to individual interpretation and potential disagreement and therefore reduces the likelihood of program acceptance.

Often organizations complain that employees are too focused on internal equity and cannot be refocused. As long as the organization keeps a job evaluation system that attempts to create internal equity across the entire organization, however, the organization is communicating to employees to focus on internal equity. In this case, the job evaluation system and the focus of pay need to change so that employees are able to refocus on what is important to the organization—results and organizational success.

The secondary focus of traditional point-factor plans is matching the point values to the labor market. The problem in doing this is that supply and demand dictate relative market value, and market value is not highly related to many of the compensable factors that are often used to determine the worth of jobs. The challenge is that major differences exist among the market values of jobs because of differences in job function. For example, engineering jobs are in a different competitive labor market than are accounting jobs, and these differences have little to do with how these jobs compare internally with each other. The market may pay an engineering job of only moderate complexity at a level comparable to a highly complex and challenging accounting job while internal equity would suggest the opposite.

In traditional point-factor plans, points are converted to dollars based on external values or external survey data that average jobs that are paid high and low in the labor market. If the plan is designed using the external labor market to regress the high-paid and low-paid jobs to a middle point, it overpays some jobs and makes it difficult for the organization to attract and retain employees that are paid higher in the labor market than the system average. If the plan is designed using internal values to determine the regression, the system may be too far removed from market realities to be relevant. Internal perceptions of job content, rather than external market realities, drive the point-factor plan.

If the traditional point-factor plan results in some functions not being paid competitively (e.g., engineering), sometimes a second, higher formula is used to translate points into dollars. Unless the original regression formula being used for the majority of employees is discounted, the organization has an overly competitive overall pay policy and overspends base pay dollars. If the original formula was developed using the jobs that are now receiving a higher formula, the original formula should be recalculated excluding these jobs. This recalculation may seem insignificant, but if the organization is labor-intensive, the difference can result in significant dollars. For example, one health care organization developed a formula and found that it could not recruit registered nurses because they were paid more in the labor market than their internal points were worth. Not only did the organization have to develop a higher formula for registered nurses—which was appropriate, given the labor market—but, because they did not reduce the original formula, they overpriced other jobs at a cost of several million dollars a year.

If comparable worth or pay equity ever becomes a reality, traditional point-factor plans that may pay higher values for the same points to male-dominated jobs than to female-dominated jobs will result in major costs—both in future pay and possible back pay. Comparable worth advocates equal pay for jobs of equal value or equal worth; it is not equal pay for equal work. For example, if comparable worth becomes legislated and if the female-dominated job of librarians is paid less for the same number of points than the male-dominated job of journey electricians, the organization will not be complying with comparable worth even though the labor market pays the two jobs differently.[6] To comply with comparable worth, organizations cannot have two pay lines to adjust for labor market considerations as described in the previous paragraphs; only one dollar value for a particular point value is acceptable. Hopefully, comparable worth will not overpower the market. The real issue to address is sex-based wage discrimination and not comparable worth because comparable worth would require the courts and the U.S. Equal Employment Opportunity Commission to use their judgments regarding the worth of jobs instead of the non-discriminatory decisions of individual employees and organizations as demonstrated in the marketplace.

It is our opinion that comparable worth should not be legislated by the United States. Comparable worth not only cannot be defined with any reliability and construct validity, but the United States cannot afford to pay jobs more than how the labor market values them and stay competitive in a global market. Also, comparable worth is solving itself as more and more women, including those who are trained in formerly male-dominated areas, enter the labor market. In fact, as discussed in chapter 1, women have been making strides compared to men in increases in income. In our opinion, the labor market, as indicated by supply and demand, is already defining comparable worth, and internal equity point systems are fraught with subjectivity and flaws.

Job Evaluation Inflation

If job evaluation committees are used, traditional point-factor job evaluation can become a strongly negotiated process. Human nature causes management to compare jobs in their organizational unit to jobs of higher rather than lower levels in other organizational units. This often sets the stage for job evaluation inflation.[7]

Traditional point-factor plans allow job evaluation inflation because the labor market for benchmark jobs (those jobs for which survey data are available) does not anchor the base pay structure. These plans permit benchmark jobs to change in value because of their internal value. The labor market for a benchmark job does not determine its pay level—the points based on internal equity do—so benchmark jobs cannot help stabilize the structure by staying permanent until the entire base pay structure is updated based on labor market considerations. If benchmark jobs anchored the base pay structure and changed only when the structure was reevaluated based on the labor market, jobs of lesser point value than the benchmark job would be kept from having their points inflated if this moved them higher in the structure than the benchmark job. New pay does not move benchmark jobs higher or lower for the sake of internal equity.

Traditional point-factor plans encourage job evaluation inflation because they are internally focused. If a supervisor is able to increase the points of a subordinate job or jobs before other supervisors can, the jobs reporting to that supervisor receive higher pay levels, and the supervisor's job itself may also receive a higher pay level because it is supervising jobs with more points. The job evaluation inflation race can only be kept in check by top management not allowing it. If top management personnel are part of the problem by inflating jobs in their own organizational units, the plan will lose credibility to the extent that job evaluation inflation is not constant across the organization. After significant job evaluation inflation has occurred, the points eventually are devalued to return pay levels to the organization's desired competitive position. In the meantime, labor costs have increased beyond what the organization had intended to be competitive.

In times when organizations need to control human resource costs, a job evaluation plan that facilitates the inflation of labor costs is a problem. Sometimes the organization cannot tolerate the inflation and replaces the traditional point-factor job evaluation methodology with another traditional point-factor plan. Unfortunately, the job evaluation inflation process continues, and the job evaluation plan becomes identified as the cause of a serious problem rather than the solution.

New Pay View of Job-Based Evaluation

New pay job evaluation involves using the labor market primarily and internal equity within broad job functions secondarily. The organization first determines its labor market and the competitive position it wants relative to the labor market (e.g., 50th percentile). Survey data are used to determine the market value of benchmark jobs. The market value of nonbenchmark jobs (jobs for which survey data are unavailable) is determined by evaluating the jobs on compensable factors that are good predictors of market value based on a model developed using the benchmark jobs. A key factor in predicting market value is the function of the job (e.g., human resources, information systems, engineering). A base pay structure is developed based on survey data for benchmark jobs and market approximation for nonbenchmark jobs to reflect the organization's desired market position.

If the organization wants to pay jobs differently from the market, a second step, strategic valuing, can be used to determine the strategic value a job has to the organization in achieving its business strategy. The strategic valuing process is separate so that the market value is not obscured by the organization's strategic valuing. This separation enables the organization to return to the market value of jobs when strategic priorities change in the future and clarifies the decision process for moving away from the market for particular jobs. This keeps the job evaluation plan from becoming obsolete due to changes in strategic direction.

Market-Based Job Evaluation

In new pay job evaluation, the purpose of compensable factors is to determine the value of nonbenchmark jobs relative to the value of benchmark jobs. Compensable factors are not used to determine the value of benchmark jobs, since benchmark jobs are valued directly in the labor market. Because the labor market is the primary consideration in new pay job evaluation, only compensable factors that are good predictors of market value are used. One of the best predictors of market value is job function, which (when combined with job level) can account for most of the market value of a job. The job functions used can reflect the organization's view of internal equity. For example, engineering can be considered as one job function or can be further subdivided (electrical, petroleum, mechanical, etc.) depending on the organization's view of internal equity, since the labor market differentiates types of engineers. If the organization views the engineering function as the unit of internal equity for the sake of simplicity, the engineering job function is not subdivided; if the organization wants to reflect the labor market as closely as possible, the engineering job function is subdivided.

Other compensable factors that are good predictors of market value are used to fine-tune the market valuing of nonbenchmark jobs—for example, type of people supervised (e.g., professional, scientific, paraprofessional) and skills required to perform jobs (e.g., oral and written communications, math).[8]

Two features of new pay job evaluation reduce the potential for job evaluation inflation. First, the labor market as measured through survey data anchors benchmark jobs in the base pay structure because benchmark jobs do not move unless labor market movement occurs. Second, internal equity is within job functions, not across job functions, so evaluation error is reduced because equity comparisons are confined to more similar jobs. A manager is less likely to inflate nonbenchmark jobs if he or she has to face employees in the benchmark jobs with the inflation.

Strategic Job Evaluation

Organizations focused on employee performance and productivity to produce world-class results by becoming customer-oriented are interested in the impact that effective human resource management can have on business strategy, profit performance, cost management, and market penetration. Some new pay organizations may want to pay both competitively and strategically for jobs or skills required to make the organization succeed.

For these organizations, job evaluation plans will need to accommodate strategic issues that may suggest paying jobs more than their market value to reflect the importance of the job or skill in positively influencing the organization's business strategy. This varies by organization but can include a job's strategic impact on customers, profits, new products or services, costs, quality, or other elements that are key to accomplishing the organization's business strategy. The organization decides from its business strategy what is critical in terms of jobs or skills and determines which jobs or skills have significant strategic value in helping the organization to accomplish its goals. Strategically valuable jobs either have higher base pay levels, are eligible for variable pay (e.g., lump-sum awards), or have greater variable pay opportunities. The cost of the strategic valuing is considered in determining the organization's overall competitive base pay policy.

Because strategic value can change, this element of job evaluation needs to be revised periodically. This revision can be done without disrupting the job evaluation process because the heart of the valuing system is the external marketplace. If strategic values change, the organization returns jobs to their original market value and is not encumbered by a job evaluation system that values jobs based on internal factors that may need to change for the organization to respond to business and competitive financial realities. Strategic valuing can serve to focus employee efforts on the issues that are directly related to effectively running the organization. The starting place is the identification of the strategic values for which the organization is willing to pay. This is a management process and can result in the following sample strategic elements:

- impact on serving customers
- impact on financial results
- impact on cost containment
- impact on quality
- impact on marketing
- impact on organizational image
- impact on future resource allocation

To keep the strategic valuing process simple, jobs can be sorted into the following "buckets" based on their degree of impact on each of the strategic elements:

- extreme impact (among the highest 10 percent of jobs affecting a strategic element)

- high impact (among the top third, but less than the extreme impact level)
- normal impact (below the top third)

Elements are weighted based on their relative strategic importance to the organization. For example, impact on quality may be 20 percent; impact on organizational change, 30 percent. Employees in jobs that have significant overall strategic impact can be paid higher (in terms of base pay, lump-sum awards, variable pay eligibility, or higher variable pay opportunities) during the time their jobs have the high strategic impact. Strategic impact is generally reviewed on an annual basis. Strategic valuing does not become an entitlement; pay eventually returns to a level competitive with the market if business strategy changes the importance of jobs to the organization.

Combining Skill-Based and Job-Based Evaluation

Based on the available information, it is possible to predict how new pay will eventually take advantage of both skill-based pay and job-based pay, add a job's strategic value, and arrive at a way to evaluate jobs and skills practically.

Neither skill-based pay nor job-based pay has a clear advantage as a practical way that any sizable organization can flexibly determine what skills and/or jobs are worth. Job-based evaluation systems are clearly the easiest and most accurate way to establish the market value of jobs and control the competitiveness and cost of base pay in the organization. As long as the concept of total organizational internal equity is avoided, job-based systems can work. The key goal is to avoid a situation where jobs of different market value are paid at the same level because of some similar scores on compensable job evaluation factors that do not correlate with the external market value of jobs or the strategic value of jobs to the organization.

Skill-based pay rewards the acquisition and use of needed skills. Clearly, the skill-based alternative is better aligned with new pay concepts because it focuses on the employee's need to grow and the organization's need to have available the skills necessary to get done what needs to be done. However, skill-based pay is not something a large organization can use to manage pay in all areas of the organization. It is not an organizationwide evaluation methodology and therefore is limited to specific applications in specific portions of the organization. Employee involvement and different organizational situations can result in inconsistent methods and results across the organization. This makes it difficult for organizations of any size to ensure that a skill or skill block in one part of the organization is paid at the proper position relative to the external market *and* relative to how it is paid in other portions of the organization. Also, because of the difficulty in defining the market price of skills, skill-based pay can result in paying more than necessary for skills that are required.

The new pay solution combines market-based job evaluation with skill-based pay. To accomplish this, benchmark jobs are compared to blocks of skills in skill-based pay applications. Subsequently, the benchmark jobs become benchmark skill blocks and are priced appropriately in the external market. In portions of organizations with skill-based pay, skills are used to progress employees from one benchmark skill block to another. In portions of the organization that do not use skill-based pay, the value of nonbenchmark jobs is predicted from a statistical model based on the market value of benchmark jobs. In this way the organization has a universal job evaluation plan that is anchored in the market. In addition, the organization can permit the use of both skill-based and job-based pay programs as methodologies throughout the organization with the assurance that benchmark jobs keep the system properly aligned with the external market.

Conclusions

Human resource policies have a critical role to play in leading an organization into a more dynamic and changing business climate. The base pay system an organization uses is generally a good way to diagnose the business's true ability to change to beat the competition. Traditional job evaluation methodologies that match the hierarchical and bureaucratic organizations of the 1960s (when most job evaluation methodologies gained their momentum) need critical study and evaluation. The need for new solutions is here. Whatever the answer to job or skill valuing is, the market value of jobs and employees' skills and their impact on the strategy and tactics of the organization must be actively and creatively considered. The answer is not likely to lie in the further evolution of point-factor job evaluation methodologies that focus on internal equity primarily and market secondarily. The comparative strategic value of jobs and skills is likely to become important in organizations striving to become customer-focused. The answer also most likely lies in more labor market-responsive job or skill evaluation approaches that permit the recognition of the skills and strategies needed to help organizations prosper.

Base Pay Adjustments

Difficulty in Rewarding Performance with Base Pay Increases

Base pay increases are the traditional reward for performance. However, base pay has limited value as a reward for performance for the following reasons:

- *Economics.* The largest portion of base pay increase dollars is consumed by the economics of responding to the organization's interpretation of competitive practice. During times when pay increase budgets are in the 5 to 6 percent area annually, there is not enough money available to grant some for economics and competitive practice and have enough left for performance that the performance portion is meaningful. If an increase budget is developed based on 4 percent for economics based on labor market movement and 1 percent for performance, the 1 percent is not enough to differentiate between levels of performance.
- *Lack of flexibility.* Base pay increase guidelines in organizations make it difficult to recognize significant differences between levels of performance. Annual pay increase guidelines distribute available increase dollars such that everyone who is even a reasonably successful performer receives an increase. This makes it necessary to give "meets expectations" performers nearly as much of an increase as "far exceeds expectations" performers, making excellence of little perceived value.
- *Permanence.* Managers hesitate to grant base pay increases that are reflective of employee performance because this has a permanent impact on an employee's pay and career. If a manager grants a small increase that accurately reflects performance but

permits the employee's base pay to fall behind, it is difficult to manage base pay so that the employee can catch up if his or her performance changes for the better. Because of this, managers feel more comfortable treating all employees similarly from a pay increase standpoint.

From the organization's viewpoint, base pay increases lack flexibility. Once given for performance in one year, the increase becomes a part of base pay and an annuity for the remainder of the employee's tenure. In some cases, the employee may be barely meeting expectations but is paid at a base pay level well above the competitive market rate for the job because of past performance. The organization is overpaying for the performance currently being received.

• *Individual focus.* Base pay is an individual pay issue. Because effective and accurate evaluation of individual performance is difficult, many managers treat employees similarly regardless of performance. Also, because complex organizations often require teamwork and collaboration, individual pay is not always well suited to a situation requiring employees to be tied together to meet a common set of goals and to be rewarded accordingly.

Due to changes in an organization's goals and needs, it is difficult to design a base pay program that effectively rewards performance. New pay requires a flexible approach to rewarding performance that permits communication of goals and objectives and the encouragement of teamwork and collaboration. Because of the focus on the individual, base pay increases do not do a good job in any of these key areas.

Making Individual Performance Appraisal Work

Some organizations want to pay for individual performance either by rewarding individual performance alone or by considering individual performance with organizational and group results in determining rewards. Because individual performance needs to be evaluated to be rewarded, the first step in paying for individual performance is a sound performance appraisal program. Performance appraisal can have two purposes: current or recent performance evaluation, or developmental planning. Current or recent performance evaluation focuses on how the employee did as compared to expected performance or results, and will be discussed in this chapter. Developmental planning determines areas in which employees need training and development and identifies promotional potential and employees with specific skills and abilities.[1] Developmental planning will not be discussed in this chapter since it is not used to determine rewards for performance.

Evaluating individual performance in an organization is difficult for a number of reasons, including the following:

- Individual performance evaluation involves many more appraisers than group performance evaluation. Appraisers typically differ in their level of skill in appraising performance, so reliability in ratings among appraisers and the accuracy and quality of the appraisals are often limited.
- It is more difficult and time-consuming to set goals and standards for individual jobs than for groups. There is less consistency in the goals and standards set for individuals because more appraisers, who often have different concepts of how difficult it should be to meet or exceed expectations, develop and interpret the standards. Individual standards also generally receive less scrutiny and hence have less consistency in quality than performance standards set for groups. Because group performance requires a more macro focus than individual performance, group performance goals are more likely to be consistent with the organization's direction.
- If pay is tied to individual performance, the individual is hesitant to evaluate himself or herself honestly during the performance appraisal, so the performance improvement process is hindered. Generally, organizations view the purpose of performance appraisal as not only rewarding performance but also improving it so that the organization can be more successful. The latter purpose may not be facilitated when pay is tied to the performance appraisal process.

Despite the difficulties, individual performance appraisal can be a valuable tool for giving employees feedback about how their performance fits with the organization's expectations. Individual performance appraisal is used to improve and/or weed out poorer performers and can help identify training needs. In this role, performance appraisal can help the organization upgrade the quality of its work force.

A *National Productivity Review* survey[2] reported that information sharing and feedback on an individual and group basis led to improved employee performance as follows:

- Employees received accurate information about their performance that allowed them to modify their performance.
- Employees like keeping score, and feedback gave them the performance information they needed to keep score.
- Organization–employee relations improved.
- Employees became concerned about performance in the areas of performance being measured.
- Employees learned what they needed to do to produce the results the organization needed.

Because of this, if performance feedback can be performed accurately and effectively, it can have value to the employee-organization partnership.

Organizations, however, often find it difficult to achieve good performance appraisal. Because pay for individual performance needs a solid foundation of performance appraisal, its credibility is reduced. Still, many organizations want to reward individual performance. If an organization wishes to improve its performance appraisal process and use it as the basis for rewarding individual performance, the following guidelines will help make individual performance appraisal more accurate and credible:

LIMIT NUMBER OF PERFORMANCE LEVELS OR CATEGORIES. Organizations can communicate a clear message if base pay increases are distributed based on three performance levels—"does not meet expectations or requirements," "meets expectations" and "far exceeds expectations." Some organizations find that making the middle performance level a combination of "meets" and "exceeds" expectations reduces the tendency to rate an employee who only sometimes exceeds expectations in the highest performance category. It also better fits with employees' perceptions of their performance, because research shows that 80 percent of employees believe their performance is above average.

Using three performance levels creates less opportunity for confusion and increases rater reliability. Appraisers generally achieve greater agreement that an observed behavior *far* exceeds expectations than that an observed behavior is rated a "five" on a seven-point scale or "four" on a five-point scale.

Corresponding to the three performance levels are three levels of base pay increases: no increase (for performance that does not meet expectations); a base pay increase approximating the movement in the labor market (for performance that meets expectations); and a larger award of some form, whether base pay increase or lump-sum award or both (for performance that far exceeds expectations). This approach clearly communicates to employees and ensures that paying for results is in effect.

PROVIDE EXTENSIVE PERFORMANCE MANAGEMENT TRAINING FOR APPRAISERS. Effective performance management involves not only training on the performance appraisal form but, more importantly, training in conducting performance review and coaching sessions. Effective training involves role-playing to ensure that appraisers are comfortable in dealing with different types of employee performance situations during the performance review. The goal is consistency among appraisers so that they appraise similarly by setting the same "stretch" or level of difficulty in the "meets expectations" and "far exceeds expectations" performance levels and by agreeing on how poorly the employee has to perform not to meet expectations.

If behaviors are evaluated, effective training involves discussions of examples of behaviors that meet, do not meet, and far exceed expectations. If goals are used in performance evaluation, appraisers develop goals for their own jobs during the training so they can learn to apply a consistent degree of stretch to the goal-setting process for the employees whose performance they appraise. If duties and responsibilities are used in performance evaluation, appraisers set standards for a job with which they are familiar to ensure consistency in the standard-setting process.

Thorough and extensive training decreases the likelihood of ratings inflation or equal ratings for all employees. If all employees are generally rated the same, the organization should consider whether it should continue to evaluate individual performance or whether the time could be better spent focusing on group performance.

Organizations give appraisers instructions on completing the performance appraisal form and conducting the performance appraisal review to increase the validity of the form and appraisers' ratings. However, the focus of the performance appraisal program is not on constructing the ideal appraisal form but on developing the skills of the appraisers.

FOCUS ON MEASURABLE RESULTS OR OBSERVABLE BEHAVIORS. The organization needs to decide what it wants to measure—output, or what is accomplished (results); input, or how duties are performed or results are achieved (behaviors); or some combination. This decision is based on the performance culture the organization wants to create.

Results compared to goals are often used to evaluate management or exempt-employee performance; accomplishment of duties or responsibilities is often used to evaluate nonexempt- or hourly-employee performance. If the organization wants to evaluate input (how duties are performed or results are achieved), performance appraisal should not be based on undefined traits—which are subject to interpretation by the appraiser—but rather on behaviors such as teamwork, communications, and leadership. Behaviors are described in terms of examples of how the organization wants the employee to perform, because examples facilitate the development of standards against which behavior can be more reliably appraised. Examples create a snapshot of the behaviors a person exhibits at each performance level. The appraiser compares the employee to the snapshots and determines which snapshot best describes the employee's behavior.

Before the measurement period, employees need to be aware of and allowed to react to the performance standards on which their appraisal will be based. Appraisers make sure that they are knowledgeable about their employees' performance or gather additional information as needed from other sources, such as internal and external clients and customers, before appraising employee performance.

The degree to which employees and others are involved in the performance appraisal process depends on the culture of the organization. The more hierarchical the organization's culture, the more likely it is that the performance appraisal is conducted by the employee's immediate supervisor and reviewed by the manager one level above. The more high-involvement the culture, the more likely it is that peers and subordinates rate the employee, that the individual employee rates himself or herself, and that the supervisor's role is to add input and to manage the process. Regardless of who is the appraiser, having the individual employee formally review his or her own performance before the performance review meeting generally facilitates the employee's acceptance of the process.

Comments on the performance of an employee who far exceeds or does not meet expectations are documented on the performance appraisal form. This facilitates developing standards and consistency among appraisers about what level of performance is required to "far exceed expectations" and what level of performance results in an evaluation of "does not meet expectations." Documenting the reasons that performance far exceeds expectations helps ensure that appraisers award this performance level only to those employees who truly perform at this level. Documenting the reasons that performance does not meet expectations is necessary for an organization to defend a termination in a wrongful-termination lawsuit. Employees are provided the opportunity to comment in writing on their performance appraisal, but appraisers document if they disagree with the employee's comments because whoever has the last word on the performance appraisal form is generally believed by courts.

STICK WITH IT. The most natural communications between people are what we call either "positive–unclear" or "neutral–unusable." Either appraisers tell employees that they are "doing well" without specifics, or they communicate in terms that makes it questionable whether communication occurred at all. It takes time, often years, to cause people to talk to each other in a direct and constructive manner that includes understandable, constructive, and corrective feedback. It also takes time to learn to coach employee performance. As a result, organizations that stick to high standards of performance management to help the process succeed get the best results.

MONITOR AND AUDIT PERFORMANCE APPRAISAL PROCESS AND RESULTS. The organization has a mechanism to spot-check and audit performance appraisal periodically for quality, timeliness, and discrimination. Performance appraisal results and the awards made based on the performance appraisal are compared for adherence to the organization's program.

HAVE TOP MANAGEMENT SUPPORT CANDOR IN PERFORMANCE APPRAISALS. Top management personnel supporting appraisers in conducting honest performance appraisals and serving as role models facilitate the development of a performance-oriented culture and acceptance of the performance appraisal process. The program needs to be not only practical and understandable but also credible to be successful.

DEVELOP A WORKABLE SYSTEM TO MANAGE WITHIN THE BASE PAY INCREASE BUDGET. Unless managed, the tendency is to overspend budgeted dollars. Appraisers tend to evaluate high; and higher-paid employees may be rated higher than lower-paid employees, thus increasing the total cost if base pay increases are based on a percentage of base pay. The organization needs to decide how to ensure that base pay increase budgets are properly managed. If base pay adjustments take the form of fixed base pay increases, spending 1 percent of payroll over budget is not just 1 percent of payroll for that year, but for every year in the future that the average employee works for the organization. Compounding this amount by future base pay increases and adding to it the increase in the cost of benefits that are tied to base pay give the real cost of one year's error in the base pay increase program.

One approach is to give managers the accountability and leeway to manage the budget, which may result in little consistency unless guidelines are clear. Another approach is to use a forced distribution, which is generally only effective if the distribution includes about fifty employees or more. However, some organizations believe that forced distributions do not create the teamwork needed for the organization to be successful but instead create competition and lack of sharing and communication. It is difficult to have employees accept a forced distribution based on a small group of employees because the smaller the group of employees, the more difficult it often is to have employees fit the distribution.

If a forced distribution is used and appraisers are only responsible for evaluating a few employees, they appraise the employees for whom they are responsible and then meet with other appraisers under the same higher-level manager to develop the distribution. Because this methodology requires communication about performance appraisal among the appraisers who are developing the distribution, it can create more consistency in the evaluation process. The effectiveness of the distribution process increases if appraisers agree on how employees from different groups will be rated and if only extreme cases are identified (e.g., "far exceeds expectations") rather than many levels of performance.

Most organizations only force a distribution above the "meets expecta tions" level of performance if appraisers generally rate high and do not force a distribution for the "does not meet expectations" performance level. As appraisers become better trained in performance appraisal and develop consistency in setting standards and determining how much above expectations performance needs to be to far exceed expectations, the need for forcing distributions decreases.

Quality performance management depends on two-way communications between the supervisor and the employee. When the quality of the performance management process is challenged, the first response is often to change the performance appraisal forms used to support the process. This forces continuous learning and relearning of methods and procedures. Instead, trouble in the performance management process is almost always due to poor-quality communications between supervisors and employees on performance expectations, progress toward meeting expectations, barriers to satisfactory performance, and changes in direction, as well as being due to lack of continuous feedback. More time and effort should be spent on the dialogue between the parties than on the procedures used.

Base Pay Adjustment Approaches

New pay provides a moderate level of base pay to employees and additional pay based on performance in the form of variable pay. This means giving employees a base pay adjustment based on labor market movement if the employee's performance at least meets expectations. Contrary to traditional base pay increase practices, new pay base pay adjustment is not a cost-of-living increase but reflects what it takes for the organization to maintain its selected competitive position in the labor market. Cost-of-living increases generally do not match the movement in the labor market. During inflationary periods, cost of living generally exceeds labor market movement; during noninflationary periods, labor market movement generally is equal to or exceeds cost of living. Labor market movement is also not the average merit increase paid in the labor market. Rather, labor market movement reflects how the price of jobs changes in the labor market from one year to the next. This change is influenced by several factors, including supply and demand for people; changes in the average base pay for jobs due to turnover, promotion, and new hires; and average merit increases.

Some organizations want to reward individual performance through base pay increases. If they have an effective performance appraisal system, the following approaches can be considered:

- realize the full cost of an individual pay increase by using the traditional base pay increase approach
- use lump-sum awards for performance above the competitive labor market rate for the job
- use a limited number of base pay levels that matches the number of performance levels in the performance appraisal

Each of these will be discussed in more detail.

The Full Cost of Traditional Individual Base Pay Increases

The traditional pay increase approach rewards an employee with a larger base pay increase for better performance. Employees tend to view the small difference between what is given to the strong performers and the meets-expectations performers as too little to be motivating; however, over time, this is a significant amount. Organizations do not get perceived value from employees for the significant cost of these small differences in base pay increases over the working career of an employee.

For example, an organization may award a pay increase of 0 percent for performance below expectations, 4 percent for performance that meets expectations and 6 percent for performance that far exceeds expectations. With 5 to 6 percent base pay increase budgets, organizations on average spend at most 2 percent from the meets-expectations pay increase for performance differences. Employees do not view this 2 percent as paying for performance. However, it provides the employee with an annuity that may be unearned on a sustained basis and is costly to the organization.

Assume an employee with a base pay of $40,000 receives 2 percent more than the meets-expectations base pay increase for performance that far exceeds expectations. In the first year, this additional amount is $800, which the employee sees as $30.77 over twenty-six pay periods before taxes. Typically the employee believes that his or her performance was not rewarded. However, the cost of the pay increase is not only in the first year; it is in every future year of employment and is compounded by future base pay increases (as shown in table 9.1). Assume in this example that for the remaining years, the employee receives no base pay increase, so there is no compounding. In five years, the additional amount paid for the one-year performance is 10 percent of the original pay of the employee during the performance year; over 10 years, 20 percent; over 15 years, 30 percent.

Compounding by future pay increases magnifies the value of the one year's performance differential. Assume in this example that for each of the remaining years, the employee meets expectations and receives a 4 percent base pay increase. In five years, the additional amount paid for the one-year performance is 10.8 percent of the original annual base pay of the employee; over ten years, 24.0 percent; over fifteen years, 40.0 percent.

Finally, the cost of benefits that are tied to base pay further increases the value of the one-year performance differential. Assume that the benefits directly related to base pay are 27 percent of base pay (as estimated from U.S. Chamber of Commerce data) and that the employee receives compounding based on 4 percent base pay increases in the future. In five years, the total additional amount paid for the one-year performance is 13.8 percent of the original annual base pay of the employee; over ten years, 30.5 percent; over fifteen years, 50.9 percent. This is a substantial payment for one year's worth of exceptional performance, although most employees would not have perceived value in it.

If the employee received a pay increase of 8 percent, compared to a meets-expectations base pay increase of 4 percent, for one year and received 4 percent in all future years, the value of the one year's additional performance is even greater, as shown in table 9.2. The same compounded, benefits-loaded example results in the one year's performance being worth an additional 27.5 percent of original base pay over five years, 61.0 percent over ten years, and 101.7 percent over fifteen years. At fifteen years, in other words, the employee has received an award for one year's exceptional performance equal to his or her full base pay for that year.

The cost of error in traditional merit-pay increase programs can be significant. Organizations need to determine the full cost of this error by multiplying the number of employees in the organization by the percentage of employees who are appraised higher than they should have been, their average base pay level, and the average percentage of base pay

TABLE 9.1
Value to Employee of Receiving 2% More than "Meets Expectations" Base Pay Increase for One Year

Year	No Compounding			Assumes Compounding of 4% per Year Due to Future 4% Annual Base Pay Increases			Assumes Base Pay-Related Benefits Cost of 27% and Assumes Compounding of 4% per Year Due to Future 4% Base Pay Increases			
	Annual Base Pay Amount	Cumulative Amount	% of Original Base Pay	Annual Base Pay Amount	Cumulative Amount	% of Original Base Pay	Annual Base Pay Amount	Annual Benefit Value	Cumulative Amount	% of Original Base Pay
1	800	800	2.0	800	800	2.0	800	216	1,016	2.5
2	800	1,600	4.0	832	1,632	4.1	832	225	2,073	5.2
3	800	2,400	6.0	865	2,497	6.2	865	234	3,172	7.9
4	800	3,200	8.0	900	3,397	8.5	900	243	4,314	10.8
5	800	4,000	10.0	936	4,333	10.8	936	253	5,503	13.8
6	800	4,800	12.0	973	5,306	13.3	973	263	6,739	16.8
7	800	5,600	14.0	1,012	6,319	15.8	1,012	273	8,025	20.1
8	800	6,400	16.0	1,053	7,371	18.4	1,053	284	9,362	23.4
9	800	7,200	18.0	1,095	8,466	21.2	1,095	296	10,752	26.9
10	800	8,000	20.0	1,139	9,605	24.0	1,139	307	12,198	30.5
11	800	8,800	22.0	1,184	10,789	27.0	1,184	320	13,702	34.3
12	800	9,600	24.0	1,232	12,021	30.1	1,232	333	15,266	38.2
13	800	10,400	26.0	1,281	13,301	33.3	1,281	346	16,893	42.2
14	800	11,200	28.0	1,332	14,634	36.6	1,332	360	18,585	46.5
15	800	12,000	30.0	1,385	16,019	40.0	1,385	374	20,344	50.9

Note: Assumes employee was earning base pay of $40,000 when increase was given. All pay amounts are given in dollars.

TABLE 9.2

Value to Employee of Receiving 4% More than
"Meets Expectations" Base Pay Increase for One Year

Year	No Compounding			Assumes Compounding of 4% per Year Due to Future 4% Annual Base Pay Increases			Assumes Base Pay-Related Benefits Cost of 27% and Assumes Compounding of 4% per Year Due to Future 4% Base Pay Increases			
	Annual Base Pay Amount	Cumulative Amount	% of Original Base Pay	Annual Base Pay Amount	Cumulative Amount	% of Original Base Pay	Annual Base Pay Amount	Annual Benefit Value	Cumulative Amount	% of Original Base Pay
1	1,600	1,600	4.0	1,600	1,600	4.0	1,600	432	2,032	5.1
2	1,600	3,200	8.0	1,664	3,264	8.2	1,664	449	4,145	10.4
3	1,600	4,800	12.0	1,731	4,995	12.5	1,731	467	6,343	15.9
4	1,600	6,400	16.0	1,800	6,794	17.0	1,800	486	8,629	21.6
5	1,600	8,000	20.0	1,872	8,666	21.7	1,872	505	11,006	27.5
6	1,600	9,600	24.0	1,947	10,613	26.5	1,947	526	13,478	33.7
7	1,600	11,200	28.0	2,025	12,637	31.6	2,025	547	16,049	40.1
8	1,600	12,800	32.0	2,105	14,743	36.9	2,105	568	18,723	46.8
9	1,600	14,400	36.0	2,190	16,932	42.3	2,190	591	21,504	53.8
10	1,600	16,000	40.0	2,277	19,210	48.0	2,277	615	24,396	61.0
11	1,600	17,600	44.0	2,368	21,573	53.9	2,368	639	27,404	68.5
12	1,600	19,200	48.0	2,463	24,041	60.1	2,463	665	30,532	76.3
13	1,600	20,800	52.0	2,562	26,603	66.5	2,562	692	33,786	84.5
14	1,600	22,400	56.0	2,664	29,267	73.2	2,664	719	37,169	92.9
15	1,600	24,000	60.0	2,771	32,038	80.1	2,771	748	40,688	101.7

Note: Assumes employee was earning base pay of $40,000 when increase was given. All pay amounts are given in dollars.

increase that the organization believes is error due to inflated performance appraisal or incorrect application of merit-increase guidelines. Add the error due to the benefit costs associated with the error in base pay increase costs (e.g., increased premiums for life insurance and disability, increased retirement costs, increased time-off costs, increased employer-paid FICA). Multiply this total base pay and benefit cost error by the average number of years employees work in the organization, and the full cost begins to emerge (on a basis that does not include compounding from future pay increases). This points out the importance of managers managing their pay increase budgets, as well as their base pay budgets in general.

If a traditional merit-increase budget is used, employees need to understand that the budget will vary from year to year based on changes in the labor market and the organization's ability to pay. Too often employees view the merit-increase budget as a promised increase that will repeat uninterrupted on an annual basis. Many organizations do not use the term *average merit increase* in their communications to employees because employees who are meeting expectations do not believe they should receive less than the average merit increase. However, in order for the employees who far exceed expectations to receive a larger increase than the employees who only meet expectations, either the average merit increase has to be higher than the increase for employees who meet expectations or there has to be a large enough number of employees who do not meet expectations and receive no increase to balance the employees who receive larger increases for far exceeding expectations. This latter approach does not fit with most organizations' performance distributions.

The difficulties in rewarding individual performance with base pay increases are such that more and more organizations are moving away from traditional merit-increase programs to programs that position base pay around the competitive labor market for employees who at least meet expectations on a consistent basis and that use variable pay to reward performance.

Lump-Sum Awards for Performance Above Competitive Labor Market Rate

The traditional approach to base pay administration is to grant increases to employees so they progress through a base pay range that has a midpoint. The midpoint is intended to represent the organization's interpretation of competitive base pay. A base pay range maximum is used to represent the organization's view of highly competitive base pay. Employees are able to receive base pay above the midpoint based on their performance. As employees proceed to the top of the pay range, base pay remains very high without the opportunity for the organization to reduce base pay as a result of changes in employee performance.

As an alternative to the traditional approach, the merit plan continues to operate, but the base pay ranges are designed so that base pay cannot exceed the market rate, which is the organization's interpretation of competitive or moderate base pay. The market rate is adjusted if the labor market shows that the external value of the job is increasing. The organization awards base pay increases based on performance to employees until their base pay equals the market rate. Above the market rate, the organization awards employees with a payment that does not become part of base pay.

Traditional pay systems consist of either base pay ranges or "step" systems that look something like this:

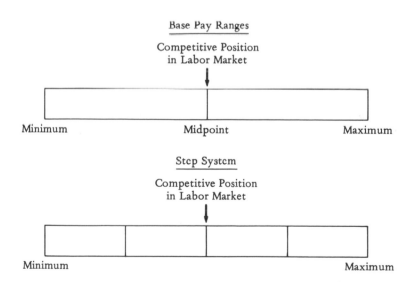

Using lump-sum awards for performance above the competitive labor market rate looks something like this:

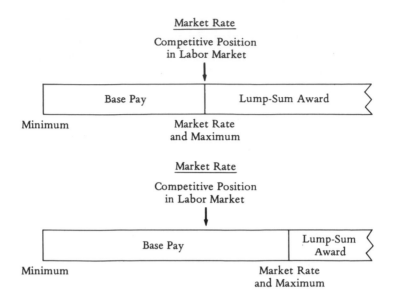

Organizations choose lump-sum awards because they want to motivate performance each year. They are paying a competitive base pay to employees as represented by the market rate, and they do not want the performance of one year to become an annuity. They want employees to re-earn pay above the market rate. Since they are not paying employees an unreasonably low base pay, organizations view the reward system as fair.

Organizations also choose lump-sum awards because managers hesitate to determine base pay as a result of performance. Lump-sum awards permit base pay to be competitive and allow managers to correct individual performance appraisal errors made in one year because the lump-sum awards do not become employee annuities.

Employees who are comfortable with performing and having their performance evaluated do not have difficulty adjusting to this type of program; employees who are not motivated to perform resist this approach. Organizations that implement a lump-sum program decide that they are comfortable with losing employees who may be unhappy with this approach, because the organization's goal is to reward performance. Some organizations view this as a way to weed out the poorer performers.

Typically, when a lump-sum award program is implemented, employees who are receiving base pay above the competitive market rate have their base pay frozen until the market rate catches up because of labor market movement. Employees whose base pay is above the market rate may either receive the full lump-sum award due to them based on performance or a reduced amount to take into account the amount they are paid over the market rate. The first alternative is more motivating to employees; the second alternative takes a total cash compensation perspective about how much the employee is worth for the performance exhibited.

The organization can pay lump-sum awards either in the form of a single payment or in equal payments throughout all or part of the following year. If the organization's cash flow can afford it, a lump sum that is paid in one payment has greater motivational value. If the organization cannot afford the one-time cash outlay, the lump sum is paid out in multiple payments, a method that has less motivational impact on the employee. In this latter case, the terminology of lump-sum award is technically incorrect because more than one payment is made.

Limiting the Number of Base Pay Levels

With this approach, the number of available base pay levels for each job is equal to the number of performance levels that the organization has established. An employee receives the base pay level that corresponds to his or her level of performance. For example, if the performance appraisal has three performance levels, three levels of base pay are used for all employees with the same market rate. If the market rate is $40,000, the base pay of employees who meet expectations on their performance appraisal may be $40,000; for employees whose performance far exceeds expectations, $42,000; and for employees whose performance does not meet expectations, $38,000.

Organizations use this approach if they want to communicate a very clear message about the relationship between base pay and performance. The employee's base pay increases or decreases based on individual performance. Base pay is re-earned each year. Employees who perform in a substandard manner have their base pay adjusted in order that they are paid less than employees who meet expectations. Employees who far exceed expectations are paid the most—a true pay-for-performance relationship.

The difference in base pay among performance levels depends on the organization's ability to appraise performance and the degree to which it wants to reward it. In the example, base pay ranged plus or minus 5 percent around the meets-expectations performance level for the other performance levels; plus or minus 7 percent could also have been used. For simplicity, the number of base pay levels set is based on the performance appraisal levels. Although the details of any pay program should be communicated before the beginning of the first performance period, it is critical to do so with this approach so employees have the entire performance period to improve their performance if necessary to avoid a base pay cut. Organizations can help employees understand their performance and thereby allow them to change their performance by more frequent performance review and coaching sessions than the annual performance appraisal on which their base pay level is set.

The Future of Base Pay Adjustments

Base pay increase systems can be used for performance management purposes. However, in most instances, organizations are not willing or able to manage pay in a strict or credible manner. Most employees do not believe they have a true pay-for-performance base pay program and do not perceive the small pay increase difference among performance levels as having the annuity value that it has. Organizations water down the impact of paying for performance by having too many performance categories. It may be that organizations do not trust their performance appraisal programs. Organizations that sincerely want to reward individual performance when it occurs and motivate employees to continue to perform should consider lump-sum awards or utilization of base pay levels that match the employee's performance.

Conclusions

Base pay administration forms the foundation for total compensation management and is perhaps in the most critical need of reform. Using base pay for what it does best is a good start. One step, described in the previous chapter, is moving toward the market as a determiner of the value of jobs and/or skills. Another step, described in this chapter, is having base pay reflect economic or labor market conditions rather than trying to reflect individual performance. For organizations that want to reward individual performance through base pay, the pay administration program should truly reflect individual performance by having pay adjustments be earned each year rather than having one year's performance increase become an annuity. Equally important is ensuring that the organization's performance appraisal process communicates the values, priorities, and goals of the organization.

PART FOUR

New Variable Pay

Principles of New Variable Pay

The Focus of New Pay

The major thrust of new pay is in the area of introducing variable pay to employee groups where most organizations pay only base pay. This means a portion of total cash compensation does *not* become a permanent part of employee base pay for employees who traditionally have received cash compensation only in the form of base pay. A second emphasis of new pay, once the variable pay decision has been made, is to measure performance in groups of more than one employee where tradition has indicated that pay would be determined only by individual performance. The third element of new pay is the partnership, wherein the employee and the organization share in the financial success of the organization. When the group or organization does well, variable pay awards are higher. When the group or organization does not do well, variable pay awards will be small or nonexistent. As a result, the combination of pay that does not all become a permanent annuity to the employee and pay that is earned based on measures determined by teamwork and performance, plus the importance of the partnership, suggests that something other than a one-size-fits-all pay solution is appropriate in many circumstances.

Tradition indicates that the only direction base pay can go under normal circumstances is toward higher levels, based on some combination of merit, competitive practice, or inflationary pressures. This means that once expended, base pay dollars become a fixed cost of doing business.[1] The primary way to reduce pay costs in this situation is to reduce staffing, since the reduction of base pay does not normally play a part in traditional base pay administration. Both the reduction of base pay and the reduction of staffing have a highly negative impact on morale and on the feeling of association the employee has with the organization.

This is because base pay cuts and work-force reductions are not an anticipated element in the total compensation strategy or plans of the organization. They are generally dramatic and radical actions taken due to negative performance or economic circumstances that are generalized or localized in nature.

Assume, for example, that an organization pegs base pay to remain no more than moderately competitive, and manages its base pay levels so that they do not increase beyond the average of external market competitiveness. Assume also that any portion of pay above the average paid in the external market is earned based on the attainment of measures of group or organizational performance that contribute directly to the financial success of the organization and are within the control of the participating employee group. This permits the organization to pay employees in the group moderately competitive base pay in times when performance or economics lag, which might help them avoid some more drastic actions such as work-force reductions or base pay cuts. When organizational or group performance is at or above financial and quality expectations, variable pay can acknowledge this by rewarding employees based on the organization's increased ability to pay as a result of the improved performance.

This combination of events involves employees earning variable pay (based on the organization's ability to pay) in addition to a moderately competitive base pay. This is an example of new variable pay. It helps form a partnership between the organization and employees so that when the organization wins, employees win; and when the organization needs support as it relates to labor costs, variable pay accounts for this by paying based on results achieved.

What Is New Variable Pay?

Variable pay is any form of direct pay that is not folded into base pay and that varies according to performance. New variable pay involves business plan gainsharing, group variable pay, winsharing, lump-sum awards, and individual variable pay. The concept of offering variable pay to employees who do not normally participate in such programs has roots in early nontraditional pay systems in the 1970s.[2] Variable pay does not become a permanent cost to the organization or an annuity to the employee. This permits control of the fixed portion of direct pay and thereby of employee benefit costs, while the variable portion of direct pay changes from performance period to performance period based on individual, group, or organizational performance. Using U.S. Chamber of Commerce information on the average cost of employee benefits, benefits that comprise 28.9 percent of payroll are not affected by variable pay if retirement is calculated using base pay, not total cash compensation; benefits comprising 23.8 percent are not affected by variable pay if retirement is calculated based on total cash compensation.[3]

New variable pay permits the organization to pay based on its ability to pay, rather than only on competitive practice or other factors that are sometimes unrelated to measures of productivity, performance, or quality. Variable pay provides the opportunity to "reuse" pay dollars from performance period to performance period to grant meaningful cash rewards that will not become fixed pay costs during performance periods that do not warrant significant performance-based financial rewards.[4]

The potential of variable pay as a business opportunity is significant. Organizations that are able to make labor costs sensitive to economic cycles may be able to reduce unemployment during a recession. This is because when organizational performance in terms of financial results falls, variable pay costs to the organization fall correspondingly, reducing pay costs without work-force reductions and thus saving jobs. For the same reason, if used by a sufficient number of organizations, variable pay may also serve to slow inflation during recessionary periods. Also, if variable pay is related to an organization's financial results, variable pay helps to stabilize earnings, particularly in a labor-intensive organization. Higher variable pay awards during successful earnings periods and lower variable pay awards during less successful earnings periods make for greater stability in an organization's earnings. An organization with such steady earnings performance can escape some of the pressure to increase financial results quarterly. This will permit the organization to focus and invest more in the long term while maintaining shorter-term financial results.

Traditional Variable Pay

Nearly all organizations use variable pay somewhere. The historical use of variable pay has been in the executive and sales incentive areas. Nearly all for-profit organizations use some form of variable pay for the executive group. Also, many not-for-profit organizations use variable pay based on some measure of performance results for executives. In addition, pay for sales professionals has traditionally included some portion of total cash compensation that varies based on a selected measure of sales success. It is unusual to find a sales compensation plan that does not involve some form of variable pay.[5]

Variable pay has been used primarily for executives in the belief that they have the greatest opportunity to influence the performance of the organization, and therefore that a portion of their pay should vary depending on the success the organization has in attaining some combination of goals and objectives. Traditional variable pay usually has the majority of total compensation paid in the form of base pay, which does not vary substantially as a result of changes in performance or the organization's ability to pay at the existing level. Traditional pay organizations most often have cultures that are well founded on base pay programs and not on variable pay programs. While they may use variable pay in some portions of the organization, in most instances the use of variable pay is extremely limited and not within the experience of most of the employee population because they do not have a view of all employees that defines them as ingredients critical to organizational sucess. This makes it difficult to change the organization from a culture of entitlement and fixed base pay and benefits to one where the organization and the employees are partners in their mutual success.

Variable Pay in the Future

The experience of organizations that are using new pay concepts—experience which is supported by the study of major U.S. companies in chapter 17—indicates that in the 1990s major changes in organizations can be expected that will have a positive impact on how pay is managed. These changes include the following:

- formation of employee–organization partnerships
- improved collaboration between organizations and employees
- primary emphasis on customer interests
- organizational success affecting all rewards
- downplaying of tenure and entitlement
- quality and customer value initiatives
- experimentation with new reward programs

These changes suggest that variable pay will play a major role in the total compensation strategy and practice of organizations that are concerned about how they will continue to compete effectively in the future.

Formation of Employee–Organization Partnerships

Leaving the customer out of the employee-organization equation is not working. The key to success is a collaborative focus on providing customer value. Where this does not exist, rewards for organizations and employees suffer. A good example of this is the American auto industry; because the unions and managers negotiated on who shared what and ignored the customer, the customers left. At the bargaining table, management would take some money for themselves; the unions would take some for themselves; and both would give some money to the shareholders. Few of these moves were related to improvements in product quality or design that benefited customers. This assumed passing on increased labor costs to customers, who were not considered to be a factor in the "who gets what" formula. As a result, customers were left out of the equation and decided that their interests might be better served by organizations that placed the customer first and then shared the results of good customer satisfaction with shareholders, employees, and management. Even the auto industry, in the instance of Saturn, is finding out that working together is better than working against each other to earn rewards. However, too few traditional organizations are forming partnerships with their employees focused on providing customer value.

Enough support from Lawler[6] and others exists to suggest that the interests of the organization and of employees must be aligned to ensure success. This involves changing from authoritarian organizational cultures to models that provide partnerships between shareholders, employees, managers, and others with vested interests in the success of the organization. This results in a better informed employee population with a stake in both the short- and long-term future of the organization.

Forming partnerships involves collaboration. However, partnerships can be effective only to the extent that the mutual interests of all parties can be benefited if some series of events occurs as a result of their efforts. Partnerships depend on the existence of ways to communicate the mutual goals to be accomplished and to share the results of attaining these goals with the parties that are instrumental in goal performance.

These sharing methodologies do not exist within the constraints of traditional pay practices. Because of this, the need to communicate and share suggests that other than traditional pay practices will constitute the future of partnerships from the perspective of tying the results of the organization's efforts to those that expend the effort and convert it into results.

Improved Collaboration Between Organizations and Employees

The entire body of information concerning how the organization is best managed is not retained within a single group of stakeholders. Shareholders provide capital and have little view of the organization's efforts and results beyond what they are told. Management has a good view from the top, but this does not give them enough information for the organization to use to differentiate their performance at all organizational levels. Employees have a very good idea about how to get a job done in the limited area in which they work, but seldom have a wide-angle view of the organization or an understanding of its goals, mission, values, and overall operations.

Since no single interested group has all the answers, it is necessary for all groups, primarily employees and managers, to exchange information in order to gain a differential advantage over organizations that do not take advantage of opportunities to exchange information. An additional opportunity exists when the organization wishes to take action based on employees' information concerning how better to achieve its clear and advantageous goals and objectives. While some of the opportunities may be actionable without collaboration between management and employees, at least those that have resulted from employee input may depend largely upon managers and employees collaborating to study, consider, test, and operationalize some of the more all-encompassing opportunities that are available. Because of this, collaboration will expand as managers and shareholders come to acknowledge the value of forming partnerships with their employees.

Partnerships will be formed with the customer at the foundation and with information and reward systems designed to determine the customer's needs and ways to satisfy them. Organizations that start with the customer and build their reward system accordingly will need to use new variable pay, because so many employees are in a position to affect how well or poorly the organization meets customer needs and thus how it performs.[7]

Primary Emphasis on Customer Interests

All organizations, whether for-profit or not-for-profit, have a customer base. For an auto company it is the driver, for the hospital it is the physician and patient, for a mortgage company it is the home buyer, and so forth. Most organizations have learned that customers have a wide range of possible alternative sources for products or services from which to choose. Exceptions are utilities and the public sector, which is the sole supplier of many services and some products. In this case, and in instances where the organization can pass the costs of ineffective performance on to the customer, a partnership is not likely to be formed because there is no driving force for change.

Partnerships founded on collaboration between managers and employees and focused on customers are best suited to produce performance results for a number of reasons. First, many employees are often closer to customers than are some managers. Because of this, employees are likely to be good sources of early information concerning customer trends, preferences, and attitudes. Once prepared to gather this information in an organized manner, employees are best suited to providing management with an accurate understanding of what customers need and some practical ways to address these needs. Second, many things that make measurable differences to customers are in the line of sight of employees. The employees are best able to put changes into action and can see the results faster than can management. Third, managers control capital allocation and are able to provide the means to operationalize the best possible opportunities identified by a wide range of employees responsible for information. Collaboration in an organization provides both broad and focused pictures of all situations, methods of analysis of information, and possible mechanisms to apply the information as needed and to evaluate the results of actions in a streamlined manner. Managers alone cannot accomplish this.[8]

Organizational Success Affecting All Rewards

Once a partnership is formed, the results of working effectively must be shared so all partners can keep score and understand how the results of their efforts are going. This means that as the results are measured, partners in the venture share in the financial results of the success (or lack of success) for the partnership to be viewed as real and important. This type of employee–organization relationship suggests that the reward systems that are used have some fairly unique features. These are as follows:

- Goals developed in the partnership form the foundation for the reward system. Goal performance determines the existence and magnitude of rewards granted. Goals are based on a realistic view of the future and what the organization needs to do to succeed in the future. Goals should be challenging but reasonable and achievable.
- The extent to which goals are missed, met, or exceeded determines the rewards granted to all members of the partnership. In performance periods when goals are met or exceeded, the rewards are distributed based on the level of performance compared to the goals.
- The group that is the foundation of the partnership is the unit of participation in the reward program. This means that reward systems are focused on the organization, business unit, or team and provide the opportunity both to win and to lose as the group's performance changes.

More traditional reward systems will be less able to respond to the new organizational strategies for a number of reasons. Some of these include the following:

- Since traditional variable pay plans are reserved for limited employee populations such as executives, managers, and sales professionals, they are not flexible enough to include all partners in the plan, nor are they strategically driven based on a diagnosis of the organization's future.
- Traditional variable pay plans are more likely to separate groups of employees than to create teamwork, because these programs create "haves" and "have-nots" within the organization. For example, executives and managers traditionally participate in variable pay plans, while other employees do not. Thus, the pay of most employees in an organization ignores a linkage with organizational results.

- Base pay programs are not able to provide sufficient variation in the size of rewards granted as a result of meeting, missing, or exceeding goal performance. Performance for one year should not necessarily continue to be rewarded in every following year of the employee's tenure, as it does with a base pay increase that becomes a permanent part of the employee's base pay. Base pay is too individualistic in nature to be the foundation for rewards based on the results of team, business unit, or organizational performance requiring collaboration. Individual performance is often difficult to measure; and when it is measurable, measuring it often creates competition between individuals rather than the desired collaboration.

This means that new variable pay will most likely be the foundation for rewards because it is highly flexible. It is able to accommodate the necessity of tying organizational success to rewards in a way that can change as the needs of the organization change to adapt to a dynamic external environment.

Downplaying of Tenure and Entitlement

How long an employee has been with an organization or what entitlements have been established over a long period of time have little or nothing to do with the results an organization can expect from the formation of an effective employee–organization partnership. This is not to say that pay systems based on tenure and entitlement are not of value to organizations. The public sector[9] seems to have goals of attendance, long service, and pay based on other factors unrelated to performance results. However, wherever the performance of employees is important to the success of the organization, the primary focus must be on results achieved, regardless of service. The objective of these strategies can be to encourage long service with the organization based on results achieved. However, to be effective, the results and service must be linked, and the right to stay with the organization for a long time a reward for demonstrated, sustained achievement and not an entitlement.

The external marketplace stands a good chance of replacing tenure and entitlement as the determiner of the level of base pay. If this is the case, base pay that is based on the labor market can be adjusted periodically so that the variable pay portion of total cash compensation can be used to align employees with the goals of the organization. However, tenure-based pay undermines the use of pay to create an alliance between the organization and the employee based on shared results. Traditional pay has many of the features of pay based on tenure and entitlement. As a result, careful modifications must be made to align variable pay with organizational results. Base pay can be moderately competitive to employees that are viewed as worth retaining, with variable pay giving them the opportunity to perform very well and subsequently be rewarded.

Quality and Customer Value Initiatives

Organizations are expending considerable effort to implement quality and customer value initiatives that give priority to satisfying customer needs. Successful results have some important features in common. Quality and customer value strategies are almost always revolutionary to an organization. Goals, both qualitative and quantitative, are organizational in nature; few, if any, are assigned only to individual employees. Teams, groups, functions, and entities must work collaboratively to meet organizational quality and value priorities. Employees become involved as members of problem-solving teams with managers as facilitators of the process so that everyone becomes an owner of both the process and the results. Additionally, the impact of failure can have negative consequences because so many other organizations are making successful quality and customer value initiatives positively affect their bottom line.

Although some advocates of quality and customer value initiatives depreciate the value of tying financial rewards to measures of quality and customer value, others, including ourselves, believe associated financial rewards are essential to making these initiatives the center of employee emphasis and to ensuring ownership of the quality and customer value process and results. To us, team ownership is more than merely empowerment. It is collaboratively taking responsibility for improving quality and customer value that helps transform the organization into one dedicated to these priorities. It involves stakeholdership not only in the results of goal performance but also in the development of the process to attain goals and measures. When the organization gains (or fails to gain) value from quality and customer value initiatives, the result is measured in financial terms. It is essential that the teams of stakeholders also share in any financial rewards the organization earns from quality and customer value to ensure an effective employee-organization partnership.

New variable pay is the natural tool to reward quality and customer value. It has the flexibility to match each quality and customer value opportunity, is able to use combinations of qualitative and quantitative goals and measures to encourage collaborative behavior, and is refreshed annually to ensure that it remains responsive to the needs and situation of the organization.

Unless organizations and employees are prepared to tie employee pay to the success or lack of success of the organization, it is not likely that any systems other than traditional ones, which do not depend on an employee-organization partnership, will stand a chance for success. This means organizational priorities for performance are critical elements in the development of more contemporary systems of financial rewards.

Conclusions

New pay cannot exist without new variable pay. This is the foundation of forming successful partnerships between the organization and its employees. Organizations that are concerned about the future will move more toward variable pay programs for employee groups that may not participate in such programs if a more traditional course is followed. The advantages of variable pay are its abilities to form partnerships between employees and the organization, to vary pay costs with performance, to create the need for high levels of teamwork and collaboration, and to support quality and customer value goals . Variable pay is a powerful and flexible communication tool that can either lead an organizational change or strongly support a cultural change led by some other initiative. As organizations need to adapt to more competitive environments, variable pay will become the primary way to link employees to their organizations.

Types of Variable Pay

Variable Pay Alternatives

A variety of approaches to variable pay are possible. The selection of the proper approach depends strongly on the organization's specific business, financial, and human resource situation and the goals developed to respond to the situation. New variable pay encourages the organization to select from the available options, use variable pay to match its business, financial, and human resource circumstances and objectives, and subsequently modify its variable pay approach as the situation changes. Classifying the best use of alternatives is difficult because generalizations do not apply. For example, while some would contend that small-team variable pay plans do a better job of paying for performance and that nonqualified cash profit-sharing plans more effectively increase the variability of total pay costs,[1] plan designers can often design small-team variable pay plans so that they do cause labor costs to vary with performance, and they can also modify the profit-sharing concept in order that it has some direct performance recognition value. The available options include any combination of the following:

- *Special recognition award*—one-time award paid to individual employees or small teams for extraordinary contributions or for significantly and consistently far exceeding expectations
- *Individual variable pay*—award paid to individual employees for achieving or exceeding predetermined individual goals
- *Group variable pay*—award funded by achievement of predetermined team, business unit, or organizational goals and paid out on a group, individual, or combined basis
- *Lump-sum award*—award to employees for performance effectiveness, paid in the form of a single lump sum that does not

roll into base pay; replaces or uses part of a more traditional merit base pay increase budget

- *Profit sharing*—award that shares a percentage of the organization's profit with each employee on a nonqualified basis
- *Gainsharing*—award that shares group improvement in productivity, cost savings, and quality with each employee in the group
- *Winsharing*—award that is funded by the profit contributions of a group and pays out based on group performance compared to predetermined goal(s) to each employee in the group
- *Long-term variable pay*—award for performance over a period longer than one year; may be group or individual in nature
- *Discretionary bonus*—group or individual award based on an after-the-fact judgment of performance, not performance compared to predetermined goals
- *Stock options*—opportunities to purchase common stock in a for-profit corporation

Each of these variable pay approaches can offer an organization something of value. Based on the strategy developed, what the organization wants to attain and what the design offers can be mixed, matched, and changed as new opportunities arise.

Measures Based on the Future or Past?

Two types of new pay variable pay plans may be considered. One type, which includes many gainsharing plans, uses past or historical experience to set measures or standards for determining awards. This is accomplished by evaluating what has been produced in the past through established practices to determine what can be produced in the future. Generally, only when capital is invested to improve performance are measures or standards changed. The problem with looking only at the past is that the past does not consider the variables that will affect performance in the future and ignores any new goals and objectives that may be more important than what has occurred before. In addition, these programs are seldom designed to be sufficiently situational to account for profit performance as well as measures of productivity or cost-effectiveness.

The second approach to variable pay plans is based on future performance expectations. In one alternative, winsharing, the organization selects the goals to be achieved and ensures that achievement of these goals is consistent with a measurable impact on profit and quality improvements. Awards granted reflect a sharing of the financial results of improved profit and quality performance. Performance expectations are based on the direction the organization wants to communicate to the employees and on an understanding of the circumstances the organization will confront in achieving the goals.

Variable pay plans founded on an understanding or prediction of the future are valuable because pay can be such a strong communicator of direction, mission, and values. Although the past performance of an organization is interesting, it is not always a good predictor of the future. It is also not consistent with the communication of a change in organizational direction or the introduction of new goals. However, basing plans on past or future performance is strongly situational. For example, union employees tend to prefer a comparison to past performance for trust reasons; organizations in a competitive and changing industry prefer flexibility in responding to these changes by comparing performance to future-oriented goals.

Special Recognition Awards

These are one-time awards granted to individuals or teams for extraordinary accomplishments clearly beyond the requirements of the job—for results that consistently far exceed expectations or for a major contribution. Special recognition awards can have two objectives. First, a special recognition award can reward performance that is better than that which might have been expected and accounted for by means of some other reward system, including other forms of variable pay. If the best performance a variable pay plan can reward is X and the employee generates three times X, it is possible to acknowledge this performance by means of a special recognition award. Second, significant unexpected performance can be recognized—for example, financial, product, or process breakthroughs that are not reasonably expected but are acknowledged as making a difference in the overall performance of the organization.

Some organizations that have a direct pay strategy consisting of labor market adjustments for base pay increases and group variable pay use special recognition awards to reward individual performance excellence. Special recognition awards can also be designed to recognize team contributions. For example, all employees in a work group that has accomplished a critical task very effectively or made some unexpected significant contribution can be the recipients of an award.

The importance of the special recognition award comes from visibility of the reason for the acknowledgment and even the size and recipient of the award. The motivational impact of the special recognition award is not only for the recipient but also for other employees, who are encouraged to seek opportunities to make unplanned and significant contributions to the organization. Organizations that are known for recognizing very significant contributions, with or without providing for them in a predetermined formal way, are likely to encourage people who can make these contributions to join and remain with the organization and to take the prudent risks necessary to earn the rewards.

Special recognition awards are often paid from a budgeted pool that provides for the recognition of very significant contributions as determined by the organization. This means contributions worthy of recognition are most often not limited to recognition of executives and managers. Rather, awards are granted to whoever makes the contribution. This communicates that major opportunities are available throughout the organization and are not limited to the management team.

To get the most from special recognition awards, the organization generally grants them close to the time of the contribution and with visible fanfare. This recognizes the contribution when and where it occurs, while it is fresh in the minds of the contributor and the organization. This is when contributions are often best observed. Awards close to the positive event encourage contribution throughout the year and do not limit recognition to the end of the year, when the rewarding of one very significant contribution may compete for attention with the recognition of other contributions.

To increase the effectiveness of special recognition awards, organizations communicate to employees the names of the recipients and the reasons for the awards. Communication facilitates employees' understanding of what the organization values. Communication can also result in improved quality of the special recognition award program because the organization will try to avoid having the program be viewed as unfair. If the organization wants more employee involvement, both management and employees can participate in determining the recipients of special recognition awards.

The special recognition award tells employees that making a contribution to the organization is not limited to employees who participate in a specific variable pay plan. Used effectively, the special recognition award can instill a sense of contribution in an organization and encourage employees to seek the opportunity to make an unexpected significant contribution.

Example of Special Recognition Awards

A large and successful organization granted special recognition awards to selected contributors following the major merger of the two organizations that were combined effectively to form the new organization. Rewards were granted for sacrifices to make the new organization succeed and for collaborations between people who were in different organizations before the merger. The objective was to recognize significantly major contributions in terms of creating a single stronger organization that was better prepared to face a highly competitive business environment.

Individual and Group Variable Pay

Most traditional variable pay plans focus on individual performance, while new pay variable pay plans focus first on groups of employees wherever practical. The purpose and design of individual and group variable pay plans are significantly different and represent a major change in the direction of variable pay in less traditional applications. Individual variable pay plans are intended to reward only individual performance. Group variable pay plans are intended to reward group performance, and an individual's contribution to the group performance may be considered secondarily if individual performance can be credibly measured.

Individual variable pay plans are a part of new pay to the extent that they involve employees who would not traditionally participate in variable pay plans and that they do not inhibit the teamwork required in an employee–organization partnership. For example, traditional organizations include executives, sales professionals, and piece-rate workers in individual variable pay plans. New pay organizations may include employees such as scientists, programmers, quality control workers, and employees who work at home.

While individual variable pay plans encourage employees to contribute to an organization as individuals, group variable pay plans encourage employees to work collaboratively to achieve goals and objectives that require teamwork and cooperation. Individual variable pay assumes that the work to be performed is not highly interrelated; group variable pay assumes that goal performance depends on two or more employees in order to achieve success. Also, group variable pay designs assume that individuals could be encouraged to compete for resources, not to share information, and to handle the easier work units and pass the more difficult work units onto others if they were rewarded only for individual performance. Individual variable pay most clearly communicates expectations for individual employees to meet; group variable pay most clearly communicates important objectives for a group of employees to achieve.

The traditional individual piece-rate incentive plan typical of manufacturing settings tends to encourage behaviors opposite to that of a partnership—for example, employees working slowly when standards are being set rather than trying to maximize performance; high administrative costs to maintain the program; supervisors functioning as record keepers rather than as facilitators, coaches, and trainers; and discouragement of employee involvement in improving processes.

Despite these difficulties in the manufacturing setting, some organizations are using individual variable pay plans for professionals whose work is not highly interrelated with others or when individual contributions can be meaningfully recognized in the body of work. These organizations typically believe individual performance should be recognized and rewarded. Goals are set, and performance is subsequently rewarded.

Many organizations have learned to include a team, business unit, or organizational component in their individual variable pay plans because they believe that organizational success is strongly contingent on teamwork and collaboration. To encourage group performance, organizations increase the portion of variable pay that depends on group performance measures and goals. For example, 60 to 75 percent of a variable pay award may be based on team, business unit, or organizational performance, and the rest on individual goal performance.

Example of Individual Variable Pay

The health care industry is plagued by shortages of qualified people for high-skill patient care jobs such as physical therapists, and organizations have great difficulty hiring and retaining physical therapists. Pay programs tend to be conventional in nature with only base pay available. If organizations increase base pay, fixed costs increase without improving performance or productivity.

Several major health care organizations have implemented individual variable pay plans to encourage productivity and an increase in caseload compared to that of other similar organizations. Physical therapists who are able to increase their productivity over current performance standards and maintain customer satisfaction (as measured by a follow-up patient satisfaction questionnaire) receive time off with pay. The amount of paid time off is granted as a percentage of additional hours of added productivity so that both the employee and the organization win. The performance–reward relationship takes into account the level of the organization's current performance standard compared to the average in the industry. These plans enable an organization to avoid increasing base pay costs, which can be quickly matched by other organizations, thus inflating competitive levels with no improved performance. Alternatively, the plan can be designed to provide a cash award or to have a group performance component in addition to the individual component.

Traditional organizations hesitate to add variable pay programs of this nature. As a result, the organization that adopts this type of plan can have a differential advantage over organizations that are not willing to be innovative. Where these plans have been used, they have resulted in both improved productivity and improved retention.

The role individual variable pay plays in new variable pay includes the following:

- Individual variable pay can make a portion of direct pay a variable cost to the organization. This makes direct pay reusable so that superior performance can be measurably rewarded when it occurs on the part of one individual during one performance period and another individual in a different performance period.
- Individual awards can be consistent with the performance to be recognized since they are not confined by the same requirements of matching competitive practice and other restrictions that are placed on base pay increases. Individual variable pay awards can be granted without loading by associated employee benefits. This nonbenefits-bearing cash compensation (i.e., excluding the impact of variable pay on certain employee benefits such as life

insurance, disability insurance, vacation pay, sick pay, and possibly retirement) gives the organization the chance to grant larger awards in exchange for performance results.

Individual variable pay may not work well in complex organizations where the need for considerable interdependence exists. This is because focusing on individual goals and measures may discourage teamwork and collaboration, which are essential in many dynamic organizations.

Using any form of variable pay is usually preferable to granting base pay increases. The possible shortcoming of individual variable pay is the inability to measure individual performance readily or to focus on the need for teamwork and collaboration, which generally makes group variable pay plans substantially superior.

Examples of Group Variable Pay

IN A MAJOR BANK. This bank is a top performer with quality leadership. The organization traditionally develops a cadre of banking professionals who are widely valued by competitor organizations. The business-banking segment is a strong financial performer that wanted to reward improvements in return on assets and pretax profit while controlling base pay costs. At the same time, the bank wanted to focus more strongly on a spirit of enterprise and make the organization attractive to employees who wanted to tie their financial fortunes to those of the bank. Additionally, improved customer value was necessary to differentiate the bank from other commercial lenders. The organization also wanted the more traditional banking professionals who were not willing to increase their performance to leave the bank.

To improve performance, several hundred commercial lenders were placed in a group variable pay plan funded by a matrix of return on assets and profit. Return on assets measures the effectiveness of the organization's deployment of assets; profit measures bottom-line financial results. Teams were formed on a geographical basis. In addition to financial measures, each team had qualitative and quantitative goals and objectives that were directly related to the specific circumstances faced by that team. Variable pay was not capped, and awards were permitted to range from very large for excellent team performance to no award for substandard performance.

In addition, career ladders were added that made it as financially attractive to remain a member of the team of lending professionals as it was to become a manager. These career ladders neutralized the historical tendency of financial institutions to add managers because it was more financially worthwhile for an employee to become a manager than it was to remain a producer. Career ladders facilitated focus on the variable pay plan, controlled increases in base pay, and removed the status and rewards that differentiated managers from professionals.

The strategy was to focus employees on overall financial goals and ensure quality through qualitative and quantitative team goals. Because lending is a team matter, the team rather than the individual was the focus of this plan, and teams of employees had to make both financial and qualitative goals, mostly in terms of both loan quality and customer value as measured by customer feedback, to earn variable pay. The variable pay available based on the overall performance of the bank could be major, making excellence worthwhile.

With this plan, the performance results over the long term were sustained high loan quality with improved asset and profit performance. The plan facilitated making employees partners in the success of the organization, encouraged teamwork, controlled loan quality, improved customer value, and made it attractive for high-performing employees to remain in productive lending jobs where their opportunity for contribution was significant.

IN A MAJOR HEALTH CARE ORGANIZATION. The president of a large not-for-profit health care organization led the implementation of a major change in pay in health care in the early 1980s. The health care industry was characterized by high base pay and an environment of little innovation and enterprise. This organization installed group variable pay for managers, funded by financial and qualitative results and including goals that encouraged horizontal and vertical integration. To earn awards, the entire organization needs to work together. Isolated excellent performance does not make up for the absence of collaboration and teamwork. Base pay is controlled at a competitive level, no higher than the average of the labor market. Although the transition was not easy and took time, the variable pay plan encouraged a change to a performance-focused culture that made it attractive for traditional health care people who were accustomed to passing on unlimited costs to their "customers" to leave the organization. A teamwork culture has become critical to the success of the organization. People think of each other when they act in order to ensure that actions taken are in the best short- and long-term interests of the organization.

Individual Versus Group Awards

The group as the primary unit of performance usually works best because complex organizations require employee collaboration to succeed. Individual performance measures may create competition among employees because collaboration and sharing of information are not emphasized. However, many organizations that have a successful culture of individual performance want to reinforce it by rewarding most those who contribute the most. In this situation, group and individual variable pay can be combined so funding is based on group or organizational performance and distributed based on individual performance. One individual measure of performance can be teamwork, which helps reduce the possibility of individuals competing with work associates rather than collaborating with them. However, it is more difficult to do this type of plan well because of the difficulty of individual performance measurement and the potentially conflicting focus between group and individual performance. The decision to reward individual or group performance depends on what the organization wants to reinforce—individual performance, group performance, or a combination of both.

Size of Groups

Groups can be defined as any formal or informal group of two or more employees who share a common goal or objective. Attainment of the objective is used to determine the extent to which any variable pay award is to be granted. Some group examples include the following:

- two or more employees working to solve a problem, develop or sell a product or service, or attain some other goal of value to the organization
- employees from different functions focusing on a customer need where the group is not limited by traditional organizational structure
- a department, division, or business unit that shares goals and

objectives and has variable pay based on the extent to which goals and objectives are met
- an entire company or entity that is seeking specific goal performance such as profit, market share, or some other valued objective that is used as the measure of variable pay determination

Larger groups (companies, entities, divisions, business units, etc.) have broader organizational goals that are farther from the line of sight of the employee. Smaller groups have goals and objectives that are more within the reach of employees. However, the concept of the partnership requires a linkage between organizational levels. For example, small teams that meet their goals and receive financial rewards and are elements of a larger group that misses its financial goals create a problem for the partnership, because the cost of awards granted in the smaller team cannot be passed on to customers when the larger group is not financially viable. Partnerships require that an important portion of any award should be based on the financial success, or lack of success, of the larger group in which the variable pay plan exists. For example, small-team variable pay plans in a plant pay off only if the plant is financially successful, so that paying a team award in the absence of positive plant results does not add to the plant's financial hardship.

Lump-Sum Awards

In chapter 9, lump-sum awards were discussed as a reward for individual employee performance when base pay is above the competitive market rate of the job. This chapter expands the discussion of lump-sum awards by showing how part of the merit budget can be formally allocated to variable pay in the form of lump-sum awards. By use of a portion of the merit budget for variable pay, organizations can move to variable pay without counting on added performance to fund it. Lump-sum awards can accommodate a small or large variable pay opportunity, based on the direct pay strategy of the organization. Lump-sum awards can also accommodate rewarding either individual or group performance.

Table 11.1 shows how an annual base pay increase of 5 percent compares with an annual 2 percent base pay increase when the remaining 3 percent annually is included in a variable pay plan. After four years of this strategy, a variable pay pool of 12 percent develops from the 3 percent annual investment in variable pay that has not become a fixed cost of human resources. This pool does not include any variable pay funding generated as a result of improved financial performance; it results from a redesign of the base pay administration program. The increase in fixed human resource costs under this alternative is 8.24 percent (including compounding), compared to 21.55 percent under a traditional base pay increase strategy. In this example, approximately the same dollars are spent under either approach; actually, fewer are spent in the lump-sum award alternative because the lump-sum award pool does not compound. The cash compensation mix between base pay and variable pay differs between the two alternatives. With variable pay, the dollars are spent to provide a meaningful reward to employees who perform each year, without the award becoming an annuity.

Allocations to base pay increases versus variable pay can vary based on the organization's ability and desire to add fixed pay costs and on labor market conditions each year. If the awards are nonbenefits-bearing, the amount budgeted for variable pay can be increased since the cost of benefits such as life insurance, disability insurance, vacation pay, and retirement may not increase as a result.

TABLE 11.1

Example of Allocating Cost to
Base Pay Increase Only Compared to a
Combination of Base Pay Increase and
Lump-Sum Award

	Traditional Approach Base Pay Increase Only		Variable Cost Approach Base Pay Increases		Lump-Sum Awards	
	Each Year	Cumulative Fixed Cost	Each Year	Cumulative Fixed Cost	Each Year	Variable Cost Each Year
Year 1	5	5	2	2	3	3
Year 2	5	10.25	2	4.04	3	6
Year 3	5	15.76	2	6.12	3	9
Year 4	5	21.55	2	8.24	3	12

Note: If lump-sum awards are nonbenefits-bearing, variable pay budget can be larger than shown and still cost the same as traditional base pay increase budget. All values are expressed as percentages.

There are many variations in the design of lump-sum award programs, based on the goals of the program. For example, an organization that wants to reward individual excellence and keep its current competitive base pay position in the labor market might design a lump-sum award program as follows: Assume a 4 percent base pay range adjustment, a 5 percent average merit increase in the labor market, and an organization with a 5 percent merit base pay increase budget. The organization allocates 4 percent to merit base pay increases in order to remain competitive with the labor market and allocates 1 percent to the lump-sum award program. This enables the organization to pay a 10 percent lump-sum award to the top-performing 10 percent of employees or a 5 percent lump-sum award to the top-performing 20 percent of employees during the first year of the program.

Another approach to funding lump-sum awards is to use some of the potential base pay increase dollars and add additional variable pay dollars that are *not* funded based on improved organizational performance. This approach may be used by organizations that are paying below their desired labor market position or by organizations that want to ease the transition to variable pay. Table 11.2 shows an example that compares a 5 percent base pay increase to a 3 percent base pay increase combined with a 10 percent lump-sum award pool each year over ten years. The employee is ahead for the first five years with the lump-sum award approach, and is really ahead for ten years given the fact that he or she has had use of the money (in this example, assuming 6 percent interest on the additional dollars). The organization is behind in absolute dollars until the tenth year; however, the organization is really behind more because of lost opportunity since it did not have use of the money for investment and growth in the business during the first nine years (unless it can demonstrate improved financial performance during this period). Other factors, such as discount rate and average length of projected employment, affect the point at which the organization breaks even. However, the analysis shows that variable pay can be an attractive alternative to fixed base pay increases from the employee's perspective.

Under this type of program, the organization needs to consider its specific circumstances and willingness to trade short-term expense for long-term gain, remembering that once embarked on additional pay expense that is not directly correlated with organizational financial performance, the organization has to stay with the program a long time (depending on the amount of add-on pay) before receiving any gain. This

TABLE 11.2
Example of Financial Impact of Add-On Variable Pay on the Employee and on the Organization

Year	Approach #1 Base Pay Only — Base Pay (5% Base Pay Increase Each Year)	Approach #2 Add-On Variable Pay and Base Pay with Lesser Increases than Approach #1 — Base Pay (3% Base Pay Increase Each Year)	Variable Pay (10% of Base Pay)	Total Cash Compensation	Difference to Employee Between Approach #2 and Approach #1 — Approach #2 Minus Approach #1	Difference to Employee at Year-End Assuming Use of Money (6% Interest)	Difference to Organization Between Approach #2 and Approach #1 (Assuming 100 Employees at Pay Level) — Approach #2 Minus Approach #1	Total Difference to Organization
1	50,000	50,000	5,000	55,000	5,000	5,000	(500,000)	(500,000)
2	52,500	51,500	5,150	56,650	4,150	9,450	(415,000)	(915,000)
3	55,125	53,045	5,305	58,350	3,225	13,242	(322,450)	(1,237,450)
4	57,881	54,636	5,464	60,100	2,219	16,255	(221,874)	(1,459,324)
5	60,775	56,275	5,628	61,903	1,128	18,358	(112,767)	(1,572,091)
6	63,814	57,964	5,796	63,760	(54)	19,405	5,400	(1,566,690)
7	67,005	59,703	5,970	65,673	(1,332)	19,238	133,191	(1,433,500)
8	70,355	61,494	6,149	67,643	(2,712)	17,680	271,196	(1,162,304)
9	73,873	63,339	6,334	69,672	(4,200)	14,540	420,042	(742,262)
10	77,566	65,239	6,524	71,763	(5,804)	9,609	580,389	323,857
Total	628,895	573,194	57,319	630,513	1,619			

Value of difference between Approach #2 and Approach #1: 9,609

Note: All values are given in dollars.

is inconsistent with the annual review approach to variable pay, in which the plan design is reviewed each year to ensure that it is accomplishing its intended objectives.

Before beginning an add-on lump-sum award program, the organization must determine what it can afford, since lump-sum award programs are typically funded as a pay expense—not as sharing gains in the financial performance of the organization. The lump-sum award program also needs to be reasonable from the employees' perspective to be successful.

Lump-sum award programs can also be designed so that the pool is generated from a combination of merit budget and financial performance. In this case, the part of the merit budget used for variable pay may be partially or totally earned when either a threshold or target level of performance is achieved. Typically, at target all of the merit budget dollars allocated for variable pay have been awarded, and the variable pay above target is funded by the gain or sharing of financial success.

Profit Sharing

Profit sharing is intended to share a portion of the organization's profit with each employee as a percentage of base pay. This approach is the original organizationwide variable pay plan and is often used as a qualified retirement vehicle because money invested is not a fixed obligation of the organization (this is discussed later in chapter 15). Rather, money is available when the organization is successful and withheld when performance is not sufficient to permit funding a retirement plan.[2] As a variable pay plan, nonqualified profit sharing pays a cash award that is immediately taxable to the employee and is based on the organization's profit and is not deferred until retirement.

Nonqualified profit sharing is a less traditional form of variable pay if it is used at an individual business unit level that has profit and loss accountability, not at the total organizational level. Usually organizations have a threshold return on investment that needs to be met before funding the profit-sharing plan, so a certain level of performance is required before the plan funds.

Nonqualified profit-sharing plans are easier to design and implement than other variable pay plan designs and are often installed with little or no involvement on the part of employees. The challenge with these plans is that they do not provide specific goals or direction on how to improve profit and ensure funding. As a result, profit-sharing plans are not very motivating to employees in large organizations. Profit-sharing plans do permit a portion of direct pay to vary based on overall financial performance and communicate the importance of financial performance to employees. However, unless the organization is small or a business unit of a larger organization and communications about how to achieve profits are well understood by employees, the profit measure is generally too far from the impact employees (either individually or as a reasonably sized group) have on the performance of the organization.

Gainsharing

Gainsharing plans share improvements in productivity, cost savings, and quality with employees who are members of a group that is instrumental in accomplishing these improvements. The employees selected for participation are generally the most meaningfully large group that has performance and quality measures the employees can influence. Awards made to employees are generally funded out of cost savings resulting from improvements in productivity and quality.

In general, award distribution in gainsharing is the same to all employees, as either the same percentage of base pay, the same dollar award, or the same amount per hour worked. Gainsharing seldom divides the employees' share of the gain based on individual performance or on any level below the group at which the plan is funded. The assumption is that the group that forms the basis for funding the gainsharing plan is the smallest unit that should be the basis for award distribution.[3] The performance period used for gainsharing is generally the shortest period in which the organization can meaningfully measure performance. In many instances, monthly measurements can be made; in others, performance can only be measured quarterly or annually.

The prime challenge in gainsharing is to provide financial value to the organization as a result of awards paid. Wise organizations ensure that the cost measure selected for funding is important and broad enough to result in meaningful overall cost savings to the organization and can be influenced by the employee group.[4] Donnelly Mirror's original gainsharing plan design is a classic example of a cost savings measure being too narrow to result in overall cost savings. Labor cost savings were rewarded in the gainsharing plan—with the result that labor costs decreased, but the organization did not achieve an overall cost savings because the expense for the diamond grinding wheels used in cutting glass increased. This happened because employees ran the machines at high speeds and quit using diamond grinding wheels before the end of their useful life since they were most productive when the diamonds were sharpest.[5]

Unless the performance measure used to provide awards to the employees is closely tied to the financial success of the organization, the organization will not want to support the plan if the funding is not otherwise consistent with the financial interests of the organization. For example, one gainsharing plan was based on an improvement in the number of items produced per labor hour. Demand for the product fluctuated because the product was closely linked to the residential housing market. During strong residential housing markets, the plan worked well; both the employees and the organization won. However, during weak residential housing markets, the highly productive employees produced products that the organization could not sell even at a price below cost. Finished-goods inventory increased, and the organization lost money while the employees received significant gainsharing awards. Plans such as this are in jeopardy because they do not create a true partnership between the employee and the organization—the employees can win when the organization loses. In this case, the line of sight was very close and motivating to the employees. However, it can be argued that the line of sight of employees should have been expanded over time (as employees influence and understand the business) in order for a true partnership to occur.

First- and Second-Generation Gainsharing Plans

The first-generation gainsharing plans are the Scanlon and Rucker plans, which measure financial results in terms of productivity improvements or cost control. These plans use historical performance standards to determine appropriate levels of performance that are worthy of reward. These plans are generally implemented for the long term and exist primarily in manufacturing-type work environments.

The second-generation gainsharing plans, such as Improshare™, measure standard hours of direct labor in each unit of output. These plans use historical standards to determine performance levels and generally exist for the long term, as do the first-generation plans. These plans tend to be implemented in manufacturing environments and cover hourly employees only.

First- and second-generation plans tend to have highly standardized implementation procedures and "rules of the road." Although these plans have had success for many years, they have some shortcomings:

- The plans are "everlasting" and assume that the circumstances are never going to change. Because of this, organizations have restricted opportunities to change the plan to meet their evolving needs.
- The plans have limited application opportunity beyond the shop floor. Standards provided are for manufacturing organizations and may not include people not directly involved in the manufacturing process.

Although first- and second-generation gainsharing introduce variable pay to the shop floor and avoid the base-pay-only limitations, they are often rigid and inflexible in design and cannot respond to economic and market changes or business needs that vary from organization to organization. Also, installation of these plans is fairly mechanical. Although Scanlon believed in employee suggestions, often installation of a first- or second-generation gainsharing plan is not founded on the formation of a partnership between employees and the organization for mutual gain, nor is it founded on employee involvement as a necessary ingredient for their success.

The lack of flexibility is much like that of other traditional pay programs that provide certain rules for organizations to follow concerning how things should be done, with little or no substantiation of why the rules are what they are. These plans did introduce variable pay where variable pay should be used. However, the future is probably in more flexible solutions that better match contemporary employee and organizational needs.

Business Plan Gainsharing

Third-generation gainsharing plans are those that follow the business plan variable pay model and use a broader range of business goals as the basis of plan funding and award determination. Rather than following historical practice concerning the development of goals and measures, these plans use future-oriented goals to determine performance measures. Business plan gainsharing is the future of gainsharing in a changing business environment because it permits the development of variable pay plans that are characterized by the features that are most likely to create success:[6]

- The future, rather than the past, is the foundation of the program. The variable pay plan is used to communicate where the organization wants to go, which may be different from where it has been.
- Participation in the plan and measures used for variable pay purposes depend on the organization's goals and the structure needed to attain the goals. Organizations may be changed in order to match the job to be done and are not limited to existing organizational structures.
- Plan design may be changed to match changes in circumstances. Plans have an annual review, which communicates that a variable pay plan will be retained but in a form that matches any changes in the goals and needs of the organization.
- Base pay may be adjusted so that a total cash compensation perspective is a part of the variable pay plan. Base pay may be placed at risk, or what could have potentially been future base pay increases may be placed at risk, if this is part of the organization's goals for variable pay.
- Employee involvement in the design of the plan may vary to match the culture and values of the organization. It is not necessary to follow hard and fast rules in order to design and implement this type of program.

The new pay view aligns pay plans with business plans. This view suggests that employees play an important role in making an organization successful. As it relates to gainsharing, matching the specific circumstances is key to differentiating traditional gainsharing from new pay, business-oriented gainsharing.

Example of Business Plan Gainsharing

A chemical manufacturing organization needed to improve cost management performance in order to stay in business. Lack of quality, in the form of major environmental problems, could threaten the existence of the business. The organization had a quality goal and a cost management goal. The organization implemented business plan gainsharing to enable employees to share half of the cost savings of performance below a budgeted cost per pound produced during the performance period. Of the employees' potential share, half is automatically earned and added to the gainsharing fund because of the cost management performance. Twenty-five percent of the potential payout is earned based on achievement of safety goals. When budgeted production levels are reached, 15 percent of potential payout is earned. The other 10 percent of the potential payout is earned by having no reportable environmental releases. This matrix of measures and goals is closely patterned after the business priorities of the organization, and this makes the gainsharing program strategic in nature.

Gainsharing accomplished some very important goals. The organization has a manufacturing process that requires cost-effective teamwork and collaboration. Combining performance measures that needed to be communicated to employees with the need for employees to communicate with each other could only be accomplished by means of a reward system that made it necessary for employees to work together effectively and achieve the group goals to earn the rewards. A combination of financial, safety, and environmental challenges could only be communicated and measured by tying the success of the organization to that of the employees.

Winsharing

Winsharing is the name we use for a specific type of group variable pay plans, so named because the other plan categories did not accurately communicate the business plan design principles that work best in certain circumstances. Winsharing grants awards funded by the contribution to profitability of a group. Winsharing pays out to all employees in the group based on group performance compared to predetermined goals. While gainsharing typically focuses on productivity and quality and not directly on profit performance, winsharing focuses on profit, quality, customer value, and productivity performance. Winsharing is different from profit sharing in that winsharing has group measures that determine funding in addition to profit.

Under winsharing, the organization is assured of a "win" because variable pay is funded out of bottom-line organizational performance. To grant awards, the organization must actually profit from the results of the employees' efforts. This is important because productivity and quality gains do not always convert into bottom-line performance results for the organization. Under winsharing, payout is based on group performance against a predetermined goal, which is often a quality modifier. The group needs to have profit and loss accountability and be small enough for the employees to feel they can have an impact or influence on performance results.

Winsharing differs from profit sharing because it uses additional measures of at least quality and perhaps customer value or productivity in addition to the profit measure and most often applies to the profit contributions of a group of fewer than 1,000 employees. Performance measures are preset at the start of the performance period based on the circumstances the organization will face during the performance period and not on what has occurred in the past. Winsharing is prospective in nature and typically based on a fiscal-year performance period, since the bottom-line win for the organization is measured most meaningfully on a fiscal-year basis. Awards are typically distributed equally to all employees as the same percentage of base pay, the same percentage of the market rate, or the same dollar amount.

The foundation of winsharing is the formation of a partnership. Both employees and the organization can win if goals are met, and employees are instrumental in meeting these goals. Profit provides a measure of the organization's economic viability in the marketplace. Most organizations using a quality modifier view continuous improvement in quality as everyone's job and believe that the cost of quality in terms of the expense of noncompliance to specifications can be significantly reduced, to the advantage of the organization's bottom line. Such organizations also believe that employees have to make the connection that customers must want to buy the organization's product in order for the organization and its employees to be successful. They believe the focus cannot only be on cost savings or productivity improvement. Since the key is the customer, who must be willing to buy the product at a certain price, the revenue side of the equation—and thus profit—must be considered. This education on the importance of the customer and quality provides a vehicle to improving profitability.

Example of a Winsharing Plan

A division of a major electronics firm had the objective of improving profit performance and becoming a world-class manufacturing organization. The organization had a history of successful participative management practices. After several years of helping the organization with recommendations and improvements, employees were asking, "What is in it for me?" The organization wanted to take advantage of a constructive environment to improve profit performance and become world-class.

The winsharing plan shares performance as measured by bottom-line profits rather than specific cost savings, which may or may not pay for the cost of rewarding performance improvements. The plan was designed so that financial awards are shared with employees once the organization achieves the business plan goal. Above the goal, 50 percent of the financial results is shared with employees and 50 percent is shared with the organization. If the organization's profit is at the level required to be a world-class manufacturing facility, winsharing distributes a greater share of the additional financial results to the employees than to the organization. Poor quality occurs when the cost of rework, rejects, and warranty expense as a percentage of volume produced is higher than the percentage budgeted. Any dollars spent due to poor quality that are more than the amount allowed are subtracted from the winsharing fund in order to focus employees on quality, on which they can have a significant impact.

To increase understanding of their impact on the bottom line, employees in each unit of the organization develop unit goals to help improve profitability. However, achievement of unit goals does not affect payout. The plan pays out to all employees in the organization based on the overall bottom line, modified by quality.

The organization developed winsharing because they believed a group focus was the way the organization would be the most successful. Winsharing is designed to create a sense of the importance of the organization's bottom line among employees. The plan is also based on quality, which has a direct impact on the organization's bottom line and which employees can strongly influence. However, the primary focus is on the bottom line.

Cash Long-Term Variable Pay

Many things that are done in an organization require a focus on the longer term. For example, many important strategic goals are performed over a two-year to three-year period rather than within the confines of a single year. Much has been said about executives managing their organizations to ensure improved quarterly or annual earnings rather than to invest in the future. Many believe that this short-term focus harms the longer-term business opportunities of an organization. As a result, because executives are believed to have the most impact on the longer term, the new pay perspective suggests that long-term variable pay should be used for the executive team. However, many other areas, such as research and development, also require a long-term focus. This means that nonexecutives should also have some longer-range measures of performance as the foundation of their variable pay programs.

Long-term variable pay awards are based on performance relative to preset performance goals for a period of longer than twelve months. The objective is to encourage sustained performance and a strong focus on more strategic goals and objectives. This type of variable pay program emphasizes the importance of long-range planning and decision making that will affect the future of the organization. Also, because the payout is typically awarded at the end of a three-year to five-year period, this type of variable pay program helps retain high-talent people. It creates a sense of proprietorship and serves as the basis for long-term capital accumulation.

Example of a Cash Long-Term Variable Pay Plan

A specialty chemical organization competes in a highly competitive market comprising many larger organizations with more resources and capital. The goal of the organization was to maintain and grow market share by new product development from the research and development organization. They wanted the research and development department to focus more strongly on applied research that fit into the organization's business plan, rather than to expend time on research that was not product related. The goal was to make it attractive for the research and development department either to improve existing products or to develop new products that had market value. In addition, they wanted to accelerate the research and development process for new products so they would not be "studied to death."

A long-term variable pay plan was implemented such that each product under development has "phantom shares." At the date of a product's commercialization, that product's shares are granted to employees based on management's judgment of their contribution to the development of the product. Each year for the next four years, the product's shares increase in value based on receiving a percentage of the product's profit for each year—for example, 2 percent of the product's profit after the end of the first year, 1.5 percent at the end of the second year and 1 percent at the end of each of the third and fourth years. Employees receive the gain in the value of the shares. Losses reduce the value of the shares, but not below the $1 original share value. For example, a share may start at $1 and increase to $2 at the end of the first year, $4 at the end of the second year, $7 at the end of the third year, and $10 at the end of the fourth year. In this case, at the end of the fourth year, an employee would receive an award equal to the number of shares he or she received multiplied by $9 ($10 minus the original share value of $1). Based on significant product improvement, additional shares may be awarded during the four years at a price equal to the value of the share at the end of the previous year. Because of the improvement, the product's profit is expected to increase so that the value of each share is not typically reduced by awarding additional shares.

Each product has its own shares, and employees may participate in a number of share plans. The plan is geared to reward employees based on the financial success of new products, in order to give them a vested interest in the results of their efforts. Significant financial awards give the employees a sense of partnership with the organization, plus the chance for capital accumulation as share value increases.

Discretionary Bonus Plans

Bonus plans, which are retrospective recognition of successful performance without prospective goal setting, are not a part of new pay because of their limited value in terms of communicating direction and focus to employees. While employees may appreciate bonuses, organizations run the risk that employees will come to expect them and view them as fixed pay—whether or not performance warrants—since there is generally limited communication about the criteria for awarding bonuses. With bonuses, the organization loses a critical value of variable pay, that of developing a partnership between the organization and employees.

Stock Options

Stock option plans offer employees the opportunity to purchase their for-profit company's common stock at some time in the future at a specific price. An employee is granted the opportunity to purchase a number of shares of common stock from his or her employer at the price of the stock at the time the employee was granted the purchase opportunity. For example, an employee is granted 500 options at the market value the day the options are granted—$10 a share. The employee is offered the opportunity to begin to exercise the purchase opportunity at the end of three, four, and five years. Fifty percent of the options may be exercised at the end of three years, another 30 percent at the end of four years, and the remaining 20 percent at the end of five years. Assume the $10 stock is worth $15 at the end of three years. The employee can purchase 250 shares at $10, which generates a taxable gain of $5 per share. The stock may continue to increase in price to $20 at the end of four years. The employee can then purchase another 150 shares of common stock at $10, resulting in a taxable gain of $10 per share. Additionally, the stock may increase in value to $25 per share at the end of five years. The employee can purchase the last 100 shares at $10 per share, resulting in a taxable gain of $15 per share.

Common stock increases and decreases in value, as we know. If an employee purchases common stock at $15 per share and the shares fall rather than rise in value, the employee can realize a financial loss since the stock has been purchased with his or her own money. Because of this, stock options represent a major opportunity for employees to place pay at risk. Many question whether or not stock options are true reflections of employee performance because so many factors combine to determine the market value of a share of common stock. However, most agree that common stock does tie the employee to the organization, because ownership does tend to cause employees to be more aware of how their organization is performing.

Traditionally, stock options were reserved for executives and senior managers because options were believed to offer stakeholder status to employees in a position to have a meaningful impact on the performance of the organization. Also, until recently, stock options offered tax advantages. This caused organizations to compete with each other to invent different types of long-term incentive plans that could provide executives with the opportunity to receive tax-advantaged pay, often without taking any risk as a result of receiving the stock options. Traditional stock options not only are limited to executives but also are generally based only on tenure. An employee who stays with the organization during the required period has the opportunity to receive any benefit the options have to offer. Performance is seldom a factor in the traditional use of stock option plans. This may be reason enough to avoid this type of pay system. New pay acknowledges the value of stock and stock options but focuses on plan designs that tie receiving options and direct stock awards to the attainment of performance goals that are within the view of employees. This makes stock and stock options a desired reward and an important element in the formation of the partnership.

The new pay solution often offers stock options to a wider range of employees so as to make many people stakeholders in the future of the organization. The belief is that owning stock in the organization helps form the partnership between the employee and the organization. To the extent the price of stock is viewed as a viable measure of performance, the employee's pay is tied to the gain to the shareholder and the performance of the organization. Some organizations such as PepsiCo believe that the way to associate the employee with the organization is by widely distributing either stock or stock options.[7]

Common stock and stock options play a role in new pay. However, according to Drucker, they should not play much of a role. Drucker states, "Stock option plans reward the executive for doing the wrong thing. Instead of asking, 'Are we making the right decisions?' he asks, 'How did we close today?' It is encouragement to loot the corporation."[8] The well-thought-out use of stock and stock options focuses on the following issues:

- *Base ownership on performance.* Employees are required to perform well to receive the options or common stock. This means the organization expects the employee to earn the opportunity to obtain the stock or stock options based on performance measures within his or her control.
- *Communicate opportunities and risks.* The organization makes it clear to employees that there is both an upside and a downside risk in owning stock. If the employee believes stock only goes up and in fact loses money on the opportunity, a positive gesture may turn into a communications disaster.
- *Emphasize performance, not avoidance of tax.* Stock and stock options are used to provide rewards for performance rather than to avoid taxes. Even though tax laws change about every three or four years, the organization should focus on ownership as a reward for results.

- *Evaluate broad-based ownership.* Some advocate distributing stock thinly to many employees throughout an organization. Distributing stock and stock options widely without concern for performance communicates a message the organization may not wish to communicate. It says to employees, "We are giving you stock to interest you in your organization. However, your performance does not determine whether or not you receive the stock."

There is nothing wrong with using stock or stock options as a reward for performance results. However, few stock and stock option plans are actually designed to reward performance because performance seldom determines the number of options granted, the ability to exercise options, or the vesting schedule.

Organizations often transfer stock to their employees by means of retirement, deferred profit sharing, or employee stock-ownership plans to accomplish a wide range of objectives other than to reward performance and create a sense of ownership. Such goals as protecting the management team from a takeover or passing on a debt-ridden company to employees at a price more than it will soon be worth are disadvantageous in terms of new pay.

Example of Options as a True Reward

A computer manufacturer had used stock and stock options as the primary reward during its initial period of growth. Many employees had become wealthy as a result of receiving stock options early in the organization's success. However, the organization had matured, and top management had come to believe that a major change in the use of stock options was necessary to recognize performance rather than to focus on tenure with the organization.

The organization decided to use stock options as an alternative to cash in the development of its pay plans. That is, the organization made stock and stock options available in situations where cash group variable pay plans would have been used. During the design process, the prime question asked was, "Would stock, stock options, or cash work best in this situation?" The answer was that in some instances cash was best, but in others stock and stock options were most effective. Although no specific rules exist for the use of cash or stock, the organization believed the following guidelines were critical.

- *Is stock understood?* If employees are granted stock, do they understand what happens when the market value of stock increases and decreases in value? Are the employees in a financial position to have the value of stock go down in value?
- *Does stock have any advantages?* Will stock ownership bind the employee to the organization better than cash? Will employees most likely retain the stock once the option is exercised? If they are likely to retain it, the organization believes it is more valuable than cash as a reward. If employees sell the stock immediately, the organization believes cash is a preferred reward.

Using these criteria as guidelines, the organization used stock in a number of ways, including in an employee variable pay plan that grants a combination of stock options and direct common stock shares when target performance is exceeded. Below the target, cash awards rather than stock and stock options are granted. This gives priority value to the organization's stock because performance standards have to be passed to grant stock and because cash was valued less than stock in the plan design.

Conclusions

Many alternatives exist in the area of new variable pay. Some, such as gainsharing and profit sharing, have considerable history; others, such as business-focused variable pay including winsharing, are somewhat new. This flexibility is very important because it permits the organization to start with the recognition of a specific challenge and pattern a viable solution that fits. Also, as the situation changes, the design can change appropriately.

Variable pay is central to new pay because of its flexibility and adaptability. Combinations of funding approaches, performance measures, design involvement alternatives, plan participation issues, definitions of groups, inclusion of qualitative and quantitative results, award distribution alternatives, differences in the period over which performance can be measured, and cash compensation mix alternatives provide a nearly endless reservoir of possible solutions to a wide range of reward strategies. Because no other form of reward has the possibilities that variable pay offers, variable pay is key to the formation of effective partnerships.

Variable Pay Design Issues

Making New Variable Pay Successful

Variable pay design provides the opportunity to give positive "winner" messages to employees. Even though the situation most often dictates what constitutes a successful new variable pay plan, some specific characteristics seem to exist more often with effective new variable pay and less often in less effective variable pay. These characteristics are as follows:

- employee–organization partnerships
- employee involvement
- relevant, simple measures
- effective communications
- short- and long-term focus
- effective balance between line of sight and organizational results
- incremental change of total cash compensation mix
- a "win" when the plan is first implemented

Each of these is important to effective new variable pay design and worth further exploration.

EMPLOYEE–ORGANIZATION PARTNERSHIPS. Variable pay works best and gives the best message when plans are designed to ensure that the organization achieves measurable financial gain when the employees receive awards. This is critical to new variable pay. This means the organization benefits on the bottom line so that the value of the variable pay plan is evident and it will gain strong support at all organizational levels. This is the importance of forming a partnership—not only do the employee participants gain as a result of variable pay, the organization also gains in measurable terms.

EMPLOYEE INVOLVEMENT. The organization involves employees in making decisions that influence how work is performed. Employees work smarter, not just harder or faster. As employees see how they can positively affect performance, their acceptance of variable pay increases, as does the positive nature of the experience.

RELEVANT, SIMPLE MEASURES. Measures used to form the foundation of a partnership are characterized as follows:

- *Relevant to both the organization and the employees.* This means the organization wins measurably if goals are made, and the goals are within the range of impact or influence of employees. Relevance of measures is not sacrificed to keep the plan simple.
- *Simple enough for the employees who participate in the plan to understand the measures, but sufficiently accurate and appropriate to measure performance as required.* More highly educated employees or those who have a more sophisticated opportunity to affect organizational results can tolerate more complex measures. However, the measures are as straightforward as possible to understand so that employees know when they are missing or meeting the yardsticks necessary for a successful partnership and understand how to affect the measures positively.

The prime value of a measure is relevance. It makes no sense to spend time developing complex measures that employees do not understand or measures that are not important to evaluating the performance of both employees and the organization.

EFFECTIVE COMMUNICATION. Whether variable pay plans are developed by an employee involvement methodology or not, it is important to provide for continual communication of the program so that employees may know the following:

- *What they are asked to do to earn the awards.* It is essential for the organization to make it possible for employees to understand what they must do to get the awards. If employees understand the relationship of the reward system to their own performance, it is likely they will expend effort to attain the goals and earn the rewards. This means setting up a process so that achievable steps can be developed and taken that will affect the measures directly or subgoals can be set that, if achieved, will correlate with success on the measures.

- *How they are progressing toward the rewards.* Goals and measures have little value if employees are not able to account for how they are progressing toward the goal until they have either met or missed it. This means feedback as often as possible, and frequently implies monthly reports on progress toward meeting the goals and objectives.

This does not mean money spent on expensive visual presentations and expensive booklets. New pay communication means that managers, supervisors, and other employees are prepared to talk to employees, show them results, exchange ideas, and coach and prepare for future challenges together. Communication is best done face-to-face without the major "dog and pony shows" that have little lasting impact on the communications process. Additional communication approaches of value include charts, graphs, or thermometers posted in the lunchroom showing performance to date, and regular articles in the employee newsletter.

SHORT- AND LONG-TERM FOCUS. Well-designed variable pay programs follow the impact employees have on organizational success. For example, executives, managers, and long-range planners and developers have an impact on the future of the organization. The organization does not want these employees to sacrifice the future for the present. The best variable pay plans in which employees participate measure success at the end of the performance period over which their efforts will affect organizational success. This means top management and others with long-range impact should have most of their variable pay based on longer-term performance measures. Enough of the reward is contingent on the future to cause these employees to sacrifice short-term gain for the longer-term benefit of the organization.

Countering this is an emphasis on short-term goals and objectives throughout the organization where partnerships can be formed that affect measures in the shorter term. Additionally, the goals and objectives of employee groups with shorter-term impact can be used as milestones for the long-term variable pay plans of employees with a longer-term focus. For example, assume increases in per-unit profit and quality are used for a plan for nonmangement employees. Unit profit and quality sustained over a three-year period can become contributing measures to a longer-term plan with management participants.

Evaluating the variable pay plan each year also ensures that a plan with a short-term focus is still consistent with the organization's longer-term strategy and direction. Performance measures and levels are reviewed annually to make sure that they are still relevant and meaningful to what the organization is trying to accomplish.

EFFECTIVE BALANCE BETWEEN LINE OF SIGHT AND ORGANIZATION-AL RESULTS. The line-of-sight issue may be defined in terms of providing performance measures that are within the direct control of employees who are variable pay plan participants. However, plans that have small teams or narrow performance measures that employees most directly affect may often pay out awards when the organization is not financially successful. The sum of the performance of small teams or of limited performance measures may not add up to the organization winning when employees win. Effective variable pay plans create a balance between the extent of control or influence the employees have on the measures and the organization's need to have overall financial success to fund the plan. Generally, effective new variable pay encourages employees to expand their line of sight both at the outset and over time as they see the bigger picture and understand how their performance affects that of the organization.

INCREMENTAL CHANGE OF TOTAL CASH COMPENSATION MIX. Employee acceptance of variable pay is more assured if variable pay is added on rather than having base pay (or the base pay increases employees have come to expect) become at risk. However, organizations may not be able to afford add-on variable pay on a continuing basis. For organizations to remain competitive, the future of pay is controlling base pay and rewarding performance with variable pay. Effective variable pay planning often eases the transition in the cash compensation mix toward variable pay by making the change over a period of time or by taking the transition into account in the way the plan is designed. A discussion of these design features (e.g., larger rewards for greater risk and use of thresholds) is included in this chapter.

A "WIN" WHEN THE PLAN IS FIRST IMPLEMENTED. The difference between moving to new variable pay when performance is good and doing so when performance is bad is remarkable. Although it is easier to get organizations to move to variable pay when times are bad, the move is colored by the other problems the organization is facing. It is always easier to install a variable pay plan when the likelihood of it paying off, at least minimally, is good. Once a variable pay plan has paid off, participants view variable pay as positive, gain confidence in the plan, and are more than willing to stick with it during lean times. If a plan is installed and payoff is unlikely, it is difficult to gain its acceptance when employees are getting only bad news from the plan. If the plan is implemented when times are poor, the organization is asking employees to share the downside of a partnership first; employees are more likely to be willing to form a partnership with both upside and downside opportunities if the partnership begins positively.

The first rule is to try to move to variable pay when the likelihood of a payout is present. At the same time, the organization honestly communicates that the plan will not pay off unless specified organizational results are achieved. It makes no sense to have employees expect variable pay awards in good periods and bad just because the plan paid off initially. Organizations have failed with variable pay when they have communicated only the positive features and downplayed the possibility of no award. When times get tough, employees who did not get the whole truth are unlikely to remain partners with the organization.

In times of pain, the wise organization seeks an important indicator of turnaround as the basis for a payout. For example, it may be worth some award to stop financial losses at their current level or to reduce costs during times of performance pressure. In this way the plan pays off for something that is meaningful to employees but still communicates that there is a very long way to go to success.

Possible New Variable Pay Challenges

Although new variable pay is important because it can be used to match the specific situation and message to be communicated, care is needed in the design of variable pay plans to avoid possible pitfalls, including the following:

- *Insufficient management time.* Effective new variable pay plans are managed on a continuing basis. While traditional pay methods can be left alone and most often are, new variable pay needs to be managed and communicated effectively to make sure it continues to meet the needs for which it was designed. Organizations that are not willing to keep new variable pay plans aligned with their business and financial strategy are likely to find their plans giving a most confusing message.
- *Overpayment.* New variable pay plans may pay for performance the organization could have received through other means such as more effective management. Because people work for many reasons, it is possible the organization may be able to get the desired performance results without the use of variable pay.
- *Double payment or conflict with base pay.* Some organizations are able to make merit pay work. If they are, these organizations may pay base pay and variable pay for the same thing. Users of new variable pay should be able to differentiate between what base pay increases are granted for and why variable pay awards are granted and to make sure these do not give conflicting messages.
- *Lack of periodic evaluation.* New variable pay programs are evaluated annually and modified as needed. New variable pay is fine-tuned to make sure it continues to perform as intended and to be responsive to changing circumstances, needs, and objectives. The review is performed annually so that the process of plan review and modification becomes customary practice.
- *Impatience for results.* Change is very difficult to institute in an organization that is accustomed to traditional pay. Organizations moving to new pay are advised to be prepared for setbacks and changes of direction. Fast results cannot be expected, because it has taken traditional pay decades to create organizations that reward bureaucratic behavior. Although it should not take decades, it will still take time to change an organization to one where people help each other and their organization perform at an excellent level.

- *Measurement challenges.* Employee performance is difficult to measure correctly. New pay requires that the organization continue to seek effective ways to measure qualitative and quantitative performance results. Organizations that have not done a good job of measuring performance in the past will need to spend time making sure measures communicate the importance of a partnership between the organization and the employee.
- *Ignoring the complexity of organizational performance.* Leaders who believe that implementing new variable pay or any other move to new pay is the sole answer to improving organizational effectiveness will be disappointed with the results they receive. Many things—such as leadership style, lack of innovation, culture, and structure—may be contributing to organizational problems. When they do, a wide range of changes is necessary to improve performance results.

While traditional variable pay plans seem to take on a life of their own, new variable pay requires involvement on the part of management and employees to ensure that it remains workable. This means new pay becomes an integral part of how the organization is managed. This level of importance means time and effort will be dedicated to making the programs work over both the long and short term.

New Variable Pay Design Elements

Many traditional variable pay plans are "imported" into organizations because they have proved successful in the organization from which they are copied. This is not the case with new variable pay, which is driven by goals specific to the organization. There are many problems with copying the practices of other organizations. One critical problem is that it is not possible to maintain a copied plan, because the reason for the plan's existence is questionable since it is not related to the copying organization's goals, objectives, and specific circumstances. Using a testimonial basis for implementing variable pay is much more destructive to the future of the organization than not implementing variable pay at all. Experience suggests that the best-conceived variable pay processes address a series of issues that lead to implementing a worthwhile variable pay plan. This experience supports new variable pay.

Plan Purpose

Why does the organization want new variable pay? What can a new variable pay plan accomplish that cannot be accomplished by some other more conventional pay plan design or traditional variable pay? The only acceptable answers to this question involve goals that cannot be accomplished better by some other solution. Acceptable reasons for utilizing new variable pay involve some of the following:

- *Group performance.* Other reward approaches cannot tie employees together to make collaboration and teamwork necessary to receive the reward.
- *Employee involvement.* Variable pay offers the organization an opportunity to have employees join management in studying the situation, considering the issues involved in improving performance, and developing a reward system for a specific application. Because of this involvement, many believe employees have a greater commitment to the performance goals and the resulting new variable pay program than they might have if they were not involved.
- *Organizational results.* New variable pay enables organizations to reward employees for contributing to organizational results. Measures in new variable pay plans are conducive to having employees take a macro view toward what the organization is trying to accomplish, rather than a micro view of what the individual is trying to accomplish. The focus on organizational results encourages each employee to think about how he or she can best contribute to organizational success. New variable pay helps employees understand what their organization is trying to accomplish.
- *Variation in pay costs.* Base pay increases can only increase total labor costs. Many organizations that want to vary labor costs with their ability to pay can accomplish this by implementing a variable pay plan that prevents awards from becoming a fixed cost to the organization without continuing performance success.
- *Failure of merit pay.* Organizations often become weary of trying to repair a merit-increase program that is supposed to pay for performance but has become predominantly a cost-of-living

program that grants virtually no difference in the size of base pay increases to the best performers compared to poor performers. Some organizations go to variable pay because performance appraisal errors do not continue in the form of high base pay; rather, they are correctable during the next performance period. Other organizations believe developing group performance measures will lead to a common understanding of performance measurement and will ultimately result in better individual performance appraisal than will continuing to focus on improving individual performance measurement.

The goal is to improve performance results that are measurable or observable. Otherwise, it makes little sense to move to new variable pay.

Plan Eligibility

Who should participate in new variable pay? Why should those selected participate in new variable pay? Again, only a few satisfactory reasons for plan participation make any sense. These include the following:

- *Impact on measures.* Employees should have impact or influence on the goals and measures to be used to generate awards for the new variable pay plan to be credible to employees and valuable to the organization. The more impact the employees have, the better; however, this is balanced with measures being broad enough to ensure overall gain for the organization. Impact does not mean under the total control of the employees; it means employees influencing the performance result.
- *New focus of efforts.* New variable pay is used to change the direction of employee effort. For example, insufficient emphasis on product or process quality may be corrected by making rewards depend strongly on quality improvement. The best example is insufficient emphasis on financial results to earn pay. If traditional pay increases pay costs for reasons that are not related to performance, new variable pay based on measured results will encourage employees to emphasize results.
- *Emphasize interdependence.* Individuals, groups, and organizations can be linked together by new variable pay

requiring teamwork and collaboration to earn awards. If individuals, groups, and organizations must work together to earn awards and these awards cannot be earned without interdependence, the rewards are likely to cause new alliances to gain the desired ends.

Organizations can gain employee involvement and commitment and a strong focus on results by placing employees in a new variable pay plan that requires employee interdependence and effective working relationships to achieve results. Even if group and individual performance are measured in the variable pay plan, the group focus is central to facilitating organizational success.

Plan Funding

Where does the money come from to fund new variable pay? Several possible alternatives are worthy of consideration, including the following:

- *Improved financial results.* The preferred justification for measuring success and granting awards is the sharing of a portion of financial results attributable to improved performance encouraged by the variable pay plan. The foundation of the employee–organization partnership is variable pay tied to improvements in organizational results. This makes the variable pay plan financially worthwhile for both the employees and the organization.
- *Redistribution of fixed pay dollars.* Some new variable pay plans take a part of what would have otherwise become a portion of fixed pay and dedicate this to variable pay. For instance, if the organization had intended to increase the fixed cost of base pay by 4 percent in a year, 2 percent can be granted in base pay increases and the rest in variable pay if a threshold or target level of performance is achieved. If this approach continues in future years, the variable portion increases to the extent that these dollars are reusable, which is not the case with base pay increases.
- *Added pay expense.* Some circumstances may justify additional pay expense. Sometimes, this is done to install new variable pay in organizations that are less than fully competitive in the area of direct pay. Rather than becoming competitive by increasing fixed

base pay, organizations add a variable pay "pool" that is tied to some measure(s) of performance.

* *Combination of redistribution or additional pay expense and financial performance.* Some plans take some additional pay expense or redistribution of fixed pay dollars to start funding the variable pay pool and then add funding from improved financial performance to create the upside opportunity.

Clearly, to be effective, the most important reason for new variable pay is an improvement in the financial performance of the organization. Success can be measured in terms of quality, customer value, and other measures that directly affect the bottom line. However, without bottom-line gain, variable pay is questionable.

Add-On Pay, At-Risk Pay, or Potential Base Pay at Risk

New variable pay can be add-on pay, at-risk pay, or potential base pay at risk, while traditional variable pay is add-on pay. Add-on variable pay occurs if the organization continues its competitive base pay position and then shares added gains over what would have been expected with the employees. If the organization reduces base pay by a certain amount (e.g., 5 percent) and offers variable pay for performance improvement, then the former fixed base pay becomes at-risk variable pay. If the organization has averaged 5 percent merit base pay increases for the last few years and now decides to average 2 percent base pay increases and put 3 percent into variable pay for target performance and more for above-target performance, base pay will still increase, but not as much as employees have come to expect. Part of the base pay that they were expecting has become potential base pay at risk. However, these employees also have more total cash compensation opportunity than they were expecting.

The decision as to whether new variable pay should be add-on, at risk, or potential base pay at risk depends on a combination of the organization's ability to pay, its current competitiveness relative to the labor market, employee readiness for variable pay, and the setting of performance standards. Generally, the greater the ability of the organization to pay, the more likely that it can afford add-on pay to facilitate the transition to variable pay. If the organization is facing layoffs, at-risk pay is an alternative. Generally, the higher the competitive position of the organization in the labor market, the more likely it is that the organization will select a potential-at-risk or at-risk model. The more ready employees are for variable pay, the more likely it is that potential-at-risk or at-risk alternatives will be selected. Normally, the higher the performance standards are set before variable pay begins to pay out, the more likely it is that variable pay can be add-on. The issue of at-risk pay, add-on pay, or potential base pay at risk is best resolved within the context of the issues of setting performance targets, the overall competitiveness of the organization's total compensation program, employee readiness for variable pay, and the organization's ability to pay.

Measures

What are acceptable measures of performance for new variable pay? The answers include measures that are within the influence of variable pay plan participants and that most often result in bottom-line gain for the organization, which is then shared with employees. Some possible measures include profit, financial ratios, quality, customer satisfaction and value, and productivity.

PROFIT RESULTS. If organizational profit performance can be placed within the view of employees participating in the variable pay plan, profit performance is important to the employee–organization partnership. Profit is preferred to cost or productivity because profit (or the excess of revenue over expense) is necessary to sustain any organization other than the government. Also, it does not need interpretation in terms of trying to determine what affects profit performance. Organizations focused on financial results often consider profit performance in the form of winsharing plan designs before considering other forms of new variable pay.

If profit is a measure, the organization is willing to communicate profit results and to grant awards when it meets its profit goal even if employees have little to do directly with the profit achievement. For example, profit may be due to a major change in the price of materials, such as the oil used to produce an oil-derived product. If funding is based on profit, the organization has to be willing to share profit regardless of how it was earned. Labor-intensive organizations where most of the cost is labor may be interested in using profit as a measure because improving productivity in labor costs can leverage significant profit gains, and because the organization cannot afford to pay out an award of any meaningful size to employees unless profit exists at an acceptable level.

FINANCIAL RATIOS. Many organizations have a number of critical measures that are important to their financial success. Financial ratios such as asset and capital performance that measure effective utilization of the organization's resources may be used if these ratios are affected by measures over which employees have direct influence. Again, the linkage is with profit results. These measures are often more distant in terms of an employee's line of sight, so they may require more communication unless the participants are financially sophisticated (e.g., commercial lenders at a bank).

QUALITY IMPROVEMENTS. The quality movement provides many opportunities to reward performance, since quality directly affects the ability to compete effectively. In combination with profit performance, quality is essential to workable winsharing plans. Also, most recently designed gainsharing plans include a quality measure. Quality is a new pay priority and an important element of new variable pay.

In health care organizations, employees value quality and may be concerned that a focus on productivity will reduce the quality of care. Some health care organizations have found it useful to focus on quality as well as productivity or financial measures such as expenses per discharge, operating expenses (only if they have flexible budgeting, since it takes into account changes in patient volume), or net operating income (because "no margin, no mission"). To the extent that improved quality can be demonstrated to improve productivity or financial performance, quality can weigh more heavily in the formula. Because of the powerful communications value of new variable pay and the importance of quality to the success of health care, quality measures are key to health care's move to new pay.

Other organizations that are concerned about long-term performance being compromised by short-term gain may take creative approaches to ensuring qualitative results. For example, an oil pipeline company with concerns about environmental and safety issues not being compromised during a time when a focus on profitability is necessary may offer "environmental funding credits." Variable pay funding is based on profitability, but receives credits for dollars spent appropriately on equipment, machinery, or upgrades that reduce environmental risk or promote safety and are classified as operating expenses. These function like the personal income tax credits individuals receive for saving energy by installing insulation in their homes. Compared to funding based only on profit, this design funds less per dollar of profit, but the funding credits provide equivalent funding.

Some believe that employees quickly understand the relationship between quality and profit or productivity and will not sacrifice quality, since profit and productivity will be affected either sooner or later. Whether quality measures are built into a variable pay design depends on a variety of factors, including the level of trust of employees, the degree of pride of employees in creating a good work product, the ability to hide quality problems, the length of time between reduced quality and impact on profitability, and the extent of communication and employee understanding of the relationship between quality and financial results. Most new variable pay plans use a measure to stress the importance of quality.

CUSTOMER SATISFACTION AND VALUE. Customer satisfaction and value will become more critical in the 1990s as organizations realize that customers want more than quality and reasonable price. As quality improves, customers will want more; for example, increased flexibility from the organization, improved delivery, improved dependability, and products and services that more closely meet the customer's needs and that are more rapidly designed or developed, produced, and introduced. New pay supports a customer-driven focus—satisfying customer needs with products and services rather than selling only what the organization wants customers to buy.

As organizations focus on the customer, they will begin to measure customer satisfaction and value. And, as they measure customer satisfaction and value, the measurement will improve and be used in new variable pay plans. Customer value, which reflects the relationship of the customers' perceptions of quality and price compared to their needs, wants, and expectations, evolves over time for a variety of reasons, including improvements in competitors' products and services. Customer satisfaction should be measured in both general and specific terms by such factors as product quality (e.g., features, reliability, performance, serviceability, aesthetics), after-sales support (e.g., speed of delivery, consistency, order fill rate, emergency response, preventive maintenance, completeness of repair or modification), and employee–customer interaction (e.g., timeliness, responsiveness).[1]

Some valuable measures are already available: customer satisfaction and value as measured through interviews and questionnaires, delivery date attainment, and lead time reductions. Service organizations use customer retention as a measure because it affects the bottom line. For most service organizations, customers generate more profit each year they stay with the organization because, among other things, the costs of initial processing, advertising, and promotion are reduced and purchases generally rise with each year of the relationship while operating cost declines. Instead of manufacturing's zero defects, service organizations can strive for "zero defections" of customers that they can profitably serve.[2] For any type of organization, a satisfied customer is an appreciating asset.

PRODUCTIVITY GAINS. Improvements in productivity indirectly affect profit performance. This is the foundation of gainsharing. However, unless it can be shown that increases in productivity are in the best interests of the organization and that the organization is not paying cash gainsharing awards for productivity improvements that cannot be "banked," the program is not likely to gain sustained support.

Productivity measures reward employees for the savings generated by performing better than an established base ratio of input to output. Examples of ratios include labor cost to item produced or service provided, labor cost to total costs, labor cost to revenues, labor cost to value added, and a variety of costs (labor, materials, supplies, purchased services, etc.) to revenues—each productivity measure having different impact and implications. If the ratio is all costs to revenues, the ratio measures profit.

If a variable pay plan starts with a narrow definition of productivity, the organization needs to determine if it is comfortable paying awards when productivity improves but profits decline. The definition of productivity can be expanded over time, as the organization and employees develop a partnership, because the employees' line of sight increases. This transition is made easier if the stated longer-term objective of the variable pay plan is to expand the employees' line of sight. Alternatively, it may be easier to start with a longer line of sight and have employees struggle a bit during the transition but achieve the result sooner so that they understand the importance of an employee–

organization partnership. When line of sight (and subsequently, the productivity definition) changes, the sharing relationship between the organization and the employee may also change. Expansion of the productivity definition is one reason why new variable pay has annual reviews.

DETERMINING MEASURES. The sustained financial performance of the organization in bottom-line terms is the most important measure of success. Without quality, customer value, and financial success, organizations cannot thrive. Unless measures selected contribute directly to or influence the overall financial performance of the organization, it is possible to grant awards that are not related to the overall financial results of the organization. Therefore, even though different goals are used, it is best that these measures not pay off unless the organization gains real bottom-line results from the performance received. This is central to new variable pay.

Productivity measures may be used at the team level as long as they do not result in awards when the organization's profit performance, quality, and customer value have not improved. Many traditional gainsharing plans are based on measures that are not contingent on the organization gaining real financial results from successful goal performance. It is best to have plans only generate awards if both the profit and productivity measures are satisfied.

If funding is not based directly on profit, the relationship of the measure used and profit is plotted graphically to determine the correlation between the two measures. If the two measures are not highly correlated, other measures may be more appropriate, or a minimum level of profit may be required for funding the plan. If the productivity measure correlates with profit some of the time but not at other times, the organization determines the conditions that produced the lack of correlation and decides if it is willing and can afford to pay out during the periods when the measure's performance is high but profit is low.

Quality, customer satisfaction and value, and other measures can be used as either funders, modifiers, or qualifiers of new variable pay. Funders operate independently of the financial or productivity measure in the variable pay plan and can pay out if the financial or productivity measure does not. Modifiers increase and/or decrease the fund determined by the financial or productivity measure. Qualifiers serve as a gate that must be passed through or achieved to receive any award funded by financial or productivity performance. The winsharing example in chapter 11 uses quality as a minus modifier. The business plan gainsharing example in chapter 11 uses volume, safety, and environmental releases as qualifiers.

If quality or customer satisfaction and value are funders, they should show a strong correlation with financial performance. Otherwise, the overall funding for all measures should be lower compared to a pure financial funding, to reduce the risk of paying out when financial results do not exist. If a plus or minus modifier is used, the organization decides what it is willing to pay for the added quality or customer satisfaction given static financial results, and may adjust the overall funding down somewhat from a pure financial funding to take into account the expected upside from improved quality or customer satisfaction and value. If quality or customer satisfaction and value function as a minus modifier or a qualifier, the maximum funding is based on financial or productivity performance so that the organization knows its exposure and is willing to be more liberal in its funding.

Whatever is measured will be focused upon. This makes it critical to select a measure for new variable pay that will facilitate organizational success. Employees want to know how to achieve the goal upon which awards are based, so communication about what affects the measure(s) and how employees can accomplish the objective(s) is critical. With financial or productivity measures, employees want to learn about accounting reports that relate to the measures. If profit is selected as the measure, employees want to learn about profitability and what leads to profitability. If the organization is uncomfortable with this level of information sharing, it determines what level of partnership it is comfortable having with its employees and designs a measure consistent with this level.

Defining the group for which funding will be determined is another issue to address. The decision is based on a combination of factors: the line of sight of employees, the group with which the organization wants to build the partnership, and the level at which the organization is comfortable funding variable pay (particularly if it is add-on).

Employee line of sight argues for funding the smallest group that makes sense. However, using very small teams may result in competition where sharing may be more helpful for overall organizational success. For example, in a hospital, individual nursing units may be the best line of sight for the employees, but nursing units such as intensive care and cardiac care need to work together to serve the patient best. Additionally, all patient care areas, including laboratory and food service, need to work together to ensure that care is coordinated in a quality and cost-effective manner.

If variable pay is funded through at-risk pay or potential base pay at risk, funding can be at the small-team level since it is funded through pay expense that could have gone to base pay. However, the wise organization considers basing upside opportunity in addition to the pay expense on a larger group basis to ensure that the organization wins when employees win.

If variable pay is add-on and is funded from financial performance and quality improvement, small teams may show financial performance and quality improvement and receive variable pay awards without the larger group showing any financial performance improvement for the variable pay expended. The organization has to determine at what level it is comfortable with funding, given the organization's need for overall improvement and the employees' need to believe they can affect the results.

Measurement is the core of new variable pay because it provides the justification for sharing performance improvements with employees. Measures are critical because they are the foundation for linking new pay with other priorities. The move to business-focused variable pay facilitates selecting measures that are important to the future of the organization and inhibits dealing only with history, which is the foundation of traditional pay in general and traditional variable pay in particular.

Relationship Between Results and Rewards

What is the organization willing to pay for various levels of contribution by employees to organizational success? Partnerships rely on organizations and employees being able to generate enough results to make the rewards meaningful. Organizations must decide what performance is worth in terms of monetary rewards to the employee. Unless the organization is able to make what it wants financially worthwhile, it is unlikely to get employees to perform as desired. Possible sharing alternatives include the following.

THRESHOLD SHARING. This is the minimum level of projected performance the organization needs before any money in the form of variable pay will be shared with the employees forming the group participating in the plan, and is defined here as close to but below goal performance. Threshold performance levels must be set within the reasonable reach of employees in the plan. Awards at this level are attractive enough to keep employees "in the hunt" for higher levels of performance while recognizing that the threshold performance should have generated profits for the organization that are worth rewarding.

Other factors being equal, the use and size of threshold awards depend on the degree to which pay is at risk. The more pay is at risk or potential base pay at risk, the more likely a threshold performance level will be used and the larger the awards can be at threshold. If variable pay is add-on, having threshold levels may not be appropriate unless reaching a target is difficult due to tough goal setting or to the possibility of significant influence by external variables.

Under most circumstances, new variable pay uses future-oriented performance levels rather than standards based on historical performance. Where circumstances suggest the application of standards based on historical performance, thresholds are not used because organizations generally cannot afford to pay employees additional dollars for no improvement over historical levels of performance.

TARGET SHARING. At this point, performance goals of the organization are attained. The organization is willing to grant meaningful awards to variable pay plan participants while still enjoying financial success that meets goals set for the plan. Other factors being equal, target awards can be larger if variable pay is at risk or potential base pay at risk than if it is add-on. If variable pay is add-on, payout may not begin until performance begins to exceed the target. If variable pay is add-on and historical performance is used to set standards, payout begins after performance exceeds the historical standard.

STRATEGIC SHARING. This is the strong performance level where the organization and employees share success. This means the organization and employees will find it financially very worthwhile to strive to achieve this level. At this level, financial measures indicate that added incremental contributions to the organization are highly worth recognizing.

The strategic sharing amount can vary based on the level of performance. For example, strategic sharing may begin at a lower percentage of sharing and have the percentage increase after a higher level of performance. A few plans may cap the strategic sharing after a certain high level of performance. However, if a cap is used, the design of the plan must ensure that employees believe they have sufficient opportunity to share in the gain to make the partnership real. The goal of new pay is strategic sharing.

The amount of sharing is determined based on what the organization is willing to share and what would be meaningful to the employees for the results generated. The organization needs a certain amount of profit to invest in the future and, if it is a for-profit corporation, to return to the shareholders. The employee needs to believe that the partnership is real. The amount of strategic sharing depends on a variety of factors, including the extent to which pay is at risk or potential base pay at risk below the strategic sharing level. Also, a labor-intensive organization may need to share a larger portion of its profit than a capital-intensive organization to make the award meaningful to employees. This is because labor costs in a labor-intensive organization are a larger portion of the costs, and all other things being equal, the same amount of profit used for awards represents a smaller award for employees in a labor-intensive organization than in a capital-intensive one.

Generally, the more the funding measure selected for variable pay affects overall profitability, the more absolute dollars an organization is willing to share with employees. This is because the closer the funding measure is to profit, the better the organization knows the impact of the funding. If funding is based on measures that are only assumed to correlate with bottom-line gain or that account for only part of the impact on the bottom line, the organization is generally more hesitant to fund variable pay with significant dollars since the organization itself may not realize any gain on which it can meaningfully rely.

Award Distribution Method

How will awards be distributed once performance measures are attained? There are a variety of possible options relating to award distribution, and these can be categorized by whether the smallest unit of differentiation is the group or the individual.

GROUP SHARING. Awards based on group performance are most often granted without any attempt to distribute the rewards further based on individual performance.

Group Sharing by the Same Percentage of Base Pay. Distributing rewards as the same percentage of base pay for all participants is common. This approach is viewed as having a similar impact on all employees because it is the same portion of base pay for each. The approach is acceptable to the extent that current base pay is viewed as fairly reflecting the performance of employees. If base pay is not perceived as fair, basing awards on base pay magnifies the unfairness.

Group Sharing by Equal Shares. When the same dollar award is granted, employees get equal shares in the fund that is available. The assumption is that all employees contribute to the results and should share equally.

This approach is especially popular in group variable pay plans where most employees are nonexempt or hourly and an employee design team decides the award distribution methodology. However, this may not always be the organization's preference, particularly when the leveraging jobs are professional and technical. For example, in health care organizations, there currently is a greater demand for professional health care workers (e.g., registered nurses, physical therapists, medical technologists) than other employee types (e.g., nursing assistants and aides). If an equal dollar amount is awarded, the impact of the award will be less on the higher-paid workers than on the lower-paid workers. The organization may view this as an inefficient way to distribute awards in a labor-intensive organization.

Another example is that of information-system professionals, who are often paid closer to their true value in terms of skills and abilities because of labor market demands. Organizations may want to reflect this in the variable pay awards for a project team by paying as a percentage of base pay.

Group Sharing by Equal Shares per Hour Worked. The equal sharing concept is also supported by awards that are equal shares per hour multiplied by hours worked. This recognizes attendance and rewards the employees who are at work while the results are being generated.

Generally, exempt workers are considered as working regular hours in the calculation, as compared to the true hours they may have worked. This approach has advantages over equal shares per hour for hours paid, which pays for times when employees are not at work (e.g., sick days and vacation days).

Group Sharing by Market Rate. If base pay is not viewed as fair and equal sharing does not reflect the impact of the job, another group sharing alternative is to distribute awards based on the same percentage of the market rate of the employee. The assumption is that market rates or base pay range midpoints accurately reflect the worth of a job. The approach can be used if employees view market rates as fair. This group sharing is based on the worth or impact of a job and makes the award equally meaningful to employees by being the same percentage of each employee's market rate.

Compliance with FLSA. If nonexempt or hourly employees participate in variable pay, the Fair Labor Standards Act (FLSA) requires that regularly paid variable pay that is not discretionary be included in the calculation of nonexempt or hourly employees' regular pay rates to determine overtime pay rates. Excluded from this requirement are "totally discretionary bonuses" (i.e., the organization retains discretion regarding whether the award will be paid and the amount of the award and retains this discretion until near the end of the performance period; and the award is not paid pursuant to any prior contract, agreement, or promise), Christmas and gift bonuses, and awards from a bona fide profit-sharing plan. Bona fide profit-sharing plans are considered as either formal (qualified profit-sharing plan or trust) or informal (paid from the organization's business profits either as a totally discretionary bonus or as percentage of the individual employee's direct pay). Included in overtime calculations are variable pay awards used to motivate employees to improve productivity, quality, efficiency, and attendance.

If percentage of base pay is used to determine awards in any type of variable pay that is not excluded by FLSA, the variable pay award needs to be calculated as a percentage of total base pay earnings (including overtime) to comply with FLSA regulations. If another approach is used (e.g., the same dollar award to all employees, award based on hours worked or hours paid, or award based on percentage of market rate), base pay rates are recalculated to include the variable pay award and overtime is subsequently recalculated to comply with FLSA regulations. This results in increased overtime costs and additional administrative work to perform the recalculation of employees' regular pay rates to include the award. If the organization cannot handle the added administrative burden, these other award distribution approaches are not feasible. Because of the administrative burden, organizations often choose to distribute awards as a percentage of total base pay earnings.

INDIVIDUAL AWARDS. After funding is determined, some variable pay plans base awards on both group and individual performance or solely on individual performance. For example, the variable pay plan may base a portion of the award on group measures and a portion on individual contributions to the group performance, or may divide the group award among the participants based on individual performance.

Individual Awards by Individual Measures. The challenge of distributing rewards based on the achievement of individual performance measures or goals set at the beginning of the performance period is that employee performance at the individual level is difficult and time-consuming to measure. However, some organizations believe strongly that they want to reward individual performance, particularly if the employees' work is not highly interrelated. The quality of individual performance measurement depends on a variety of factors that were discussed in chapter 9. Also, the greater the proportion of plan participants with the same basic duties (e.g., lenders as participants in a variable pay plan), the more likely it is that individual performance can be measured in a quality manner, since fewer different sets of goals or standards need to be developed to measure performance.

Individual Awards by Performance Review. Often, organizations try to distribute awards at the individual level as the result of a subjective performance review. The success of this approach depends on the quality of the performance review. Sometimes this is best accomplished by using a peer rating system, where evaluation is performed by the variable pay plan participants so the people closest to the actual work performance can determine who contributed most to results achieved.

Levels of Individual Performance. Organizations that want to reward individual performance often find that the fewer performance levels used to measure individual performance, the easier it is to administer variable pay and the better the employee acceptance. It is easier to define three performance levels clearly so they are understood than it is to define four or more. Most organizations can only clearly and credibly define three performance levels.

The simplest individual performance differentiation is a "go–no go" gate. If the employee at least meets expectations, the employee receives an award. If the employee does not meet expectations, no award is granted. Some argue that they do not want to pay an award to an employee who is not contributing to the performance results. However, as discussed in chapter 9, the quality of the performance appraisal results and the ability of the appraiser to make honest judgments determine whether the identification of employees who do not meet expectations is done effectively and thus whether this group is worth differentiating. On the other hand, some argue that this go–no go gate is not necessary because peer pressure will either encourage the poor performers to improve their performance or weed them out. And still others argue that other management tools are more appropriate for commenting on and dealing with an individual employee's below-expectations performance.

If the organization wants to reward the outstanding performer, three levels of individual performance can be used—no award for performance that does not meet expectations, an award for meeting expectations (which is what most employees earn), and a significantly larger award for those employees whose performance far exceeds expectations and would be viewed as outstanding by most employees familiar with the performance in question.

The popular and most straightforward solution is group sharing to encourage all participants to contribute to the goals and objectives assigned. However, some organizations believe that individual performance plays an important role and attempt to define individual criteria that make sense and are credible to the participants in the plan.

Performance Period

Over what period should performance be measured and evaluated? Generally, performance periods are dictated by the ability to measure. For example, either seasonality or a long production cycle argues for longer performance periods. Sometimes the extent to which pay is at risk or potential base pay at risk combined with the competitiveness of base pay is considered. If more pay is at risk or potential base pay at risk and the competitiveness of base pay is lower, a shorter performance period may be used, providing performance can be meaningfully measured. Some alternatives include the following.

MONTHLY. This is often the shortest period over which results can be measured. Although motivational theory argues for frequent performance periods and reward opportunities, performance measures often work better over longer periods than a month since monthly contributions may not add up to any sustained gain for the organization. If a monthly performance period is used, it is set in the context of the period that will be used for payouts (e.g., partial payment for monthly performance after the end of the month, and the remainder of the payment reserved until annual performance results are determined). Modeling of past performance is used to determine the extent of monthly fluctuation and the extent to which awards need to be reserved.

QUARTERLY. Often, performance can only be measured relevantly at a minimum on a quarterly basis. This gives plan participants the opportunity four times a year for considering where they are compared to goals. Often this is enough to help the plan participants increase their focus on results.

ANNUAL. Depending on the employees' perspective and motivation, this may be too long a measurement period. However, it matches the organization's fiscal-year planning and budgeting. At the end of a year, results can be reviewed; but if the plan is to pay off at the end of a year, midcourse corrections are not possible without more frequent reviews.

LONG-TERM PERIODS. For jobs that have an impact on some measure of long-term performance, two-year, three-year, or longer performance periods are possible. However, milestone performance periods are generally needed in order that corrections in direction can be instituted. Long-term focus is a priority of new pay.

PERIOD THAT MATCHES PROJECT OR RESULTS TO BE ACCOMPLISHED. Some variable pay awards need to match the period of the project or the results to be accomplished. For example, an information-systems department that is converting to a new system needs to continue to complete current projects, as well as work with consultants to ensure the smooth installation of the new system. On-time completion of milestones may be rewarded, with the major award given for the smooth running of the new system by a certain date, provided other projects are completed in a quality, timely, and cost-effective manner.

Performance measures are critical to determining the performance period. In general, the best choice is a performance period consistent with the measures and the time focus that the employees should have. The ability to measure performance in a relevant and practical fashion affects how frequently performance can be measured, although rewards granted close to the contribution are usually most meaningful to employees.

Frequency of Payout

How often should awards be granted? Most often this answer is provided by the performance period over which performance will be measured for variable pay. However, some differences exist for consideration. Alternatives include the following.

SAME AS PERFORMANCE PERIOD. The payout period can be the same as the performance period if the performance measures are not subject to fluctuation due to business cycles and are difficult to sandbag (i.e., to shift performance into different periods so that one performance period is strong and then is followed by a poor performance period).

USE OF RESERVE FUND. A reserve fund allows the organization to pay awards frequently but hold back a portion of each award until the end of the year in order to balance the account for annual performance results. This reduces the impact of monthly fluctuations, where a few months may be strong but the whole year may be weak. If the reserve fund is positive at the end of the year, the employees receive their share of the balance. If the reserve fund is negative at the end of the year, generally the organization takes the loss.

PAYOUT OVER TIME AFTER END OF PERFORMANCE PERIOD. Part of the award may be paid out at the end of the performance period (e.g., at the end of the fiscal year), and the remaining part of the award paid out over a period of time in one or more payments (e.g., at the end of the second year and at the end of the third year). This approach is generally used either to retain employees or to acknowledge the longer-term sustenance of the results produced during the original performance period. In the former case, the amount retained has to be significant enough to serve the intended purpose of retention. In the latter case, criteria need to be developed to determine if the retained award increases or decreases in value. For example, a lending officer responsible for real estate joint ventures between a bank and other organizations may achieve an award level for the joint ventures developed during a fiscal year but receive the award over a longer-term period of three years based on the success of the joint ventures.

Matching performance periods to rewards is the place to start in determining how often rewards are granted. The payout approach depends on the degree to which performance measures will consistently reflect performance over time, the organization's administrative capability, and what will motivate employees.

Conclusions

Organizations have reason to expect a good level of return from investments in new variable pay. Employees also deserve positive recognition when they help the organization succeed. Although new variable pay is a potent ally of business, financial, and human resource goals, new variable pay plans work most effectively if they are patterned after principles that have a track record of success. New variable pay confronts not only the complexities of organizational change but a number of other challenges as well. As a result, how new variable pay plans are designed, implemented, communicated, and managed matters.

New variable pay accomplishes a wide range of objectives better than base pay and indirect pay because of its flexibility. However, this flexibility requires care so that programs are responsive to the proper organizational goals, offer rewards to people that can help make goal performance a reality, are structured to employ relevant measures, and grant rewards that link employees to organizational success. Communication and frequent monitoring are also needed, making it likely that new variable pay will cause management to spend more time on employee rewards than before new pay became a reality. Above all, this must be an employee experience that gives organizations something to celebrate because all parties are winners.

PART FIVE

New Indirect Pay

Principles of New Indirect Pay

The Role of Indirect Pay in New Pay

Organizations moving to a total compensation strategy that emphasizes new pay find that over the years indirect pay plans have evolved that are too inflexible to pattern after necessary changes in the organization's business circumstances. Indirect pay or benefits include retirement and welfare plans (e.g., health insurance, life insurance, disability, pension and profit-sharing plans), pay for time not worked (e.g., vacation, holidays, sick leave, personal absence pay, and rest, break, and lunch periods), miscellaneous benefits (e.g., dependent care and educational assistance) and legally required payments (e.g., Social Security, workers' compensation, and unemployment compensation). Indirect pay provides employee protection without regard for performance, flexibility, or changing challenges to the business. The U. S. Chamber of Commerce reports that in every year since 1985, benefits (excluding those provided to retirees and former workers) have ranged between 36.2 and 39.3 percent of payroll.[1] Traditional indirect pay strategy involves spending more money on employee benefits to remain competitive without expectation of a measurable return on the investment.

Because indirect pay is traditionally driven by tenure and entitlement, it is difficult to implement a contemporary human resource strategy that recognizes issues such as teamwork and collaboration and not be able to change the total compensation program to communicate with employees about new circumstances and directions. Indirect pay is traditionally not sufficiently flexible to permit organizations to redirect pay expenditures easily to new pay areas where the opportunity exists to communicate more effectively concerning the organization's priorities. Indirect pay is traditionally determined by the practices of others rather than by the needs of employees in a specific organization or by the circumstances in which an organization finds itself.

The new pay view of indirect pay is to contain indirect pay costs to free dollars to spend on direct pay, particularly variable pay, where the organization can get more return from its investment by rewarding performance consistent with the goals of the organization.[2] New pay contends that indirect pay provides a basic level of employee protection for major life and health problems and provides benefits that help employees come to work and be productive at work (such as child care), as well as other benefits that are attractive to the organization's employees but may not be offered by other organizations. Employees share in the responsibility for financing that protection.

New pay organizations determine the level and cost of benefits they are willing to provide. They maintain that level with active cost management and cost sharing with employees to keep indirect pay from rising disproportionately to cash compensation. They work to manage health care providers. New pay organizations are not concerned with being competitive on benefits because the cost of benefits, the true financial value in benefits, and employees' perceptions of value and preferences for benefits have a limited relationship. Instead, new pay organizations want to get the most perceived value for indirect pay dollars spent by managing these costly programs wisely and, wherever possible, providing programs that encourage regular attendance and satisfactory performance and give the organization a differential business advantage. Employee benefits can be used for retention, provided the poorer performers are humanely weeded out of the organization through other human resource programs.

The Importance of Indirect Pay

Most agree that organizations have an obligation to help employees provide for their health and welfare. Because of the tax advantages granted indirect pay and the group purchasing opportunities that are available, it is more economical for the organization to provide the employee benefits on a pretax basis. If benefits are taxed, this circumstance will change.[3]

Benefit entitlement continues into the 1990s in many organizations. Indirect pay has become an expensive and important element of total compensation. Many factors have caused indirect pay to increase in cost and importance; some continue to pressure organizations to expend even more total compensation dollars on indirect pay. In the past, federal wage controls encouraged increasing levels of indirect pay. Also, Social Security has become more important by providing survivor, disability, and health benefits in addition to the original retirement benefits that were the foundation of the program. Tax policy has been most influential by permitting organizations to provide indirect pay to employees without the tax obligations that are incurred by direct pay programs. To avoid the tax consequences of direct pay, organizations moved more of their total compensation dollars from direct to indirect pay. Employee benefits proliferate when organizations are more willing to increase indirect rather than direct pay costs or taxation policy makes them more advantageous.

Social legislation has affected indirect pay by causing the many plans to correspond with strict regulations that prohibit patterning indirect pay programs after changes in employee or organizational priorities. In each instance, legislation and regulation have increased the cost of providing indirect pay. Union involvement in determining employee direct and indirect pay has also affected indirect pay. Unions are strong advocates of one-size-fits-all total compensation planning that ignores the need to manage health care costs and respond quickly to changes in employee needs and in the environment in which the organization must compete.

New pay advocates are interested in the reasons for increased indirect pay that are within the control of management. They believe indirect pay growth and costs must be slowed and reversed where practical. More total compensation dollars need to be focused on direct pay. At the same time, is it important to recognize that employees value some elements of indirect pay highly. Offering more than reasonable levels of indirect pay, however, does not result in increased satisfaction, performance, or productivity. It is direct pay that can ensure the organization's ability to compete effectively by communicating performance priorities to all employees.

Three major factors contribute to the level and type of traditional indirect pay programs. One is the role of outside experts who advise organizations on benefit practices. Another is the role of competitive practice, or what other organizations do. A third is the pressure to respond to employee needs and demands and to keep pace with union-negotiated benefits. Traditional pay provides that competitive practice should determine the amount organizations spend on indirect pay.

External advisors have gone so far as to design elaborate methods of evaluating the comparative level of employee benefits in one organization to those of others in terms of both the cost of benefits and the specific benefit provisions. Techniques such as actuarial value analysis tell organizations that something is missing unless they increase expenditures on benefits to correspond with competitive practice. In effect, this is a high-technology form of me-too indirect pay planning. However, these analyses and employee perceptions of the value of benefits do not necessarily correlate. As a result, benefit dollars may be wasted. New pay suggests that organizations look for reasons for both direct and indirect pay programs that are related to the business, financial, and human resource strategy of the organization. The focus is on seeking an appropriate new pay role for indirect pay that is not based primarily on some definition of competitive practice.

Impact of Competitive Practice

When organizations cannot identify a business, financial, or human resource reason for an indirect pay program, they often call upon the competitive practices of others to compare the level of their indirect pay. Competitive practice is not a cost issue unless it causes an organization to become noncompetitive from a labor cost perspective. Consider two organizations in the same business and same location with similar labor force needs. Assume one of these organizations is less financially successful than the other. Competitive practice would say that both should have similar indirect pay programs in order to be competitive in the market. However, because one organization is less financially successful than the other, a new pay strategy suggests that competitive indirect pay is less important than competitive financial performance. Therefore, the goal is to become more competitive from a business perspective. Once financial results are comparable, comparable benefit costs can be considered, if necessary.

Traditional pay principles provide that indirect pay be competitive from a cost standpoint with other organizations competing for the same labor pool. Indirect pay costs escalate, assuming that what one organization does in the human resource area is adopted by other organizations. Competitiveness assumes that employees in an organization that does not offer levels and types of indirect pay programs comparable to those offered by other organizations will be disadvantaged. In addition, practice assumes that the organization offering less than fully competitive levels and forms of indirect pay will also be disadvantaged.

New pay looks at the competitiveness, cost, and capabilities of total compensation rather than isolating the competitiveness of indirect pay. Total compensation expenditures are focused on the elements that have the best chance of helping the organization meet its goals and objectives. This means spending more time, money, and effort on direct pay programs in general and on variable pay specifically. Although there is some evidence that employees will not work for an organization that does not provide a basic indirect pay program, there is no evidence to suggest that organizations with the most liberal indirect pay programs have an easier time of getting and keeping the very best employees. Employees appear to be less sensitive to differences in indirect pay among organizations than they are to differences in direct pay. All employees are interested in the direct pay they will receive when they consider joining an organization, but fewer ask questions about specific levels of benefits and the portion of benefit costs they will be required to pay.

New pay contends that an organization should determine its total compensation mix and the level of benefit costs that it is willing to expend, and then manage benefits accordingly. Focusing on the competitiveness of specific benefit provisions is not necessary. Employees do not generally leave organizations because of benefits, nor do employees join organizations solely because of benefits. In addition, employees' perceptions of benefits and the cost of the benefits do not often equate. For example, most employees value defined contribution plans more than defined benefit plans. New pay suggests that organizations get the most value for the dollar expended, and this means providing benefits that employees value in a cost-effective manner.

New Pay View of Indirect Pay

In new pay, base pay is the foundation for variable pay and is the less flexible of the two. Indirect pay programs are less flexible than direct pay programs and therefore need special attention. New pay provides that indirect pay is designed to provide a basic level of employee protection from major life and health problems that considers the organization's ability or willingness to pay. New pay views indirect pay as follows.

HEALTH CARE. Cost sharing is key to forming a partnership with the employee relative to providing health care benefits. This means using deductibles and coinsurance that require employees to share costs. Also, it includes employees helping to pay for dependent benefit costs. The reason for cost sharing is to communicate to employees the cost and value of health care. Organizations that pay all health care costs are not viewed as communicating the proper cost/benefit values to employees or getting employees involved in questioning or managing the cost of care provided to them. Case management, which controls the cost of health care to insured people who need extensive care, is key to controlling costs.

LIFE INSURANCE. Life insurance is traditionally offered as a multiple of base pay, with higher-paid employees receiving larger insurance policies than lower-paid employees. Since life insurance needs vary by employee (e.g., a single employee with no dependents versus a sole wage earner with a family of four), new pay organizations—to get the most value for their indirect pay dollars spent—will offer basic coverage and give employees the opportunity to purchase additional term life insurance at their option.

DISABILITY PROTECTION. The new pay view considers this to be critical because disability is more likely to occur than death during an employee's working career. As a result, new pay organizations often offer longer disability protection, coupled with rehabilitation protection, so that employees have some financial security in the event they are not able to work. New pay organizations make sure that not working is not more financially attractive than working; the objective is to provide rehabilitation and career alternatives as appropriate to encourage employees to reenter the work force to the extent that they can. New pay organizations have a longer waiting period for disability coverage to serve as a retention vehicle for employees and to ensure that the employee is a "keeper" and has earned disability protection by giving value to the organization through working before disability protection is provided.

RETIREMENT. New pay organizations are concerned about being able to manage poorly performing employees out of the organization in a prompt but humane manner. Liberal retirement programs of the defined benefit variety communicate to the employee that remaining with the organization for a long career is highly valued. This is no longer practical or desirable. In addition, it is equally desirable to be able to hire older workers without the organization having the burden of funding a defined benefit plan.

New pay supports the continued development of the concept that organizations fund retirement by taking steps to minimize their defined benefit programs and to move toward defined contribution programs, such as profit-sharing plans, that avoid future fixed promises of retirement benefits and communicate the value of overall organizational financial success. A profit-sharing plan that is funded based on the organization's profitability creates a long-term partnership with the employee wherein the employee's retirement funding increases only with the sustained success of the organization.

Many organizations choose not to provide defined benefit retirement plans for a variety of reasons, such as maintaining their entrepreneurial spirit, having employees fund their own retirement based on successful performance that is reflected in direct pay, and having more of total compensation dollars be performance based. For example, Apple Computer does not provide a defined benefit retirement plan but provides a matching 401(k) plan in part because it wants to maintain its entrepreneurial employee spirit.

PAID TIME OFF. The new pay strategy suggests organizations should attempt to structure paid time off so that most vacation time is actually taken annually and not accumulated and/or paid for. Also, new pay rewards those who take minimal sick leave. Labor-intensive organizations focus on the high cost of paid time off and make it attractive for employees to be at work when not on vacation and to return to work quickly following illness. Employees cannot perform unless they are at work, and working must be much more financially attractive than not working.

EXTRA BENEFITS. New pay organizations are attempting to make non-management career paths as attractive as management career paths to prevent excessive organizational levels and layers constructively. Many are also moving away from extra management benefits and toward the use of cash awards in the form of variable pay, which can change from performance period to performance period.

Although new pay design efforts are most strongly focused on direct pay, a new pay perspective of indirect pay exists. In the next two chapters, the traditional and new pay views of indirect pay will be reviewed to compare and contrast these perspectives for evaluation and consideration.

Role of Indirect Pay Objectives

Employees often "understand" that they have been "promised" a specific level of retirement benefits at a certain age or a specific level of medical or dental protection from their benefit program. Indirect pay programs are difficult to change unless these changes provide more liberal benefits to the employees. Whatever the reason for reducing the level of indirect pay, or asking employees to share in the cost of indirect pay plans, these changes are often viewed as "takeaways." This makes it difficult to reduce the level of any indirect pay plan. If benefits are to be reduced, a preferred strategy from an employee-relations viewpoint is not to reduce benefits but to maintain the current level of benefits at the organization's current cost, have employees pay any additional costs, and have the organization actively manage benefit costs. This will slowly shift total compensation costs away from indirect pay.

Organizations have the opportunity to consider three distinct postures relative to indirect pay communications objectives:

- The organization is vague and inconsistent, and the employee is left to figure out what the human resource objectives are and what role the organization serves relative to the employee.
- The organization serves as the employee's keeper from harm's way and protects the employee from all risk.
- The organization serves as the employee's facilitator by providing the opportunity for the employee to become a partner with the organization and have the employee accept some responsibility for the protection that benefits provide. At the same time, the organization aggressively manages the costs of benefits, such as the financial relationship with health care providers. This is the new pay view.

Obviously, this is a mix-and-match situation, with opportunities existing among these postures. However, organizations tend to remain fairly stable relative to their indirect pay objectives without regard for the situation in which they find themselves. New pay organizations do not believe the employee's-keeper policy is consistent with the interests of either the organization or the employee. Rather, they believe that if employees are lulled into feeling that they will be sustained without concern for the fortunes of the organization, it will not be possible for them to behave like partners during economically difficult as well as successful times. New pay organizations believe that the organization's obligation is to inform employees of their benefits and that employees should take responsibility for making informed decisions based on the information provided.

A vague indirect pay policy and correspondingly vague objectives create problems that may be similar to an employee's-keeper philosophy. If employees do not know their role as it relates to the organization, it is unlikely that they can either be lulled into a sense of well-being or become partners. Because of this, new pay organizations elect to implement clear indirect pay objectives and communicate these objectives aggressively and continuously in an understandable manner. If it becomes necessary to change the indirect pay objectives, employees have a starting point of understanding and an information basis on which to compare the magnitude of change. Also, they have not been promised something that the organization can no longer deliver.

New pay organizations prefer the role of facilitator of the employee's opportunity to contribute to organizational success and to benefit as a result from his or her association with the organization. This means providing employees with a road map that honestly defines the rewards and the opportunities to contribute to short- and longer-term goals and objectives and empowers the employee to be successful. Given the road map and honest opportunities to succeed, the employee has the chance to become a partner with the organization and share in both the wins and the losses the organization faces. If the direction of the organization and the values of the employee are not consistent, the employee can find another organization with values that are consistent with his or her own.

This position is most consistent with the direct pay planning process because direct pay can be more easily changed to match specific circumstances. However, it is of critical importance in the indirect pay area as well. It is important that employees not be permitted to assume that because of the inflexibility of indirect pay plans, these plans will never be modified to reflect changes in the circumstances that encourage people to influence organizational performance positively.

Strong Employee Considerations

If changing base pay is a challenge, changing employee benefits is an even larger challenge. This is why communicating and conducting annual reviews of benefits and making changes as needed is important. Visible annual reviews will communicate to employees that benefits are not forever and can be changed. The challenge to implementing change in the indirect pay area is with traditional indirect pay communications. Seldom is the fact that indirect pay may change ever communicated to employees. When organizations are faced with economic or competitive pressures to have employees share indirect pay costs or when levels of indirect pay need to be reduced in order to increase expenditures on direct pay, this is viewed as a takeaway and a breach of a promise to the employee. Honest employee communications are critical if partnerships are to be credible. Although indirect pay may stabilize eventually, change is to be expected for some time.

To move to new pay and implement the needed changes to indirect pay, the following are suggested.

ANNUAL REVIEWS. During the next decade it will be impossible to promise employees that there will be no change in the composition of their total compensation program. Because of this, communications will help employees understand that indirect pay programs will be reviewed on an annual basis to determine the extent to which they continue to meet the needs of employees and the organization. Consistent with this, employees will need to understand that the possibility of change exists. It is a management responsibility to communicate this honestly to employees. The presence of an annual review requires that the organization remain in touch with employees to prepare them for changes in indirect pay program content and direction.

INVOLVEMENT. New pay implies a role for employees. New pay requires more than merely involvement in choice making in a flexible benefit plan. It implies a role in providing input to management concerning the overall design of benefits. For example, if costs are to be shared, how this will occur should involve employee input. If dollars are directed to variable pay, employee involvement in the redistribution of expenditures will facilitate acceptance. Employees are important to making change work effectively, and involvement is a key issue in the area of indirect pay.

COMMUNICATIONS. Often, benefit dog-and-pony shows are a part of indirect pay communications. This is not lasting, and it does not respond to employee needs to understand how they are affected by change. Communication means supervisors understanding indirect pay and communicating with employees face-to-face rather than sending them to the personnel office for answers. This implies two-way communications so that supervisors can listen to concerns as well as answer questions and thereby become more meaningfully involved in the change process. It also involves providing employees with benefit statements that show clearly the features and values of their benefits.

TWO-TIER CHANGE. Changes can be made by "grandfathering" senior employees and changing the benefits of those with less tenure. This is best approached with care because it introduces the possibility of creating have and have-not employee groups, and must be viewed as secondary to a complete change that would affect all employees.

INCREMENTAL CHANGE. Changes can be implemented over time. This may lessen their negative impact, or it could draw out a change that would be best accomplished more quickly. The organization may need to move rapidly, making a smooth transition over time impossible.

The preferred strategy is to get employees involved and prepared for change. During the change, organizations ask employees to help make the change work. Based on this approach, employees become partners in the change and understand why it is necessary and how it affects them. Two-tier change or incremental change can work but introduces challenges and complexities.

Role of Business and Financial Strategy

Indirect pay can play a role in helping the organization attain business and financial goals. Some examples of the role business and financial goals play in influencing indirect pay planning include the following:

- *The organization diversifies by means of acquiring a business that has a lower profit margin and higher labor costs than the primary business.* Adopt a profit-sharing plan rather than a defined benefit plan as the method of funding retirement for the newly acquired business. This will permit a "pay as you can afford it" perspective for funding employee retirement.
- *A tight labor market places the organization in a position of strong competition for local talent in female-dominated jobs.* Adopt a day-care center to make the organization a more desirable employer. This can be a way to gain a tactical advantage over others; the day-care center can contribute to employee retention because employees may not want to disrupt their child's environment by switching jobs and causing a change in child care providers. Place an annual review provision on the policy so that it can be changed in the event the labor market supply changes.

  Another alternative for this tight labor market is to offer a reimbursement account in which employees can set aside a portion of their pay on a pretax basis for child care expenses. Reimbursement accounts are described more fully in chapter 16 on flexible benefits.

The challenge is not always to redistribute indirect pay expenditures toward direct pay. Actually, the objective can also be to use indirect pay to address a specific business need. The challenge is to make the addition of an indirect pay program something that need not last forever. Even indirect pay need not become an annuity. In this way a program that is added to respond to a specific problem can be changed when circumstances change. This is often very difficult and is why new pay organizations most often view direct pay as a better strategic business and financial tool than indirect pay.

The Evolution of New Indirect Pay

In spite of the momentum created by the indirect pay practices of the 1960s, these approaches to pay management are becoming troublesome. Progressive organizations faced with growing business competition and increased financial pressures realize that traditional indirect pay is not viable when they can no longer pass on high human resource costs to their customers if these costs are unrelated to organizational or employee performance or product or service quality. Executives and boards of directors are inquiring about alternative approaches as a possible competitive weapon. Cost pressures, and not the need for organizational performance, have forced many organizations to explore opportunities to gain an added advantage from total compensation expenditures. Enlightened managers realize that all employees count in the success of an organization. They also find that about 25 to 30 percent of their total pay costs are indirect pay costs and are not focused on employee performance and productivity. This has caused indirect pay programs to be evaluated in a constructive manner.

Conclusions

The future is very uncertain as it relates to traditional employee benefit plans. This is a time for cost sharing and cost containment. It is a time to evaluate the possible advantages indirect pay plans provide and to manage employee indirect pay like any other aspect of business. Organizations are interested in keeping people at work so that they can be motivated to perform. This means vacation, sick pay, retirement, and health care plans need to be restructured so they support and coordinate with other pay plans that help focus employees on the strategy and tactics of the organization.

Traditional indirect pay programs are expensive and based only on entitlement. The new pay view recognizes the organization's obligation to protect the employee from a certain level of unexpected expenses. However, protection is more closely tied to performance and contribution than merely to tenure.

Health Care Benefits
Under New Pay

Overview of Health Care

If employees are asked to identify which element of indirect pay is most important, they will say health care protection. This is because health care benefits are the most used benefit. Unfortunately, it is the benefit that is most quickly increasing in cost.[1] Retirement and life insurance programs are not as close to the employees' stream of consciousness as a benefit they and their families have used many times. In most instances, health care involves protection for expenses related to hospitalization, surgery, and general medical expenses. In some instances these plans additionally cover dental care, eye care, and prescriptions.

Health care protection is available in a number of forms, including comprehensive plans, self-insurance of some or all of the potential protection liabilities, and managed care contracts (health maintenance organizations and preferred provider organizations).[2] Some of these alternatives have important cost implications, while others limit the possible physicians or hospitals available to the employee.

Comprehensive Plans

Most health care programs began as products sold to organizations by insurance companies. The insurance carrier can either insure all of the employer's risk of exposure as it relates to health, disability, and death or share the risk with an organization that is willing to self-insure a portion of the health care cost exposure. Insurance companies can also provide claims processing to an organization that elects to self-insure.

Comprehensive plans offer considerable flexibility to organizations in the design and risk assumptions involved in their health care protection. The employee has the opportunity to elect the care provider of his or her choice, and the insurance company provides benefits consistent with a specific schedule or as a percentage of the health care expenditures incurred by the employee.

Self-Insured Plans

To manage health care costs better, larger organizations self-insure all or a portion of their health care costs. Because many additional burdensome state insurance and federal benefit regulations apply to insured programs but not to self-insured programs, organizations that are financially able to self-insure are moving to do so. This movement is taking a number of directions. One is to self-insure most of the costs and to purchase a stop-loss policy from an insurance company. The stop-loss insurance program can be applied to the total annual claims exposure of the organization or to each covered individual. In this way, the organization is able to predict the implications of the risks assumed.

Some organizations are beginning to contract directly with health care providers for discounting if they have sufficient leverage because of a large employee population in one area. These contracts provide preferred pricing while ensuring quality of care.

Organizations funding all or part of their health care benefits usually elect to have either the insurance company or a third party handle the claims. Often, the reasons for the organization not handling claims processing itself are cost management and containment; the processor's ability to provide the organization with network and case management, UCR (usual, customary, and reasonable charges) data and trend data; the processor's assistance in legal compliance issues; and the processor's credibility with employees, who seem to prefer having an "insurance-like" organization handling claims and claim processing.

Managed Care—Health Maintenance and Preferred Provider Organizations

The health maintenance organization (HMO) requires employees to use the physicians and hospitals provided by the HMO. The HMO may be either a group practice model, which employs physicians and uses its own hospitals for subscribers, or an individual practice association (IPA) model, in which the HMO contracts for services with physicians who are not its employees and with hospitals that it does not own.

HMOs are attractive because they provide very cost-effective health care and are motivated to keep the employee well since the HMO is generally obligated to provide complete medical service to the employee in the event of need. In addition, HMOs know a patient's history and generally offer well-integrated services (or "one-stop shopping") for the employee who can get complete medical service at a single or at most only a few locations.

Preferred provider organizations (PPOs) offer more range of choice to the employee than HMOs and can be cost-effective to the employer who contracts with a PPO. PPOs enlist hospitals and physicians into their program at discounted rates. Employees can avoid or have a reduced deductible cost if they elect to receive their medical service from a physician or hospital that is a member of the PPO. However, the employee can elect to go to a nonmember hospital or physician and still receive the same coverage, with the understanding that in this case, they will have to pay for a larger portion of the health care cost themselves.

One difficulty with HMOs and PPOs is that an employee's preferred physician may not be on the panel of the particular HMO or PPO that the employer provides. This may be an issue in recruiting an employee who has, or has a family member who has, a long-term relationship with a physician for the care of a specific medical problem. Employees often ask the physician to join the PPO, thus having the physician participate in the health care changes that the United States is undergoing. Also, some HMOs offer employees the opportunity to purchase a "swing-out option," in which limited coverage is provided for a specified person to be treated outside the HMO for a specific health condition.

Hospital, Surgical, and Medical Plans

Group health care plans cover hospitalization expenses and physician fees for services performed in the hospital. Plans protect employees and their families against major medical expenditures. Because the plans originally paid only for treatment in hospitals, employees went to hospitals for medical care. Later, plans began to cover treatment in a wider range of outpatient facilities.

Often the typical comprehensive plan covers nearly all hospital costs and reasonable and customary surgical fees plus specific medical expenses, including physician visits to the patient in the hospital. The plan generally pays after a deductible amount has been charged on an individual or family basis each year. Subsequently, the plan pays for approximately 80 percent of medical charges and office visits, prescriptions, lab fees, and other treatment. The remaining 20 percent of the charges are paid by the employee. Usually, the amount the employee pays is limited to about $1,000 when the plan pays all the charges permitted by the plan. When hospital charges are exempt from the deductible, the design encourages overutilization of hospitals for health care; most plans now include hospital charges as part of the deductible.

Cost Savings Opportunities

Two-income families have created a situation where duplication of health care coverage is possible.[3] The objective of cost containment is to prevent more than 100 percent of expenses from being paid. Most plans provide for coordination of all benefits if an individual is covered by more than one plan so that the responsibility for paying benefits is assigned. The plan that covers expenses for an employee is the primary coverage, and the duplicate coverage is the secondary plan. Dual coverage makes it difficult to involve employees in cost containment since they know they will receive full coverage.

As a result of providing less liberal health care benefits, organizations can contain health care costs in dual-income coinsurance situations because the employee is encouraged to obtain primary family coverage from his or her spouse's employer's more liberal benefits. For example, the California aerospace industry generally has more liberal health care benefits than the banking industry. As long as the aerospace industry continues to provide liberal health care benefits, the banking industry is able to shift some of its health care costs to the aerospace industry. This practice may stop as organizations with more liberal health care plans get smarter and require employees to pay an additional amount for coverage of spouses who do not use their own employer's plan.[4]

To contain health care costs, organizations have looked to alternative funding arrangements such as HMOs and PPOs. These systems offer competitive protection with all other providers of health care coverage. The advent of competition among health care providers has given organizations the opportunity to contain costs. In the future, the issue will be not just cost containment but a combination of cost containment and quality of care. Insurers will favor those health care providers with lower costs plus good quality of care as measured by morbidity rates and other clinical and service indicators.

To control costs, insurers and organizations are restricting mental health care benefits with higher coinsurance and low annual and lifetime maximums. Alternatively, mental health care costs can be controlled by case management and employee assistance programs (EAPs) that provide employees with a limited number of inexpensive visits to a mental health professional.

In addition, organizations are redesigning health care plans to provide cost savings opportunities. Some of these opportunities include the following:

- deductibles (increasing the deductible from $100 to up to $500 so that the employee pays for initial and reasonable expenses and is covered for major expenses)
- coinsurance ratio (increasing the employee's share of the expense to more than 20 percent and adding a stop-loss that protects the employee from major losses)
- annual stop-loss (increasing the annual stop-loss from $1,000 to up to $5,000 to provide a higher level of cost sharing by the employee)
- employee premium contribution (increasing the employee contribution for personal coverage and charging the employee a realistic amount for dependent coverage)

In any of these alternatives, the organization has responsibility for a minimal level of coverage and the employee shares in paying the cost of very expensive health care. New pay encourages all of these strategies because they are geared toward cost sharing and having employees understand the cost of health care and play a role in managing costs.

Effective claims administration offers a major opportunity for savings because claims often involve considerable waste by poor eligibility checking, neglecting to apply benefit coordination, neglecting to obtain third-party recoveries, improperly applying deductibles and copayments, not observing plan maximum limits, or not detecting overcharges by the health care provider. Employees are less likely to call attention to an overpayment than they are to an underpayment. As a result, errors cause only increases in costs to the organization. Organizations and insurers work hard to detect errors by training claims processors and offering variable pay for high-quality cost control.

Insurers are controlling costs by requiring precertification for hospitalization and surgery, second opinions before surgery (to reduce unnecessary surgical procedures), outpatient surgery where appropriate, and utilization review at the hospital to ensure the most cost-effective use of health care.

Organizations are undertaking communications programs to show employees why cost containment is needed and how they can benefit from cost-effective benefit administration. Some organizations make an ombudsman available to help employees manage their inpatient and outpatient health care efficiently and cost effectively. The ombudsman is technically qualified in health care cost-benefit issues and plays an objective role in ensuring reasonable cost and quality care.

Wellness programs educate employees to participate in preventive or remedial programs. Some of these programs involve stopping smoking, nutrition, exercise, stress control, and related programs. As more organizations take a stand for employees to keep well, it is probable that these programs may eventually have some positive impact on the cost of providing medical protection. The cost justification of wellness programs should be determined. A true wellness program will provide for lower contributions from employees who practice good health habits than those employees who do not and will still result in health care cost savings.

A major opportunity for health care cost containment is case management. Much of the cost and most of the savings can be achieved by managing special cases—those people who have a major health care need, such as premature babies, bone marrow cancer patients, or AIDS patients. Case management companies assist insurers or organizations in managing a patient's care from preadmission review through posthospital care to determine the most cost-effective care for the patient. This includes setting up appropriate care outside the acute care hospital as soon as is practical. For example, the case management company may obtain an exclusion waiver for a companion that will allow a patient living alone to come home sooner at less expense than hospitalization. In most cases this is a win–win situation since the patient would prefer to be at home.

Postretirement Health Protection

Employees are retiring before age sixty-two, when Social Security retirement benefits become effective, and before age sixty-five, when Medicare coverage becomes effective. The primary business reason for an organization to consider offering retirees health care protection is to encourage early retirement, thus reducing staff without the disruption of involuntary terminations. Beyond the incentive to encourage retirement, no true business reason exists for offering postretirement health care protection.

New Pay View of Health Care

Wise organizations manage indirect pay aggressively and effectively. This is especially true for health care, which must be managed now or national health care programs will take the responsibility for management out of the hands of organizations and employees. Instead of simply administering health care benefits, organizations need to manage them as they would any other expense. Organizations that are serious about cost containment will need to go beyond usual cost management and focus on utilization and case management.

Some organizations are working hard to solve the cost problems of health care. *Industry Week*[5] indicates that there are major challenges to an organization's ability to manage health care costs effectively:

- *Cost shifting.* Health care providers price services 30 percent higher than necessary to compensate for people without health care insurance and to account for the limits the government has set for people covered by Medicare and Medicaid.
- *Little control over delivery of health care.* The RAND Corporation estimates that 25 to 33 percent of all health care services are not medically necessary. This indicates that standards for determining the necessity of procedures do not exist.
- *Unhealthy life-styles.* Hewitt Associates estimates that 7 percent of employees account for 70 percent of all health care costs and that 71 percent of people with medical protection have claims for less than $500 annually.
- *Cost sharing.* Organizations have caused employees to share in

the costs by means of higher deductibles, higher premiums, and copayments, since wellness programs have not changed employee use of medical plans.

- *Ineffective managed care.* Organizations stop controlling health care costs once they negotiate a discount from health care providers instead of focusing on utilization and case management.

To many large and small organizations, managed care has taken on the intensity of a "crusade," according to the *Industry Week* article, and this level of activity has paid off financially. Some of the actions that these organizations have taken include the following:

- To avoid having health care providers pass on costs to small organizations that they can no longer pass on to larger organizations, some small businesses have formed a single health care buying unit to control health care costs.
- One major organization has taken physicians to court over fees and has often won. The objective was to control costs and gain public visibility of excessive physician fees. Because the organization was not able to pass on unreasonable costs to its customers, it believed physician costs should be controlled.
- One organization gathered utilization information and increased cost monitoring, and this helped them learn to manage prenatal care to avert premature births, determine what could be treated through outpatient surgery, and decide when bypass surgeries were necessary. The major change was the development of an information base upon which to make educated decisions. Until the organization had the information, it was not able to manage health care costs effectively. Insurance companies did not retain the organization's information because the average organization tended to change insurers every two years in its local area.
- A major organization retained the training group of a local football team to eliminate office-visit costs of up to $150 for athletic-type injuries and to return employees to work sooner. The organization chose an alternative to compete with local health care providers in order to control costs.
- One large organization arranged to have local physicians who were primary providers join the organization's PPO and accept payment based on the number of patients they had rather than

for the number of times they saw each patient. They paid hospitals on a per diem basis, not on the actual services given to a patient. This reduced unnecessary health services and limited costs dramatically.

- An organization made it financially unattractive for employees to use local primary physicians that were not in its PPO. As a result, 95 percent of this organization's employees changed their family physicians.
- An organization gives each employee a $100 credit for preventive health services not covered by the plan and gives more if the employee exhibits none of the following risk factors, which affect health and can be modified—high blood pressure, diabetes, high cholesterol, smoking, and excess weight. This rewards good health practices.
- Some organizations are separating the assessment and evaluation process from the treatment process. An independent physician or health care advisor is responsible for the employee's health but does not have a financial investment in the frequency or course of treatment. These organizations have clinics or use primary care physicians to make the diagnosis and then refer patients for treatment elsewhere.
- Some organizations are hiring a medical director to develop standards of necessity and define appropriate care. Based on these standards, organizations negotiate with providers.
- Some organizations are opening their own clinics in order to control health care and avoid some hospitalizations. They are taking the health care services out of the human resource organization and having them managed as an independent cost center. The clinics are in competition with local health care providers as a cost control move. For malpractice liability reasons as well as cost efficiencies, opening a clinic that provides more than basic services would seem to be limited to large companies with large employee populations in one concentrated area.
- In-house pharmacies are being set up by some organizations to control the expenses of prescription drugs by providing them at cost to employees.

The *Los Angeles Times*[6] reports that organizations have taken specific actions to manage health care costs:

- AT&T, Southwestern Bell, and Allied-Signal adopted preferred provider organizations where physicians and hospitals are assured a flow of patients in exchange for cost concessions.
- Goodyear Tire & Rubber and Tenneco provide in-house clinics for employees. Goodyear provides an in-house drugstore; Gillette provides in-house X-rays.
- Southern California Edison implemented a comprehensive managed care system involving 10 in-house clinics, an in-house claims payment system, and a preferred provider organization.
- Johnson & Johnson, U-Haul, and Adolph Coors Co. have various forms of wellness programs. Wellness programs may involve routine checkups, an emphasis on healthy habits, or lower premiums or a lower employee coinsurance ratio for employees with no controllable risk factors compared to other employees.

The above sets of examples illustrate how specific organizations responded to a challenge. It is possible that other organizations will find different local solutions. However, unless they look for solutions, they will not find them. The major change in these organizations is from being merely payers of bills to being actively involved in reducing their health care costs. The thrust is to define the limits of reimbursement for health care providers and ask them to respond accordingly. The focus of these organizations is to free total compensation costs for direct pay. They understand that a dollar spent on health care is a dollar they cannot spend on forms of pay that are better suited to making the organization a success.

Providing reasonable protection for employees and focusing on the control of health care costs is central to the effective management of costs. New pay suggests that organizations focus on communication with employees concerning the costs of providing protection. When cost savings are possible, the savings are shared with the employees to make it worthwhile for them to contain costs.

The partnership means that employees and the organization are in it together to succeed or not to succeed. This applies to issues of health care cost containment. If claims are higher than expected and premiums increase, employees share a portion of the premium increase. Organizations are also willing to share the savings from aggressive and successful attempts to contain costs by means of effective claims administration, management and employee intervention, and wellness programs. This means using a general financial sharing program that shares the reduction in health care costs from year to year with employees. At the individual employee level, some organizations have a "wellness dividend" that returns a portion of the employee's contribution toward his or her health insurance premium if the insurance carrier does not pay any claims for the employee.

The focus on containing costs is part of the equation of improving bottom-line performance. If the advantage of performance is to be shared, so can the savings from containing costs. Sharing is important because it places the responsibility for containing costs on the employee as well as on the organization. Getting people back to work is sometimes most effectively done by coworkers when it is advantageous for all parties to the partnership.

Conclusions

Health care is a major U.S. priority during a time when organizations are struggling under heavy costs of providing health care. Organizations are bombarded by legislative initiatives regarding health care. Because health care plans are important to employees and costly to organizations, they are central to forming a partnership between the two. Both organizations and employees are focused on sharing the costs of benefits and seeking opportunities to conserve costs and minimize unnecessary plan usage under new pay.

Major opportunities exist to provide measurable levels of health care protection while focusing on effective cost management. Unless both employees and organizations manage health care effectively, government intervention is imminent.

Other Employee Benefits Under New Pay

In addition to health care benefits, organizations and employees are concerned about the effective management of other important benefit areas.[1] These include the following:

- sick leave and disability protection
- life insurance
- retirement
- time off

Under traditional pay, these benefits have been taken for granted. Under new pay, they offer opportunities to strengthen the employee-organization partnership.

Sick Leave and Disability Protection

Disability Protection

Everyone misses some time from work due to sickness or injury, since employees are more likely to be ill for an extended period than they are to die during employment. Disability coverage is a concern to employees. The challenge is to ensure that the organization protects employees against the possibility of loss of income due to disability without making it more attractive to be ill than to return to work. In other words, disability benefits should not reward employees for staying away from work.

Social Security and state workers' compensation laws provide statutory benefits for temporary disability. Wise organizations consider the tax-provided benefits as a baseline of protection, with the benefits provided by the organization a secondary level of protection.

It is important to note that disability plans that protect an employee from the complete loss of income can create long-term problems for the organization because much of disability payments are not taxable. Workers' compensation, Social Security, and disability payments for which the employee has contributed premiums are not taxable. Offering the same level of after-tax income during disability as during work creates a disincentive to return to work.

Sick Leave

There are two different views of sick leave that occur in traditional pay organizations. Some employees view sick leave as an alternative to vacation days, while organizations see them as an insurance benefit to be used only if needed. To this end, production and clerical employees especially believe that sick pay accumulates into an account that they can use for personal time off as a reward for not being ill. However, from the organization's standpoint, days of absence for illness and those as a "reward" are equally costly because of their unplanned nature.

Managing Sick Leave and Disability Protection

Sick leave and disability are major management challenges to organizations and present considerable opportunities for effective management. The primary focus for management is effective communication with employees. A second approach is to ask for physician verification of employee illness. However, neither methodology has proven to be very successful as the cost of providing protection to employees continues to increase, due in part to inappropriate usage of the benefits. New strategies are required to manage better the costs of time off for illness and disability.

New Pay View of Sick Leave and Disability Protection

The new pay perspective offers rewards for the cost-effective use of time off for illness and disability. This makes the employee and the organization partners in saving money on sick leave and disability costs, with employees placing pressure on fellow workers to take only necessary sick time off. Some of the options used to focus on cost containment include the following:

- Share in the cost containment gain by setting goals for use of time off for illness and disability each year and share the savings when goals are exceeded between employees and the organization.
- Create a paid time-off account. This may be the answer, since time off for all reasons is combined without being differentiated as vacation, sick time, or personal days off.
- Give cash awards in the form of visible and highly acknowledged contributions to the organization for not using illness and disability time off.
- Use the peer pressure from group variable pay plans to reduce absenteeism. Variable pay goals cannot be achieved without everyone working, so the plan itself becomes a reason for reducing absenteeism. When variable pay plans are evaluated, a successful variable pay plan is often related to reduced absenteeism. Usually the connection is not made explicit in the plan design; in a few group variable pay plans, the plan design either makes the distribution of awards to individuals contingent on the employee having fewer than a certain number of sick days or bases the awards on hours worked, not hours paid.

The objective of new pay is to keep employees at work and to make it financially worthwhile for them to stay at work. New pay programs are designed to make it more rewarding to work than not to work.

Life Insurance

Overview of Life Insurance

Basic term life insurance is the most broadly applicable form of coverage and is used by most large organizations. This is the core of life insurance benefits since it protects against death loss, does not accumulate cash value for the person covered, and is inexpensive. Most establish coverage as a multiple of base pay, with the most common provision being twice the annual rate of base pay for professional and administrative employees. Production workers generally receive a common level of coverage, around $10,000.

Supplemental term life insurance is generally made available to employees on a contributory basis since an employee's taxable income must include the cost of employer-paid group term insurance coverage that exceeds $50,000. Employed people are a better insurance risk than the general population, so premiums for this type of coverage are lower. Premiums are not as low as they are for basic noncontributory insurance because employees with health problems are more likely to pay for the additional insurance than are employees with lower health risk, and because rates are usually age banded.

Accidental death insurance is included as an employer-paid benefit in most instances. This type of coverage is generally fairly expensive for the risk covered, and the probability of accidental death is low compared to the risk of death from sickness. Because of this, many organizations are considering moving away from providing a general level of accidental death coverage for all employees, and instead offering accidental death coverage to employees based on business need due to extensive travel or other increased risk of accidental death.

Business travel accident insurance is offered for business-related accidental death. Some organizations offer a benefit of between two and five times base pay when an accidental death occurs related to business travel. Again, the cost is high compared to the risk, and some organizations consider the additional coverage to be extremely expensive for the value received.

New Pay View of Life Insurance

The least expensive form of life insurance is term insurance. This type of insurance protects the employee's family in the event of loss of income. Other forms of insurance have objectives other than those that are related to replacement of income in the event the employee dies (such as capital accumulation). Group term insurance is the preferred insurance coverage, with other forms of coverage offered for specific business reasons other than income replacement.

The new pay view suggests that term life insurance in reasonable amounts is the best investment of all insurance products. This is the most economical way to provide survivor protection.

Retirement

New pay advocates partnerships based on associating the financial results of the organization with employee pay. The challenge of new pay is to form a partnership that helps the employee provide financially for years after he or she is no longer working while still retaining the ability of the organization to reward excellence and manage those who do not perform well out of the organization before retirement becomes an issue.

Qualified and Nonqualified Plans

Qualified pension plans cover many employees and meet the requirements of the tax code in order to receive favorable treatment. When an organization wants to cover its work force or a large group of employees, qualified plans are the most often used retirement vehicle. With a qualified plan, the organization receives an immediate tax deduction for the amount contributed to the plan, and the plan participants pay no current income taxes on the amount contributed. The nonqualified plan offers no special tax treatment because employer contributions cannot be deducted until benefits are paid or until the plan funds and the participants are taxed.

Nonqualified plans are used for a special group of employees to provide benefits in addition to those provided by the qualified plan. Because the combination of a qualified plan and Social Security replaces more of the income of lower-paid employees than higher-paid employees, the nonqualified plan can be used to supplement the qualified plan in spite of the tax consequences and provide retirement benefits to higher-paid employees that are comparable to those paid to lower-paid employees.

Defined Benefit and Defined Contribution Plans

Defined benefit plans produce assured and continuing income for retirees. Defined contribution plans or capital accumulations plans may have many investment options and are generally profit-sharing or 401(k) plans. In recent years, more organizations have adopted defined contribution plans and have terminated defined benefit programs. This is generally because defined benefit plans are heavily regulated by law, much more so than defined contribution plans.

The 1986 Tax Reform Act stipulated that qualified plans should provide retirement income and retirement savings rather than lump-sum distributions and early withdrawals. Numerous tax penalties were placed on premature employee withdrawals from defined contribution plans, as well as an excise tax on employer reversions of excess assets from terminating defined benefit plans.

SOCIAL SECURITY INTEGRATION. Until 1986, Social Security integration allowed the combination of the pension plan and Social Security to generate the desired income protection. Social Security favors lower-paid employees, and integration provides the organization with the chance to equalize the benefit levels of the more highly paid employee group. However, tax changes in 1986 had a negative impact on the opportunity to integrate with Social Security and meet the organization's retirement goals. Because tax laws constantly change and keep the area of indirect pay in constant turmoil, wise organizations are on the lookout for any change to again use Social Security integration to save dollars spent on retirement.

DEFINED BENEFIT PLANS. Often, retirement benefits are viewed as a reward for organizational service. Under this assumption some plans accrue benefits as a flat dollar amount for all employees for each year of service. However, this approach is not responsive to the goal of maintaining the employee's standard of living at the time of retirement.

Most defined benefit plans determine benefits using a formula that includes earnings as well as service. Earnings often include both base pay and variable pay. In recognizing service in the benefit formula, it is common to weight the computation in favor of the final three to five years of service, when earnings are generally the highest. These costly provisions are intended to make pension plans replace realistic amounts of preretirement income.

Most defined benefit plans are noncontributory, because most employer contributions are tax deductible while employee contributions are made on an after-tax basis. Inflation has been viewed as eroding postretirement income, and some organizations increase benefits after retirement. This is usually done on a voluntary basis rather than being indexed to changes in the cost of living.

Many defined benefit plans are overfunded. The overfunding can be used by the organization in one of two ways. The plan can be modified so that the overfunding can be used to provide future benefits; or the organization can terminate the plan, pay excise and income taxes, and use the overfunding for variable pay to reward performance more immediately.

DEFINED CONTRIBUTION PLANS. Historically, most plans have been defined benefit programs because employees can plan for a specific level of retirement income and a promised benefit after retirement. Organizations that prefer defined benefit plans suggest that this lets them plan funding over many years, recognizes the loyalty of long-service employees, and combines with Social Security to provide an excellent level of retirement for employees.

Organizations are now considering defined contribution programs as retirement plans. The prime reason is the financial risk of being able to meet future funding obligations under a defined benefit program. In addition to the risk, some organizations believe retirement credits should be earned rather than be an entitlement and also believe that the employee should bear the risk of the investment performance of the assets in the program.

Presently, the tax code limits contributions for each employee participant to 25 percent of income up to $30,000 per year for all defined contribution plans. This limit is scheduled to increase in 1993 or 1994.

Profit-Sharing Plans. Tax-deferred profit-sharing plans have a great deal of appeal. Profit-sharing plans permit employees to participate in the profits based on a formula for allocating among the eligible employees and for distributing accumulated funds at retirement or upon termination. Generally, organizations are permitted up to 15 percent of employee cash compensation. The IRS limits the amount of annual cash compensation that can be taken into account under IRS Code Section 401(a)(17). Plans may also permit employees to participate on either a pretax or after-tax basis, depending on the plan design. Participants in profit-sharing plans often have a variety of investment alternatives. Employees who terminate their employment before retirement usually receive their vested benefits as a cash disbursement and have the opportunity to roll over the disbursement into an IRA or other qualified retirement plan within sixty days of receipt in order to avoid additional tax.

If the organization chooses to provide a basic retirement contribution, a profit-sharing plan can have minimal funding regardless of the organization's performance. The majority of the funding, however, can be determined by the performance of the organization to make the performance–reward linkage. Although the partnership is less direct than with variable pay, profit-sharing plans encourage employees to view themselves as long-term partners with the organization.

401(k) Plans. These plans are becoming increasingly popular as alternatives to defined benefit plans. Employees are able to reduce a portion of cash compensation on a pretax basis and place this money in a qualified retirement plan. These plans can be combined with employee savings plans, with the organization matching contributions. Plans permit several choices of investment funds. The IRS limits the maximum annual cash compensation deferral that is subject to cost-of-living adjustments under IRS Code Section 402(g). 401(k) plans also must pass a nondiscriminatory test to ensure that highly paid employees are not taking greater advantage of this benefit than lower-paid employees. Often, organizations use matching on the pretax contribution to encourage participation so that the nondiscriminatory test is passed.

Money Purchase Plans. Organizations make contributions based on a percentage of cash compensation in the range of 2 to 10 percent. The organization may also provide for voluntary employee contributions on an after-tax basis. All contributions to money purchase plans are held in trust funds, and the employee can generally elect from several investment options with different degrees of risk and growth potential. Employees who terminate their employment before retirement have their vested benefits held in trust and continue to appreciate in value until the date of early retirement eligibility.

Savings Plans. With savings plans, employees can elect to contribute through payroll deduction a portion of cash compensation to be administered in an individual account by an outside trustee. Organizations usually do not restrict the amount of employee contributions up to a prescribed maximum percent. In some instances, organizations match a portion of employee contributions to the savings plans; some also match based on years of service or the profitability of the organization. In most instances of matching, vesting is quite rapid. Employees are offered a number of investment alternatives and can invest the money as they see fit.

Savings plan withdrawal and loan features are similar to profit-sharing plan features. Organizations often impose time limits and periods of suspension from plan participation for withdrawals of employer contributions. Employees are encouraged to use the savings plan as a retirement supplement by a number of tax provisions. At retirement the benefit is generally paid as a lump-sum distribution or converted into an annuity.

Employee Stock-Ownership Plans. Employee stock-ownership plans (ESOPs) can provide employees ownership in the organization or can also be used with leveraged financing to benefit the organization. The organization establishes a tax-exempt trust that borrows funds from a bank based on the organization's credit. The funds are then used to buy company stock, which is placed in the trust. The organization makes tax-deductible payments annually through the trust to repay the bank loan. Concurrently, the trust distributes stock equal in value to the payments to the accounts of employee participants in the ESOP that the trust administers.

The leveraged employee stock-ownership plan is a tax-efficient way to raise capital. It shares management with employees. This is an important consideration as long as it is not used to "sell" an organization to employees for an inflated price or under conditions that don't really let employees run the organization. Compared to other forms of defined contribution plans, ESOPs have the disadvantage to employees of having only one organization's stock in their portfolio. The success of the plan depends on business results and the valuation of company stock in the market.

New Pay View of Retirement

Organizations understand that they cannot get performance and productivity from retired employees. Organizations are interested in paying for reward systems that make it attractive for employees to continue to perform effectively during their entire careers. This means preventing entitlements without concern for employee or organizational performance. In simple terms, retirement is contingent on sustaining productive value for a complete career. Expensive retirement plans are a challenge to organizations. In the future, the "here and now" will gain additional attention unless retirement protection can become more contingent on results produced than on how long the employee is with the organization.

New pay views retirement as an important earned result of successful organizations and successful employees. The strategy is to tie the funding of retirement to the organization's ability to pay and the receipt of benefits to employee performance. Because qualified retirement plans cannot discriminate based on employee performance, other rewards will need to communicate to employees the role they play in the future of the organization. In the meantime, funding vehicles other than those in the defined benefit family more closely match the new pay retirement strategy, in which organizational performance affects funding and the employee accepts some responsibility for his or her own future financial security.

Effective retirement programs reward productive employees but do not encourage substandard employees to remain in order to "put in their time" and earn retirement. New pay suggests that employees should have their performance judged all through their careers so that the first time they are found to be performing below job expectations is not at a time when they are strongly vested in an expensive retirement plan. When it is not possible for an employee to perform at the meets-expectations performance level, corrective action is taken as early in the employee's career as possible. This prevents the problem of discovering a poor performer with many years of service who has always been a poor performer and should have been terminated years ago, and who may now be protected under the Age Discrimination in Employment Act.

Time Off

Overview of Time Off

Paid time off is one of the most expensive employee benefits an organization provides. According to the U.S. Chamber of Commerce,[2] payments for time not worked average 13.1 percent of payroll, which includes vacation, sick leave, holidays, personal time-off allowances, jury duty, paid rest periods, and paid lunch periods. Little emphasis is customarily placed on the effective management of paid time off. However, the new pay view suggests that paid time off must be an urgent focus. This is because before an organization can use new direct pay programs to encourage employee performance, the employees must be at work. Paid time off must not be more attractive than paid time at work.

WHERE IS THE FOUR-DAY WEEK? At one time, employees worked until the job was properly done and results were achieved. Over the last 100 years, the reduction in the workweek has not been contingent on sustaining a specific level of employee productivity and performance. Rather, humanistic goals and a developing competitive practice that provided the short workweek as a standard were the driving forces behind it. Employee pay increased on an hourly basis over this time period. The focus was to pay for time and attendance and not performance and results produced. This was an important factor in the declining level of work-force performance and productivity.

The shortened workweek was advocated as an opportunity to accommodate employee needs for more time away from the workplace. Some futurists said that the 1990s would be the "leisure times" in the workplace. This has certainly not come to pass. A number of organizations have experimented with four ten-hour days per week as an approach to staffing. Because employees did not lose any money on a four-day workweek, the only result was that the organization's schedule changed to accommodate the availability of the employee. However, the organization's customers also were required to accommodate the shortened workweek. As long as they were willing to receive service based on the employees' schedule, the organization stood a chance to maintain a mutually satisfactory relationship with their customers. Where the organization lost performance and productivity is where performance and productivity were required during time periods when employees were not available.

While the shorter workweek has provided more leisure time off, it does not provide any advantage to organizations in terms of performance and productivity. Many exempt employees commonly work a five-by-ten workweek instead of the standard five-by-eight workweek. A change to four days would probably not result in a four-by-twelve workweek because of fatigue. A shorter workweek is an important benefit for employees who are interested in more time away from work. Employees staying at home and not performing do the organization little good except to enable it to recruit and retain those employees who are interested in working short workweeks.

WHERE IS THE FLEXIBLE WORK SCHEDULE? Flexible work scheduling was designed to accommodate employees' personal schedules and obligations. Some predictions indicate that the United States is in store for a shortage of employees with needed skills in the 1990s. This may be the primary human resource challenge organizations will face. However, in parallel with this, strategies will be needed to improve the performance and productivity of existing employees so that fewer additional employees may be required. If organizations move to flexible work schedules to attract new employees, present employees will need to be offered similar opportunities to customize their scheduling.

The enlightened view of the flexible schedule is the empowerment of the employee. This means the employee works with the organization to determine how his or her personal needs and the organization's need for performance and productivity can be mutually accommodated. This shared-goals-and-objectives perspective, where the responsibility for getting the complete job done is not left with the organization alone, is characteristic of new pay.

WHERE IS JOB SHARING? Job sharing involves a single job being shared by two or more employees. The objective is to accommodate the employee's desire to spend only a portion of his or her time in the workplace. In most cases, this is an attractive alternative for employees with family responsibilities. This is usually accomplished by one employee working two or three days a week and the other employee working the other two or three days. Job sharing often requires some duplication of effort to coordinate the job.

The new pay view of job sharing is productivity based. The employees are accountable for sharing the job without loss to the organization. Employees invest in communications and integration of the job without creating more cost for the organization than would be the case if only one person had the job. The organization is important in its role of matching the two individuals who share the job so that productivity is not lost with either incumbent and so that the "personality" of the job is sustained with both incumbents.

VACATIONS. Traditionally, vacations are offered as rewards for service and in recognition of the employees' need to rejuvenate to be more productive during the time they are at work. Although strong conflicting opinions exist about the performance and productivity of employees who take more vacations compared to those who take less time off, no evidence is available to show that a liberal vacation practice is related to employee productivity. However, time off is highly valued by employees, raising the question of whether the climate provided by organizations is consistent with job satisfaction.

The trend is to provide more vacation to professional and administrative employees than to production employees for any given level of service to the organization. See table 15.1 for a 1989 U.S. Department of Labor, Bureau of Labor Statistics,[3] report of paid vacation days per year.

TABLE 15.1

Average Number of
Paid Vacation Days Per Year

Years of Service	Professional/ Administrative	Technical/ Clerical	Production/ Service
6 mo.	6.6	6.0	5.3
1 yr.	11.1	9.9	7.5
3 yrs.	12.2	11.2	10.3
5 yrs.	14.9	14.0	12.1
10 yrs.	17.8	16.9	15.6
15 yrs.	19.7	19.2	17.7
20 yrs.	21.4	20.6	19.7
25 yrs.	22.4	21.7	20.9
30 yrs.	22.8	22.0	21.3

New pay views vacations as an encouragement for performance rather than an entitlement for years spent on the job. Different factors determine vacation time:

- *Calculation of the basis for pay.* New pay perspectives include income from variable pay in the form of incentives, gainsharing, and lump-sum awards in vacation calculations when pay is at risk to encourage the use of variable pay where variable pay constitutes a major part of cash compensation. When variable pay is a minor part of cash compensation, variable pay is excluded from the calculation; this is to encourage a larger expenditure on variable pay. New pay organizations tend to omit shift differential and overtime payments since they are related not to performance and productivity but only to time spent on the job.
- *Scheduled hours or hours actually worked.* Because of the cost of vacations, organizations interested in getting people to work base vacations on the time actually worked rather than on the time employees are scheduled to work. This rewards those who work the most rather than those who are off from work.
- *Pay in lieu of vacation.* Organizations focused on performance may selectively offer pay in lieu of some vacation to

excellently-performing employees. These organizations are more likely to offer employee-preferred options to employees who comply with organizational goals. If pay in lieu of some vacation is attractive, the organization will gain in exchange for the right to trade vacation days for cash, since this benefit option is expensive to the organization.

- *Vacation offset for other time off.* Organizations that want people to come to work ask employees to take vacation if they are away from work for reasons of personal business (as contrasted with true vacations) unrelated to the job.
- *Vacation as a reward for performance.* Organizations may vary vacation days based on performance. This can be an attractive reward in organizations with few vacation days and an employee population with short tenure, and for some employees such as members of a dual-income family. The award for performance needs to be tempered with the organization's need for the strong performers to be at work performing.

One organizational objective is to have employees take vacation in the year in which it is earned. However, another objective is to keep employees at work when they are productive. Progressive organizations are permitting employees to be paid cash instead of taking some vacation days or to defer a specific portion of vacation to retirement or termination. They do insist that before employees do this, the employee must have taken sufficient time off to return to work in a productive manner. The cost of deferring vacation is considered since the cost is typically determined at the rate of the employee's pay when it is paid. This is usually higher than the rate when the vacation was earned, so new pay organizations that pay deferred vacation tell employees that they will be paid at the rate when it was earned.

HOLIDAYS. In most organizations, ten holidays are common. Some organizations permit employees to take "floating" holidays to correspond with their personal preferences. Holidays are not related to increasing organizational performance and productivity.

New Pay View of Time Off

Organizations vary in the amount of time off they provide. Paid time off must be well managed since there is a double cost of having someone off work. The first cost is the organization paying for time not worked; the second is the loss of the employee effort during the period of absence.

Tracking paid time off is an important element of monitoring overall employee productivity. Because of the predicted shortage of skilled employees, it is critical to get those an organization has to work as much as possible.

Conclusions

There was a time when books on pay merely reported on what other organizations were doing in the area of employee benefits and suggested that this was what the reader should do. Now, although indirect pay is an important element of total compensation, it is best viewed as a supplement to cash compensation. Indirect pay programs are wisely designed with an understanding of how they can support cash programs that are better able to bind the employee and organization to what is to be accomplished.

In the future, organizations will not be liberalizing indirect pay as a matter of course. Rather, they will take a total compensation view and use indirect pay only where it does a better job of responding to a need than does direct pay. Indirect pay will likely play a more secondary role until innovators find how indirect pay can do a better job of responding to the communications and flexibility goals of organizations.

Flexible Benefits

What Are Flexible Benefits?

The concept of flexible benefits is that employees are provided the opportunity to select between alternative benefits that are made available to them by the organization for which they work. The organizational reasons for these programs range from responding to differences in employee needs and desires to controlling various costs of benefits as the result of providing employees with what they need and want (and not with benefits in which they do not have interest) and as a result of defining the organization's role as providing a level of contribution rather than a level of benefit provisions.

Flexible benefits provide the opportunity to elect from choices in a number of alternative areas. Some of the nontaxable benefit areas include the following:[1]

- uninsured medical expenses
- health and accident insurance
- disability
- dependent life insurance
- child and elder care
- term life insurance

In addition, the following taxable benefits are often included in a flexible benefit plan:

- cash
- excess dependent and term life insurance
- vacation days

Also, deferred compensation in the form of elective employee deferrals under a 401(k) plan can be included in a flexible benefit plan.

Generally, organizations begin a flexible benefit plan by providing a few choices. As programs evolve, additional choices are provided.

The Origins of Flexible Benefits

Social scientists such as Nealy[2] provided the foundation for flexible benefits by suggesting that employees more highly valued direct and indirect pay when they had the opportunity to influence the design of their programs. This was an extension of suggestions that employee involvement in decision making made employees more satisfied with those decisions than if they did not have the opportunity to participate.

The Research at TRW

Research at TRW, initially conducted in Redondo Beach, California, explored whether employees were interested in selecting how to allocate the money TRW was spending on indirect and direct pay among a number of alternatives. At the time, the corporate human resource staff of TRW was contemplating liberalizing the defined benefit retirement plan because the pension program was not viewed as competitive. In the 1970s, the employee mix at TRW was such that younger employees were working in the high-technology areas of the business and older employees were working in the low-technology areas. Because TRW had one pension plan for all employees and because the corporate human resource staff was in Cleveland, Ohio, close to the low-technology areas of the business, the retirement plan was liberalized in spite of the fact that employees in California wanted cash and not an increase in pension provisions.[3]

Later, TRW in California undertook a pioneering flexible benefit project that offered employees choices from a number of possible alternatives. This resulted in a program of flexible benefits without a cash option even though employees preferred cash to most forms of indirect pay. The TRW experience and an unrelated undertaking at Educational Testing Service led to considerable early program development.[4]

New Pay Reasons for Flexible Benefits

Organizations that are moving to flexible benefit programs for what might be called new pay reasons are interested in not only patterning choices to match employee preferences but also containing indirect pay costs. Effective flexible benefit programs consider both employee choices and cost containment.

By 1989, over 1,000 flexible benefit plans existed in the United States.[5] Although many organizations are now moving to flexible benefits because of their prevalence, others are considering flexible benefits for reasons that are valid from a new pay perspective. For example, employees undervalue the cost of their benefits. Flexible benefits cause employees to think about the benefits they are getting and the cost of those benefits. Employees are able to choose those benefits that are important to them, so the organization gets more perceived value for the dollars spent. Because flexible benefits give employees more control over their benefits, they are also a sign that management trusts them with an important decision—which may help strengthen the partnership between employees and the organization. Additionally, employees' awareness that their benefit choices affect the cost of health care may be one route to the control of costs. And finally, flexible benefits redefine the organization's commitment to a specific contribution instead of a specific program of benefits.[6]

The Strategies of Flexible Benefits

A number of possible solutions are available to organizations that decide to move to flexible benefit programs.[7] Some of these are simply base pay reduction plans, while others are elaborate choice-making systems. Whenever employees have the opportunity to select from a number of possible direct and indirect pay alternatives, a form of flexible benefits is in effect. Which alternative design approach is selected depends on what the organization wants to gain from the program of flexible benefits.

REIMBURSEMENT ACCOUNTS. As of 1991, the tax code provides that employees may be permitted to set aside a portion of their pay on a pretax basis for nontaxable benefits. Employees agree to set aside a portion of their income at the start of the calendar year into a reimbursement account. For example, an employee making $40,000 can elect to place $5,000 into the account; subsequently, the employee's taxable income is reduced to $35,000. The employee then has the opportunity to purchase benefits on a nontaxable basis up to the amount placed in the reimbursement account. For example, day care or elder care may be purchased, or out-of-pocket medical expenses may be reimbursed, for up to $5,000. In the event the employee does not spend the $5,000 during the year, the unspent amount is lost to the employee. Spending over the amount in the reimbursement account is done on an after-tax basis.

Plans of this nature permit employees to purchase benefits that are necessary and/or attractive to them on a pretax basis. The program can be easily managed and provides the opportunity to pay for medical and dependent care expenses.

ADD-ON PLANS. These are programs where current benefit levels are not changed or reduced. Employees are provided with flexible credits that they can use to purchase additional benefits. The flexible credits are granted to employees based on factors such as tenure, performance, or a percentage of base pay. Using these flexible credits, employees can buy additional benefits such as insurance and health care.

In the new pay perspective, any add-on plan is viewed as resulting in increases in costs. This is a useful strategy for an organization that has a less than competitive indirect pay program and is interested in more closely matching the external market. However, few organizations with a strong benefit program are interested in liberalizing benefits further.

MIX-AND-MATCH PLANS. Under this approach, employees may pattern their programs after their own specific needs and objectives by electing different levels of coverage within a selected number of benefit areas. Credits from electing lower levels in one area may be used to elect higher levels of coverage in other areas. These plans are often coupled with base pay reduction plans if employees want more of one type of benefit than is available by reducing another benefit area.

CORE CARVE-OUT PLANS. A core carve-out plan provides a baseline of coverage in health insurance, life insurance, and other protection areas that an organization believes represents coverage that all employees should have. Universal benefits are reduced to the carve-out or baseline level; employees are then offered the opportunity to focus on their preferred benefits.

The carve-out provides the organization with a reduced fixed benefit program and the employee with the opportunity to purchase additional benefits on a pretax basis. Employees can direct expenditures on a personalized basis to benefits that they highly value.

MODULAR PLANS. External advisors are providing organizations with "canned" flexible benefit products. These plans have two or three modules of benefit choices. One module may have certain levels of health and life insurance, another different levels of health and life insurance, and the third a still different mix of benefit choices. Employees have the opportunity to elect a specific module but cannot custom design their own benefit program. If the module costs are not equal and the employee does not pick the least expensive module, the employee pays the excess.

The New Pay View of Flexible Benefits

New pay permits employees to participate in the organization through their pay program. One way to do this is to use variable pay based on employee performance. Another is to provide flexible benefits. Clearly, new pay involves a role for flexible benefits if they answer an organization's business, financial, or human resource strategy. However, organizations often install flexible benefits just because other organizations have them.

Considering flexible benefits under certain important circumstances seems appropriate. First, the organization should enjoy a substantial human resource advantage from permitting employees to influence the design of their benefits. The organization must be willing to allow employees a say in the benefits they receive. Second, employees must be believed to be capable of understanding the choice-making opportunity. This means the employees are able to evaluate their personal situations and make choices within the parameters provided. It is the organization's obligation to determine whether employees understand the consequences of their choices. This can only be done in face-to-face meetings with employees to discuss their choices; sending employees a written description of the choices does not ensure understanding. Third, the organization should understand that claims that it will save money as a result of flexible benefits may not prove to be the case, for the following reasons:

- Flexible benefit plans often provide for a common baseline of benefits that all employees receive. Unless the organization is willing to reduce this level of benefits below the level it had before it implemented flexible benefits, flexible benefits result in increased indirect pay costs.
- Adverse selection, in which the poor risks participate and the good risks do not, raises overall costs by increasing the cost of providing a specific benefit unless steps are taken to minimize its impact. Such steps include restricting employees' eligibility for higher coverage or switching coverage, combining or bundling options, developing pricing strategies to encourage good risks to participate, and providing only core coverage while offering supplemental benefits with minimal or no employer subsidies.

Flexible benefit plans can be used to contain benefit costs to make money available for direct pay in general and variable pay specifically. This, of course, is the value of a total compensation strategy that focuses scarce pay dollars where they can get the most value for the organization and employees. In this instance, the focus is on the partnership by making dollars available to the variable pay plans that permit the organization to reuse dollars based on results achieved and permit the employee to receive significant financial rewards for generating the desired results. To become an effective new pay vehicle, flexible benefit plans would be designed as follows:

- Benefits are viewed from the cost and employee perspective, rather than only from the perspective of benefits provided. The objective is to do no more than redistribute current expenditures. Cost reduction is a goal. Flexible benefit plans are not developed by starting with employee preferences and then seeing what this costs. Cost limitations are first developed; subsequently, choice modules are developed that pattern what is offered after what it will cost to provide the benefits.
- The concept of the partnership is applied to flexible benefits. The organization determines the maximum it is willing or able to expend on benefits, and employees pay the remainder. As benefit costs increase, the organization determines what it can or will pay and the employees are expected to pay the differential or to reduce their benefit levels.

- Modules are designed to take into account the fact that employees will select what they will use. For example, young employees prefer dental plans and older employees want more life insurance. Placing both of these options in the same selection module will balance the cost to the organization and minimize the impact of adverse selection.
- Flexible benefit plans often have high initial costs because organizations hesitate to reduce the level of existing benefits to install a flexible benefit plan and because start-up costs are high. However, the organization can have long-term savings if the focus remains on containing benefit costs to free money for variable pay (and thus variable costs) based on performance.
- A possible new pay flexible benefit plan would start with a basic benefit plan that is not subject to choice. This plan would have a medical plan that provides employees with protection from high medical bills, moderate life protection, a disability plan that encourages prompt return to work, and perhaps some additional basics of critical importance. Beyond this, modules permit employees to expend whatever additional organizational funds are available, plus some required and optional employee contributions, in a balanced manner. This plan is paired with a defined contribution retirement plan of some type to provide a sound benefit program. As costs rise, employees share these costs to the extent that the organization must not be inhibited from redirecting indirect pay dollars to direct pay dollars.

It is essential that organizations remain in a position to focus pay dollars on programs that have high potential motivational value. Unfortunately, this does not generally include indirect pay programs because benefits are difficult to allocate based on results achieved.

The new pay solution suggests that the organization permit their benefit program to fall below competitive levels by not increasing benefit provisions and by controlling benefit costs to the extent possible. Subsequently, the organization considers benefit flexibility so that the baseline of benefits plus choice making results in total benefit costs that are not disadvantageous to the organization.

New pay organizations look for ways to tie performance to flexible benefits. Some organizations award flexible credits based on job performance; others tie job performance to earning employer benefit contributions. For example, one organization shifted sole responsibility for the cost of benefits to employees. Using a flexible benefit plan, employees earn and re-earn the employer contribution based on six-month performance review ratings. This makes an individual employee's performance count and links performance with indirect pay.

The new pay view suggests that if the organization moves to flexible benefits and the employee population is capable of making informed decisions, flexible benefits offer cash as an option. The use of cash in a flexible benefit plan increases the program's flexibility. Even though the cash is taxed, employees can develop their own total compensation strategy on how their pay dollars will be allocated. For example, a healthy young employee may choose to develop his or her own core carve-out plan with low health and life insurance and use the extra cash to help in the purchase of a home. If the flexible benefit plan offers insurance benefits in which the cost to employees is based on the real individualized cost, the true cost of benefits per employee—and thereby the total compensation per employee—is more accurate from the organization's view. Younger employees will have more dollars freed to spend as they choose, and it will be equally desirable for organizations to hire older workers.

Conclusions

Flexible benefits began in the 1970s as a way to give employees a say in how their benefit plans are structured. When combined with effective cost management, flexible benefits offer attractive involvement opportunities. Care is necessary to ensure that flexible benefits are used to help form an employee–organization partnership rather than to increase benefit costs and add complexity and confusion.

Many organizations are moving to flexible benefits without concern for the role that benefit choice making plays in their total compensation strategy. This makes flexible benefits a me-too pay planning solution. It is time for an annual review process to begin in many organizations around the subject of flexible benefits to measure gain and cost savings. Many flexible benefits plans have been in effect for many years without a thorough analysis. The 1990s may be a good time to evaluate the continued effect of these programs.

PART SIX

New Pay in Major Companies

Survey of Pay Practices

Over the last ten years, our studies of pay and organizational performance in labor-intensive organizations have included financial institutions, high-technology firms, and health care organizations. We found that the labor-intensive organizations that performed best financially were more likely to use group variable pay and other new pay programs to focus the organization and its employees on achieving higher levels of performance and productivity.[1] While these studies do not claim that pay management is the cause of differences in financial results, the better-performing organizations do report that new pay facilitates the process of setting standards for sharing performance results, encouraging teamwork and collaboration, and providing a scorecard concerning expectations and results achieved.

Top management has broadly acknowledged that this information supports a total compensation strategy that encourages experimentation with new pay and places a stronger focus on performance results.[2] In the surveyed financial, high-technology, and health care organizations, often 50 percent or more of total costs have been labor costs. After seeing these results, other organizations have been interested in whether these conclusions apply to organizations that are more capital-intensive. This caused the investigation of total compensation strategies and philosophies in major *Fortune* 100 companies.

Study Methodology

A sample of sixty major U.S. corporations was selected by a client organization, based on the fact that they were large, high-visibility, capital-intensive corporations. Thirty-eight provided information consistent with our quality standards by answering all of our questions candidly and objectively, contingent on our promise to keep their individual organization information confidential. Information was gathered from a combination of direct executive contacts, public information, and members of the American Compensation Association. In many instances, the top human resource or compensation executive was involved. To ensure that the organizations were all asked the same questions, a patterned interview was used. Opportunities to obtain additional information that might be relevant to the study were explored. Exhibit 17.1 provides the list of survey participants:

Exhibit 17.1
Survey Participants

AT&T	GTE
Allied-Signal	Hewlett-Packard
American Cyanamid	Honeywell
Apple Computer	IBM
Boeing	ITT
Caterpillar	Lilly
Coca-Cola	Martin Marietta
Deere	Merck
Digital Equipment	3M
Dow Chemical	Motorola
DuPont	NCR
Eastman Kodak	Raytheon
Emerson Electric	Rockwell International
Exxon	Union Carbide
Ford	United Technologies
General Electric	USX
General Mills	Westinghouse Electric
General Motors	Weyerhaeuser
Georgia Pacific	Xerox

The purpose was to find some measure of trends to test the correctness of general beliefs and contentions about pay.[3] After the information was obtained, organizations were placed in two groups: one group of eighteen organizations that employed or experimented with new pay (new pay or NP companies) and another group of twenty organizations that employed primarily traditional pay (traditional pay or TP companies). In some NP companies, philosophies, strategies, and practices that are more aligned with the new pay approach to pay management existed throughout the corporation; in others, it existed only in some major elements of the corporation. Subsequently, financial analysis was performed to determine whether any difference existed between the categories based on earnings per share, return on shareholder equity, return on assets, and profit margin.

The study explored the areas in Exhibit 17.2 in detail. During the information-gathering process, overlap was found among the issues. Because of this, some of the issues were combined and others were explored in some detail.

Exhibit 17.2
Survey Questions

Total Compensation Philosophy/Strategy

- What is the organization's total compensation philosophy/strategy?
- How is the business/financial plan used in the total compensation planning process?
- What is the purpose of the total compensation strategy?
- How is employee total compensation viewed?

Human Resource Organization's Role

- What does the human resource organization do relative to total compensation?

Base Pay Programs/Practices

- What is the role of base pay versus variable pay?
- What unit of human resource performance is used for tying pay to performance (individual, group, etc.)?

(continued)

- How is the value of jobs determined?
- How is employee performance evaluated?

Variable Pay Programs/Practices

- How are variable pay plans designed?
- How is variable pay funded?
- What performance goals and measures are used for variable pay?
- Who is eligible for variable pay?
- What is the variable pay emphasis (individual, team, business unit, organizationwide, etc.)?
- How do variable pay award sizes vary?

Indirect Pay Programs/Practices

- What has happened to indirect pay lately?
- What has happened to pensions?
- What has happened to profit sharing?
- What about flexible benefits?

Executive Pay Programs/Practices

- What has happened to executive compensation?

Study Results

NP companies are generally better financial performers as a group than TP companies. This is not to suggest that new pay causes the financial success; rather, a relationship exists between better financial performance and the experimentation with and use of new pay. Although it is much less prevalent, new pay also exists in organizations that perform poorly. As a result, new pay is not likely to be the sole solution to improving performance at an individual organization. NP companies fared better financially on average based on financial measures than TP companies, as shown in table 17.3. The summary results of the study are shown in table 17.4.

Although it would make no sense to adopt new pay strategies and programs just because large, successful organizations use these programs,

TABLE 17.3

NP Companies and TP Companies: Performance Comparison

Measures	NP Companies (Average)	TP Companies (Average)
Financial growth		
Earnings per share (EPS)—annual growth over three years	13.8	8.9
Return on shareholder equity (ROSE)—annual growth over three years	6.3	2.0
Return on assets (ROA)—annual growth over three years	1.9	−3.9
Profit margin—annual growth over three years	4.1	−1.4
Productivity growth		
Profit per employee—annual growth over three years	10.2	5.7
Cash flow per employee—annual growth over three years	8.8	3.5

TABLE 17.4

Summary of Survey Results

	Total Compensation Philosophy/Strategy	
	NP Companies	*TP Companies*
Total compensation strategy/philosophy	Focus on key organizational goals and objectives to get a differential advantage; emphasize excellence	Focus on fairness, competitiveness and equity; emphasize "good pay practice"
Purpose of total compensation	Communicate, reward, and differentiate between individuals, teams, and business units; encourage top performers to contribute	"Attract and retain"; no strong statement of purpose; focus on competitiveness of all programs

(continued)

TABLE 17.4 *(continued)*

	Total Compensation Philosophy/Strategy	
	NP Companies	*TP Companies*
Plan design	Customize approach to meet the specific goals and circumstances; be practical and use sound business judgment	Copy practices and levels of others; uniform practices across organization
Reward focus	Recognize and encourage desired results, behaviors, and innovation	Granted for uncertain reasons; people treated similarly without strong performance focus
Attitude toward new approaches	Experimental, looking for a better way; using variable pay and other solutions where advantageous	Stick to historical practices, follow others; experimentation viewed as risky
	Human Resource Organization's Role	
Role of human resource organization	Facilitate solutions that match the challenge or situation, aligned with business and financial goals of organization	Propagate "one size fits all" solutions; not partners of line organizations in seeking better ways
Approach to total compensation	Problem solve, innovate, collaborate as partner; try to improve programs and results	Defend and attack, keep programs uniform; negative to innovation or change
Contribution to organization	Consult, reach consensus, develop practical answers; welcomed by line organization	Administer direct and indirect pay, conduct surveys; sometimes adversary to line organization

TABLE 17.4 *(continued)*

	Base Pay Programs/Practices	
	NP Companies	*TP Companies*
Role of base pay	Respond to economics of market and serve as foundation for variable pay where appropriate	Constitutes the only widely used form of direct pay
Job value	External labor market, some skill-based pay experimentation	Mostly internal equity with external market as starting place
Performance basis	Based on results, behaviors, and goal performance	Emphasis on performance of tasks, duties, and traits of employee
Level of base pay	Moderately competitive, sometimes less than competitive	Based on industry comparisons, higher than "average"
Reason for base pay increase	Economic and competitive realities of market; many variable pay plans to supplement base pay	Merit increases to base pay; few variable pay programs lower in organization
Primary reward	Variable pay alternatives where this makes practical sense	Merit base pay increases consistent with corporate-set guidelines
Performance categories	Few categories, flexible to meet situation	Many performance levels, often five or more, many new "forms" each year
Evaluating employee performance	Management accountability; heart of direct pay program	Accountability is inconsistent; often viewed as "human resource problem" by line management

TABLE 17.4 *(continued)*

	Variable Pay Programs/Practices	
	NP Companies	*TP Companies*
Role of variable pay	Communicate organizational strategy, goals, requirements, and values; use where it works; looking for a "better way"	Use only where practices suggest, such as sales jobs; very limited usage; little experimentation
Plan design	Where it makes sense, based on goals, measures of value to shareholder; potential base pay at risk or additional earned reward; change plan as needed to stay meaningful	Only where historically used by other organizations; no new ground breaking
Funding	Quantitative and qualitative goals within control of participants	Quantitative based on broad measures of profit or sales
Eligibility	Where variable pay makes sense, often deep in the organization; based on need	Executives and senior managers, sales jobs, some others but very few
Basis for variable pay	Individual, team, or business unit as situation dictates; based on circumstances	Individual only; little emphasis on teamwork and collaboration
Award size and distribution	Vary from large to zero; based on preset goals, measures, or expectations	Some variation but limited; focus on being competitive more than on results achieved; discretionary awards to individuals

TABLE 17.4 *(continued)*

	Indirect Pay Programs/Practices	
	NP Companies	*TP Companies*
Role of indirect pay	Secondary to direct pay; not an area of growth	Equal in importance to direct pay
Current focus	Control and redirect future additional expenditures and resources to direct pay	Follow competitive practice
General emphasis	Not important focus for 1990s; cost control under way	Cost is major concern for future; still want to be competitive

	Executive Pay Programs/Practices	
Role of executive compensation	Focus executives on shareholder, customer, and public interests	Copy the practices of others, little variance from industry practice
Changes under way	Hold executives more accountable, no "windfalls"	Follow practices of competitors, remain competitive, no innovation
Base pay	Moderately competitive, serve as platform for executive variable pay; less important than variable pay	Controlling executive base pay levels where possible; concerned about negative press about lack of focus on shareholder interests; high base pay, often above 75th percentile
Variable pay	Move toward longer-term cash variable pay based on performance other than stock performance; retain existing stock plans and add performance measures to vesting provisions; higher variable pay leveraging	Stock options are primary long-term variable pay, "profit-sharing" approach to annual variable pay; no innovation

NP companies are most likely to experiment with and use new pay programs. Even conventional wisdom supports looking for a better way to manage total compensation.

Strategies, philosophies, programs, and practices differ between the two groups of organizations. NP companies report total compensation strategies or philosophies that encourage a strong focus on issues such as performance/productivity, teamwork, commitment to quality, employee involvement, quality of work life, recognition of excellent results, focus on the customer, encouragement of innovation, and shared values and common goals as elements in their programs and practices. These organizations are either experimenting with or have already adopted new direct and indirect pay programs—primarily variable pay programs below the executive and senior management levels—and report success with these experiments. NP companies are more likely to ignore industry practice where they see advantages in using less customary pay programs. Experiments often become more permanent solutions that are used selectively throughout the organization.

TP companies stay primarily with traditional pay and seldom experiment with practices that do not exist extensively in organizations they view as business and labor market competitors. These organizations often lack a clear statement of total compensation strategy or philosophy. In addition, where variable pay or other programs are used, they are not part of a general plan of action but instead are isolated instances where something is tried without any methodology for evaluating program success or failure. Sponsorship for other than traditional pay practices comes from isolated middle managers or human resource representatives, rather than from executive strategy or philosophy.

Total Compensation Philosophy/Strategy

As indicated by the previous discussion, strategy and philosophy affect direct and indirect pay programs. But what are the primary strategic and philosophical elements that cause direct and indirect pay programs to be what they are? Whether the total compensation strategy or philosophy is a formal corporate document, an informal but widely communicated and understood commitment, or a part of a total business, financial, and human resource strategy, the differences between NP companies and TP companies begin with the answers to this question.

NP COMPANIES. NP companies most commonly have total compensation strategies that outline goals for the design, implementation, and evaluation of effective direct and indirect pay programs based on the value they add to organizational success. In cases where NP companies have performed at a satisfactory financial level for a period of time, the common strategic and philosophical statements define pay to encourage employees to play a role in extending progress, continuing gains, and expanding on existing organizational advantages. In instances where the goal in an NP company is to regain performance excellence, the focus is on having pay reward employees for helping regain lost ground, reestablish momentum, and restore progress toward the organization's goals and objectives.

NP companies view total compensation as a key communications vehicle that serves as the primary tool for sharing the rewards of success among the shareholders and the employees, as well as a tool to hold employees accountable for results. Pay is important in these organizations because they believe reward systems are powerful determiners of behavior (i.e., employees will work to earn rewards).

Some of the statements coming from NP companies concerning the role of total compensation from a strategic or philosophical perspective are as follows:

- Reward employee and management involvement in solving problems of financial performance, productivity, quality, and customer service. Encourage trying new ways and permitting mistakes that ultimately result in better solutions.
- Communicate with employees concerning the organization's goals as they relate to what makes the organization successful and what role employees should play in this success.
- Help manage change by rewarding employees who achieve results by creating synergy among individuals, teams, functions, and groups that must work well together.
- Reward the generation of ideas, the increase of performance of capital equipment, and the reduction of operating costs. Make it worthwhile to seek credible performance measures and provide employees with a scorecard regarding how they are doing.
- NP companies believe they have excellent people. However, they believe in the "rule of threes." This means one group of employees is aligned with the organization and does not need

rewards to perform well, another group will not perform well no matter what the organization does, and a middle group is important because it can be encouraged if rewarded for desired behaviors. For the top group, pay is recognition for excellence over a sustained period of time; for the middle group, pay is a reward for focusing on desired behavior and results. For the lower group, pay gives employees a chance but moves them out of the organization if their behavior and/or performance does not change.

NP companies indicate that the human resource strategy, including the total compensation strategy, is of equally high quality as the financial, marketing, business, and other general strategies and philosophies.

TP COMPANIES. Few TP companies have formal total compensation strategies; if they do, they are more slogans than statements of shared values. As a result, their pay strategies must often be interpreted from pay practice. Practice focuses on the importance of direct and indirect pay to the attraction, motivation, and retention of employees. In addition, the internal fairness of pay is emphasized. Although paying for performance is viewed as important, the focus is most strongly on paying the individual employee for effort expended, behaviors demonstrated, and results achieved by means of merit-oriented base pay.

Some of the strategic statements about the role of pay include the following:

- Attract, retain, and motivate high quality personnel (without saying how to do this).
- Pay as well as, or better than, other quality organizations in their industry and locale (without saying how liberal direct and indirect pay relates to results achieved).
- Provide fair and equitable direct and indirect pay that make the organization one of the outstanding places to work in the United States (without saying how this helps improve quality or performance).

TP companies do not indicate that pay is a communications tool for performance expectations. Rather, they are interested in the fairness and equitability of direct and indirect pay and make few statements about it as a reward for results other than the "pay for performance" slogan. Also, the few existing formal TP company total compensation strategies and philosophies are not part of the organizations' overall business and financial strategies.

The Human Resource Organization's Role

In all companies surveyed, the human resource organization plays a role in the development and administration of direct and indirect pay programs and strongly influences the total compensation strategy. However, the role differs greatly between the two types of companies.

NP COMPANIES. In NP companies, the human resource organization shares accountability for direct and indirect pay with the line organization. Human resource staff members consult throughout the organization and focus strongly on ensuring that pay programs and practices are flexible, responsive, and properly aligned with the organization's business, quality, financial, customer, and human resource strategies. Among the roles played are the following:

- participating with line management to develop total compensation strategies that parallel business and financial strategies
- consulting throughout the organization on the development of direct and indirect pay programs that recognize differences in businesses, strategies, types of employees, and other variables
- providing guidance concerning the development of variable pay programs, survey participation, and policy development and administration

In this role, the human resource organization becomes an active participant in the formation of the employee–organization partnership. Accountability for results achieved becomes a shared responsibility of both line and staff personnel.

TP COMPANIES. Direct and indirect pay are viewed as either costs to be effectively managed or as employee-relations challenges to be managed fairly and competitively, rather than as helping the organization meet long- or short-term goals that require a role for employees.

Several important issues are common to the role of the human resource organization in TP companies:

- Direct and indirect pay plans are centrally developed and common to the entire organization, even when more than one business is represented within a large organization.
- A single job evaluation plan based on internal equity applies to the total organization.
- Uniform pay administration practices apply to the entire organization, including base pay budgeting.

The focus is on good pay practice, interpreted as competitive and uniform practice with a strong emphasis on internal equity. The view is from the employee's perspective and not from the organization/employee/shareholder/public perspective.

Base Pay Programs and Practices

The perspective of base pay in NP companies is more integrated with other organizational priorities, while in TP companies base pay is viewed as totally a responsibility of the human resource organization.

NP COMPANIES. NP Companies view base pay as the starting place for other programs. They manage base pay to be in a position to add variable pay or other programs where and when appropriate.

Role of Base Pay and Variable Pay. NP companies indicate that base pay is limited as an effective communications tool. They are seeking alternatives to the merit system and are experimenting with and expanding the use of variable pay programs. NP companies believe variable pay can supplement other human resource programs and organizational prerogatives because it is more flexible than base pay programs. They generally feel that a check for $2,600 has a greater impact on an employee than a $50 weekly pay increase. Also, some believe that because they have many white-collar "knowledge workers" where output is less tangible, where nonlinear processes require analysis and creative thought, and where the organization is struggling with how these knowledge workers provide added value to the organization, variable pay is more suited (as a more flexible reward system) than is base pay alone. They believe they can more readily use variable pay than conventional merit-pay plans to reward knowledge workers for well-designed, high-quality products and services, insightful financial statements with sound recommendations, well-defended lawsuits, and excellently performing computer programs.

Unit of Pay for Performance. NP companies may still *try* to use individual performance, productivity, results, and organizational contributions as the foundation of their reward programs. However, they believe that what needs to be accomplished often requires collaboration among different functions and groups to gain the best results. Because of this, they believe that using only individual measures and rewards sometimes inhibits teamwork, collaboration, and a broader organizational perspective that requires an individual to share rather than perform alone. NP companies measure performance for reward purposes based on the goals to be attained and are not limited by the constraints of individual rewards. These organizations are the most likely to be experimenting with or using reward programs that limit base pay to dealing with the economic or competitive aspects of pay management and employ variable pay and group or organizational measures to communicate goals and to reward results achieved.

Determining the Value of Jobs. NP companies define the labor market in terms of their competitors for talent. However, they are only interested in what financially successful organizations pay. They say they pay only average base pay and use other valuable things about their organizations to make them attractive places to work for the best people. Some NP companies are moving to skill-based pay and job valuing approaches that start with the external marketplace.

The value of NP company jobs is based on the market. Equity is defined in terms of paying employees based on their job's worth in the labor market rather than the pay of some other job in the organization.

Base Pay Management. NP companies are defining the external market in terms of the average or the 50th percentile of competitive practice. To these organizations, this has meant reducing fixed base pay over time so that having competitive base pay means being paid an average salary or wage based on some external comparator. Some NP companies have structured their base pay ranges in order that the most an employee can be paid in the form of base pay is somewhere near the 75th percentile of competitive practice. Some have limited base pay to the 50th percentile of competitive practice.

More NP companies are seeking alternatives to base pay ranges and their negative connotation of communicating inflexibility of pay management. Although they have not yet always found the alternative, they are moving to more restrictive base pay progression, where possible, combined with some form of variable pay.

Performance Basis. Wherever performance is evaluated, it is judged based on either the results the organization expects from performance or desired behaviors the organization wants from employees and based on preset goals in order that the employee knows what is expected. Performance evaluation is a management responsibility. Often, how well employee performance is evaluated is used to judge manager performance. Even in instances where only observed performance is possible, the manager is accountable for evaluating performance based on the best methods available.

TP COMPANIES. These organizations view base pay as the primary direct pay element and focus their efforts on managing base pay as effectively as possible. Although some TP companies do use variable pay lower in the organization, this is not a part of a plan to determine whether other forms of financial rewards will eventually be used to supplement base pay if proven beneficial.

Role of Base Pay and Variable Pay. TP companies follow or determine industry practice, and their industries generally use base pay primarily. Also, in some instances these organizations are industry trendsetters and are copied by others much more than they copy others. They seldom investigate or experiment with new practices to determine if they are better than current practices.

Unit of Pay for Performance. Individual merit-pay programs focus only on individual performance. These organizations experiment extensively with how to evaluate individual performance better by changing the forms, performance level descriptions, and evaluation methods used. They believe that base pay is the only way to design pay programs for most employees and that individual performance is the only way to determine the portion of base pay that is founded on merit.

Determining the Value of Jobs. TP companies primarily use internal equity to determine job value. When internal equity and competitive practice conflict, internal equity prevails if the result is placing the job at a higher value. When external competitive practice indicates a higher value than internal value, "comparable" jobs with historical internal relationships that lack the higher external market value are placed in a higher base pay range. Most of these organizations use a point-factor methodology, where jobs are assigned points by a committee process based on job descriptions.

Base Pay Management. Conventional base pay ranges with minimums, midpoints, and maximums are used to manage pay. Progression through the range is based on interquartile or midpoint control, which helps determine the size of any merit increase granted. The organizations address issues of employees paid "over the maximum" and other issues such as how large increases should be for the same level of performance for employees above or below the midpoint of the range. Typically, TP companies indicate that their base pay is somewhere between the 60th and 75th percentile of competitive practice.

Performance Basis. TP companies tend to attempt to design the "ideal" general-purpose performance review form based on the tasks, duties, and traits of employees required to perform each job in the organization. Performance evaluation is viewed as a complexing human resource problem that is the subject of extensive time and effort. The absence of good measurement criteria is used as a reason the organization does not hold managers accountable for distributing base pay increases according to performance differences that are observed or measured. Performance review results are often similar throughout the organization with little differentiation—making the performance appraisal program a credibility problem.

Variable Pay Programs and Practices

Variable pay includes group and individual incentives, gainsharing, lump-sum awards, and other cash compensation programs other than base pay. Variable pay is a major difference between NP and TP companies. NP companies believe they cannot get the entire pay job done without the use of variable pay. They report that variable pay works in circumstances where base pay does not. They use variable pay successfully on an as-needed basis at all organizational levels. TP companies reserve variable pay primarily for executives and senior management, plus certain special plans for sales and other jobs where variable pay has traditionally existed.

NP COMPANIES. These organizations normally have a strategy for the management of direct and indirect pay. The total compensation strategy includes understanding the limitations that exist for base pay and benefits. The strategy defines an important role for variable pay to make up for the limitations of base pay and benefits as communications vehicles and as rewards for results and behaviors that are consistent with organizational goals.

Designing Variable Pay Plans. Human resource organizations help line organizations lead the design and implementation of experimental as well as continuing variable pay plans. Plans have annual review provisions that indicate when plans are to be evaluated and redesigned or ended as appropriate so they can be improved based on additional experience in the specific situation. Variable pay plans are changed or eliminated when they are less effective than base pay–only programs as performance rewards, communications vehicles, or sources of individual or group recognition.

Funding Variable Pay Plans. NP companies fund variable pay plans based on a wide range of measures that are important to the performance of the organization or some business unit of the organization. Often, measures of financial performance are used, and these measures vary widely according to what the organization or business unit wants to accomplish. Nonfinancial measures are employed to focus on issues of customer service and product or service quality. Plans are most often funded by measures over which the employee, teams of employees, or employees in the business unit have some direct or indirect control.

Performance Goals for Variable Pay Awards. Many different quantitative and qualitative measures and goals are used by NP companies for granting awards to employees who participate in a variable pay program. Plans distribute awards based on behaviors, goal performance, teamwork, collaboration, results, and whatever the organization believes are viable business, quality, and economic reasons to use variable pay. NP companies report they do not extensively use special-award programs that provide a fund of money for executives and managers to award "on the spot." These organizations say that they do not believe this adds lasting value and that they prefer well thought-out plans driven by preset goals and performance measures.

Variable Pay Plan Participation. NP companies have a wide variety of employees in variable pay plans. However, few have all unionized employees participating in variable pay programs. Many variable pay plans are being tried that involve cross-functional teams, knowledge workers, groups of exempt and nonexempt employees, and entire work units from manager to clerical support. In addition, individual-contributor variable pay plans are employed when the opportunity exists for a single employee to accomplish some measurable breakthrough.

Participation in variable pay is generally deep and wide in portions of the organization where it is used, and is based more on the goals and the situation than on some predetermined rules about variable pay participation.

Variable Pay Emphasis. Because NP companies report difficulties in credibly measuring or observing individual performance, much of the experimentation with variable pay below the executive and management areas is with approaches that include more than one employee. The plans measure the worthiness of plan participants based on some measures or goals that require employees to work effectively as a group.

Award Variation. Many large awards and many zero awards characterize variable pay in these organizations. If variable pay begins to become an annuity, NP companies view this as a sign that variable pay is not working. This is why the plans have annual review provisions and can be modified or terminated if necessary.

TP COMPANIES. Variable pay and executive and senior management variable pay are synonymous to TP companies. These organizations most often use top management variable pay funded by overall financial performance. They commonly distribute awards to individual executives and senior managers retrospectively. These organizations use variable pay in the form of gainsharing in some production locations because the plans were championed at a local level. However, base pay is the primary focus, and variable pay is not a priority.

Designing Variable Pay Plans. Involvement in the design of variable pay plans is limited in TP companies, while existing variable pay plans have been in effect for many years with little or no change. Most often, measures used for variable pay do not change even though the circumstances surrounding the group in which variable pay is found have changed. Variable pay plans often are developed in the financial organization with the assistance of line and human resource professionals. Few TP companies provide for the continuing development and experimentation with less traditional pay systems. Human resource organizations in these companies do not often lead experimentation with variable pay, but rather support organizationwide uniformity.

Funding Variable Pay Plans. Since mostly executives and top managers participate in variable pay in TP companies, measures of profit performance are used to fund variable pay. Executive variable pay often pays out in both good and poor performance years. Where variable pay is used below the executive level, plans tend to be discretionary in nature.

Performance Goals for Variable Pay Awards. In TP companies, once variable pay plans are funded, the money is often distributed to all participants without the benefit of evaluating group or individual results based on goal performance. Variable pay is most often driven by competitive practice, meaning that the TP company often starts with the competitive total cash compensation rate and designs the variable pay plan to generate that amount of awards. If organizations they view as comparable use variable pay in a specific area, TP companies are likely to use variable pay to respond to competitive practice. When they do, plan design and performance measures are most often copied from prevailing practice.

Variable Pay Plan Participation. Executives and senior managers are the primary variable pay plan participants. Also, sales employees participate in variable pay plans. A few other variable pay plans may be used, but they are generally employed only where an established precedence for the use of these plans exists in other organizations.

Variable Pay Emphasis. Executive variable pay is most often based on some combination of measures of overall organizational performance. Where sales variable pay exists, awards are based on preset quotas or objectives for revenues or sales.

Award Variation. Most often, award size varies only moderately on an individual basis. Since TP companies often work back from total cash compensation competitive practice to determine awards, variable pay represents a fairly common percentage of the individual executive's base pay.

Indirect Pay Programs and Practices

Nearly all TP companies surveyed indicate that they are focusing more on direct pay than indirect pay because they believe they can get more mileage from direct than from indirect pay, because they want to reduce the cost of indirect pay, because they are presently fully competitive in the indirect pay area and do not want to extend these programs any further, or because they are in the process of undertaking a move toward increasing the portion of indirect pay costs that is shared with employees. Even the most tradition-bound organizations are beginning to investigate indirect pay closely because of the cost and legislative changes that confront them.

NP COMPANIES. NP companies are either exploring variable pay or have completed their exploration and are in the process of implementing variable pay. They believe such actions provide them with an advantage. These organizations view direct pay as the most important element of total compensation and are not presently focusing on indirect pay.

Indirect Pay Trends. NP companies have studied or are studying the cost implications of indirect pay programs. They have increased or plan to increase the portion of benefit costs paid by their employees. They are looking for ways to manage indirect pay costs, especially medical costs, more effectively.

Pension and Profit Sharing. NP companies are concerned about the future of their pension plans because of the possibility of additional restrictive legislation or because they believe pension plans cause people to try to spend a full career with an organization when some people should be encouraged to leave. They are not liberalizing existing pension plans and express a preference for deferred profit sharing. Where these organizations add retirement benefits, they add programs in the profit-sharing or 401(k) model because they believe that this does a better job of tying the economic future of the employee to organizational success.

Flexible Benefits. Many NP companies have some form of benefit flexibility or are in the process of developing and implementing programs in this area. The goal is cost containment in the nonretirement areas of benefits. In addition, these organizations view choice making as a way for employees to understand the value and cost of benefits and to make decisions that impact their total compensation. Flexibility is reported to be a step these organizations take only after they have done all they can to contain benefit costs.

TP COMPANIES. Probably because TP companies have had more financial performance "dips" than did NP companies, TP companies are either studying benefit reduction or are now reducing benefits and sharing cost increases with employees. Few organizations are making indirect pay programs more liberal. At most, TP companies are only keeping the current benefit levels.

Indirect Pay Trends. TP companies are trying to stay competitive in the indirect pay area, to keep implied "promises" to employees, and to address benefit cost problems. None are considering improvements in benefit levels. Many are studying reduction or are actually reducing benefits—primarily in the medical/dental area, where they believe costs are out of hand. The trend is clearly toward cost reduction or at most staying where they are and passing more costs on to employees.

Pension and Profit Sharing. Most TP companies are not changing retirement plans that are presently in place. However, many have the programs under study and are concerned about future funding requirements and legislation that they believe may have a negative impact on the cost of retirement plans. Many have both pensions and profit sharing, and others have only profit sharing. Cost containment is the strategy for TP companies.

Flexible Benefits. Many have flexible benefits or are in the process of developing or considering these plans. TP companies are moving to this type of plan based primarily on the practices of others rather than on the implementation of an organizational strategy.

Executive Compensation Programs and Practices

Executive and senior management compensation in NP companies is reported to be closely aligned with the organizations' business and financial plans. In TP companies, executive total compensation issues relate mostly to the competitiveness of pay plans, pay levels, and the organizations or industry groups used to compare levels and forms of executive compensation.

A typical strategy in an NP company is to tie executives to certain long-term measures of performance or goals that are viewed as valuable in addition to stock price. A typical TP company would say the strategy or philosophy was to pay at a given percentile of some industry or organizational group.

NP COMPANIES. The total compensation strategies of NP companies start with executive compensation, so these survey participants make the strongest statement about how executive compensation is managed. While NP companies explore variable pay in other areas of the organization, true variable pay aligned with shareholder value is reported to be the prevailing goal. NP companies say they pay executives based on results. This means goals and objectives are set for each executive; unless the executive performs well to preestablished goals and objectives, the executive receives no award.

Executive Base Pay. NP companies believe that while executive base pay can serve as the starting place for sound total executive compensation plan design, it is not flexible enough to help the organization focus on the performance results that are desired. Base pay for executives is moderately competitive in order that room exists for substantial variable pay based on performance. Base pay at the average of industry practice is common, with major upside opportunities equal to several multiples of base pay as a result of long-term and short-term variable pay. NP companies say they believe a combination of short- and long-term variable pay aligns executives with shareholders and is flexible enough to vary with shareholder interests.

Executive Variable Pay. The major issue in NP companies is the focus on more nonstock long-term variable pay in addition to the use of stock plans. These organizations report the increased use of restricted stock plans with performance requirements added to the lifting of restrictions. NP companies are adopting more cash and restricted stock long-term variable pay for a number of reasons:

- NP companies acknowledge the importance of stock price and stock ownership among their executives. However, they believe that stock price is not the only measure of success as it relates to executive performance. They want executives to deliver goal performance in areas where they have direct impact.
- They believe tenure is only one issue related to making options and stock available to executives. They also indicate that more direct measures of executive results should be used as requirements before the executive is able to gain from stock appreciation.
- They believe executive cash variable pay should focus on longer periods than one year because they are interested in sustained executive performance. They believe a single year may not be as valuable a measure of success as the longer term.

The interest in NP companies seems to focus on evaluating executive performance based on measures in addition to share price and also on extending cash variable pay over performance periods of longer than a year because of the belief they have in focusing executives on the longer term. Some organizations report that to set an example of true "merit variable pay," they had to hold executives accountable for getting certain jobs done. For example, operating executives have quantitative and qualitative operating goals, financial executives have qualitative and quantitative goals for their organizations, and marketing and sales executives and human resource executives also have specific goals that are included in variable pay plans.

TP COMPANIES. Perhaps because more of these organizations than NP companies were experiencing financial challenges during the time the survey was conducted, they are staying put relative to executive compensation.

Executive Base Pay. TP companies often have executive compensation programs that include base pay above the 75th percentile of competitive practice. This makes them high payers of executive base pay. Lately, some of these organizations have been criticized in the press and by shareholders concerning their high fixed base pay, which prohibits variation in total cash compensation according to the fortunes of shareholders. As a result of this negative publicity, some TP companies are trying to control base pay. This is inhibited by the fact that their annual variable pay plans often pay out when shareholders are doing less well.

Executive Variable Pay. Annual variable pay is often based only on global performance measures of organizational success and lacks goals and objectives for individuals or groups of executives. Stock options remain the primary executive long-term pay tool when combined with the annual variable pay plan. TP companies are often focused more on the practices of industry counterparts than on the performance measures or goals of executive compensation. However, they are also worried about what their boards will approve in terms of the competitiveness of pay levels, rather than what makes sense to the organization.

Variable pay plans are viewed as not working when they fail to pay off. Cash plans are limited to an upside opportunity of something in the area of 100 percent of executive base pay, and few executives receive zero awards. TP companies have difficulty changing from high base pay and fairly automatic annual executive variable pay to moderate base pay and variable pay that offers substantial opportunities for earnings if shareholders are benefited, because industry practice locks them into a less flexible strategy.

Conclusions

New pay is more likely to be used by one of the better financially performing *Fortune* 100 companies than it is to be used by a *Fortune* 100 company that is not performing as well financially. However, this does not mean that pay methods alone cause differences in performance results. Organizations that use new pay do so because they cannot get the same advantages from traditional pay. It seems that some important "winners" are changing their reward systems in significant ways. Although new pay does not alone cause the differences in financial performance among organizations, the bureaucratic characteristics of traditional pay seem much less likely to facilitate excellence than do the features of new pay.

The chapters on variable pay, base pay, and indirect pay are experience based and are confirmed by this study of major capital-intensive organizations and our other studies of labor-intensive organizations. It is because the conclusions are based on such a wide range of organizations that the future of new pay looks encouraging.

PART SEVEN

The Future of New Pay

Linking Employees and Organizations

Productivity, Customers, Quality, and New Pay—Strategic Linkage

American organizations are fighting hard on a global basis for business. At the same time, productivity in the United States has dropped dramatically during the life cycle of traditional pay. It is not likely that pay concepts of the 1960s will support the goal of regaining worldwide economic leadership.

New pay makes practical sense for America because it helps focus organizations and employees on customers, business competitors, financial results, productivity improvement, and quality, which are national objectives. The universal goal is to help employees understand that the success of their organization depends strongly on how well they satisfy customer needs, including such issues as flexibility, delivery capability, dependability, and lead time for product development, modification, and production, in addition to quality, price, and products and services offered. The concept of partnership must include the employee, organization, customer, and supplier. The rewards the employee receives must depend on the performance of the organization, which is affected by how well the organization responds to the requirements of customers.

The customer's role in new pay will increase as an extension of the quality and customer value initiatives. This will create the need to refine measures of quality and customer satisfaction in order to include specific information concerning customer desires into all decisions made by the organization. This will make it impossible for organizations merely to develop products and services that they want and subsequently sell these to customers. Instead, customers will provide the foundation for products and services, and customer attitudes toward these products and services will be used to determine whether the organization prospers.

As Band says in *Creating Value for Customers,*

> The difference between a bureaucratic organization and a customer-responsive one is like the difference between an elephant and a shrew. The elephant, which is relatively secure in its environment, has a small surface-area-to-bulk ratio, which makes it slow, cumbersome, and relatively impervious to external stimuli. The shrew has a large surface-area-to-bulk ratio, which makes it extremely sensitive and agile in responding to changes in its environment.[1]

We agree with Band and propose that the United States needs more shrews than elephants.

The quality and customer value movements contend that rewards that make people, groups, and organizations competitive should be turned from win–lose to win–win, whereby everyone would gain—employees, stockholders, stakeholders, customers, and suppliers. The quality and value movements say that the total organization depends for its success on its parts, which include teams, people, machinery and suppliers. All parts must first be concerned about the entire system and then focus on how quality and value issues within their special purview contribute to total results. New pay attempts to make everyone a winner. New pay and the quality and value movements are partners in the success of organizations. The fact that quality and value are so essential, as well as the role new pay plays in communicating the importance of quality, will help make new pay grow.

New pay focuses on a wide variety of performance measures in addition to profitability and productivity, including the elements of quality and customer value. It acknowledges that organizational performance is complex and unique to the specific circumstances, while traditional pay emphasizes the individual and encourages the individual employee to compete with others in the organization for scarce assets. Teamwork, collaboration, and overall organizational success are not the cornerstones of traditional pay. This means traditional pay will not be a partner of the quality and customer value movements, while new pay is critical to making these movements a success.

Leaders pressed by competition and in a position to make changes are realizing that better solutions exist. They are discovering that new pay closely matches their need to improve productivity, customer value, and quality. This process will encourage new pay and discourage the further expansion of traditional pay.

New Pay Is Just Starting

Many high-visibility organizations are finding that traditional pay solutions are unresponsive to the challenges they are facing. New pay focuses human resources on financial and nonfinancial goals and objectives that change periodically and sometimes dramatically. The very flexibility of new pay makes it responsive to times like the present when the need for adaptability is critical.

Although there will be some failures and setbacks for new pay as a result of experimentation and ill-conceived designs, there will also be many successes. Each venture into new pay will provide experience in how to match the proper pay solutions to specific circumstances. As the body of information grows, it will become easier to select the solutions that will most likely generate the desired results for a given situation.

Getting Past New Pay Blockades

Change is difficult and often causes organizational disruption. The organization's ability to deal effectively with disruption depends strongly on whether or not sufficient support for change exists. This support often depends on whether the organization is in "pain" because of poor performance or productivity, whether the organization is changing before it is in pain to help ensure continued excellent performance, or whether the organization is merely experimenting with new pay because traditional pay is viewed as having a negative impact on organizational success.

Organizations in pain because of lagging performance and traditional pay programs that are unable to support new priorities and directions have no problems getting through the blockades of pay programs that have been in effect for many years. Change is needed, and corresponding action is taken. In this situation both leaders and employees can understand the relationship between pay and results achieved, and considerable momentum supporting change exists. However, the challenge is to maintain communications and to make sure that as the turnaround is experienced, employees share in the success if they have been expected to share in the downside.

Where performance is good and the organization wants to ensure its future, pain does not exist to drive program change. However, new pay is most likely to work if initiated when organizational performance is good because the employees' first experience with new pay involves sharing success. Later, if downsides occur, the employees have a better understanding of the concept of sharing in both the ups and the downs of organizational performance. Constant contact with and involvement by employees and managers are needed to establish ownership of the change. Periodic communications and discussions with employees to show the impact of "before" and "after" the change are important, as is the continuing commitment of managers to lead the change process.

Experimentation offers the opportunity to show the impact of change on a selected basis, since the organization may move to new pay strategies incrementally. However, employee ownership is critical, and employees can become advocates for new pay programs as they gain experience with them.

Employee Involvement

Organizations are finding considerable value in encouraging employees to participate in the evaluation, design, implementation, and administration of pay programs. Organizations with employee involvement cultures must implement pay plans that can tolerate close evaluation and scrutiny by employees. Traditional pay will not be able to stand the critique of a participative process. For example, while it is rather easy to claim that merit-oriented base pay works, it is difficult to demonstrate this fact to employees who are involved in an actual review of the details of the program.

Employee involvement is a more comfortable partner with new pay because new pay is based on involvement, partnerships, teamwork, and collaboration. New pay is designed to change as the circumstances change. This makes it possible to have employees help improve the programs. Under traditional pay, the organization must sell, defend, and justify the pay systems to employees. With new pay, employees can help improve the programs during the program evaluation or annual review period, and management can behave positively toward their contributions.

A Little Help from Our Friends

The private sector can adopt new pay without assistance. However, it would help if governmental agencies provided some support for pay systems that match existing circumstances. The largest employer in the United States, the public sector, has avoided anything other than tenure-based pay and highly liberal benefit programs. This sets a poor example because public organizations that need high levels of performance often attract employees who wish to avoid evaluation. It is important for our nation's largest employer to attract high-talent, highly motivated, and high-performing employees rather than often being forced to retain employees who would have difficulty finding jobs elsewhere.

Public organizations should be required to adopt new pay. If the U.S. Postal Service were required to place all increases in postal rates in a pool based on measures of customer value rather than on more base pay and benefits for the highest-paid semiskilled employees in the United States, employee and organizational productivity could be enhanced. Merely putting more fixed direct and indirect pay dollars into an organization where 83 percent of expenses are fixed pay costs will gain nothing. To ensure prompt and quality service, the paychecks of postal employees could be disguised and mailed to them from cities other than the one in which they work. For example, the checks of Los Angeles workers might be mailed from New York City, and vice versa. Although this suggestion is a bit tongue in cheek, this practice would create employee interdependence and encourage attention to quality issues.

Suggestions for Further Study

More work needs to be done on the role that pay plays in the performance of organizations. It is necessary to determine whether there is any causal relationship between pay design and performance results. This is important because it appears that the characteristics of new pay are more likely to exist in circumstances where goals are attained than where goals are missed. So many issues contaminate the impact pay changes have on organizational results that a closer look in more controlled circumstances is necessary.

More before-and-after research is needed that tracks the impact of changes in specific pay practices of low-performing organizations. This should be fairly easy to do, because new pay plans have annual reviews during which they are critically evaluated. Investigators have the opportunity to evaluate new pay as a normal part of the pay management process and to parallel research with practical plan evaluation and improvement.

Cleaning Up Pay Management

Never have more opportunities for pay innovation been available. Slumping productivity and potential loss of economic leadership make the United States the ideal place to try methodologies that can provide organizations with the opportunity to gain a differential advantage.[2]

New pay offers some strong advantages to organizations that are facing an increasingly competitive business environment. It is important that some changes be implemented to keep new pay from being placed at a strong disadvantage versus traditional pay. Many changes can be initiated by management with employee involvement. Others could be legislated in order that new pay does not need to overcome the tax breaks granted to some elements of traditional pay that are encouraged merely for these tax advantages. Still other changes can be made by members of boards of directors and trustees by supporting management changes to new pay.

Some of the nationally legislated changes that would support new pay include the following:

- change tax policy
- require new pay in public sector
- encourage new pay in government contractors
- resolve comparable worth in a practical manner
- encourage long-term pay programs

At the board level in both for-profit and not-for-profit organizations, directors can encourage management to implement a total compensation strategy that is supportive of new pay. Some areas of emphasis include the following:

- ask for a total compensation strategy
- restructure executive pay
- increase equity ownership
- encourage group variable pay

- encourage control of fixed base pay and benefits
- understand the employee–organization partnership initiative

In combination, these actions will place new pay on a equal footing with traditional pay, and this will create an opportunity to see how these changes affect the performance of organizations and people.

Legislated Changes

With tax laws changing constantly, some organizations continually struggle to shelter ordinary income from taxation. In the process, organizations make it impossible for pay to be linked to performance. Pay should be managed to reward desired performance and not to gain tax advantages. In addition, important legislative changes should be undertaken as follows.

CHANGE TAX POLICY. Employee benefits are not taxed. This encourages organizations to increase indirect rather than direct pay. Encouraging organizations to spend more on benefits, which some say are more likely to retain poor performers than excellent performers, is not consistent with the need to identify organizational results closely with the pay employees receive.

Tax legislation should support pay alternatives that have the opportunity to contribute positively to organizations' ability to compete. Pay should encourage employees to perform to earn rewards. Direct pay can be managed to reward differences in performance, while employee benefits must be offered to excellent and marginal performers alike. Direct pay, especially variable pay, is more flexible in terms of communications and reward value.

Tax treatment should vary based on the pay component's ability to reward performance. This means that base pay should receive better tax treatment than indirect pay, and variable pay should receive advantaged tax treatment over base pay. A second alternative is to give equal tax treatment to the three total compensation components, since every total compensation dollar affects the price of a product or service equally, and this will facilitate organizations and employees determining where dollars should be best allocated. A third alternative is equal tax treatment for base pay and indirect pay and more favorable tax treatment for variable pay because, of the three, variable pay is best able to respond to performance differences and reward performance improvement. An improvement in the performance of organizations will provide a solid foundation for improvements in other areas of life in the United States.

REQUIRE NEW PAY IN PUBLIC SECTOR. Our largest employer is the public sector. In public organizations, the words *merit system* mean an automatic pay increase system based on tenure and internal equity. The newest "innovation" the federal government is implementing is area differentials based on what the private sector pays employees in one part of the country compared to other parts of the country. The geographic comparability is based only on cash compensation and does not include employee benefits, where federal employees clearly outstrip the private sector. This means that in some parts of the country (and where the majority of federal employees are located), the federal government will pay higher fixed pay levels to people in the public sector than they do now. It seems likely that new pay must be legislated in the public sector to get pay focused on results achieved and value received by the taxpayer. Public organizations should be required to set the example of pay for performance and productivity for the rest of the country—the opposite of how the public sector is currently viewed.

ENCOURAGE NEW PAY IN GOVERNMENT CONTRACTORS. Many organizations that sell products and services to the government would like to consider the use of certain elements of new pay. However, they are discouraged from recovering many costs of new pay from their customer because the government wants contractors to pay employees as the government does. Contractors are not encouraged to employ streamlined organizations or to use skill-based pay or variable pay. Rather, they are encouraged to mirror the bureaucracy of the federal government. This means government contractors cannot readily use variable pay and expect reimbursement from their customer. Government contractors should be able to implement variable pay based on their own performance and the value and quality of the products and services provided to the government.

RESOLVE COMPARABLE WORTH IN A PRACTICAL MANNER. After many long reports and books on the subject of comparable worth, it seems impossible to define comparable worth in any reasonable manner and with any validity to the construct. It is clear that the "Canada solution" is not for the United States. In fact, the actions taken in Canada are resulting in increased labor costs without concomitant productivity, placing Canadian companies in a disadvantageous economic competitive position relative to the United States.[3] Creating artificial markets, thus inflating the financial value of some skills and jobs and deflating the value of others in the name of comparable worth, will give us more of what wage controls produced. Comparable worth and market value must be defined as the same thing to encourage people to acquire skills that are more valued in the market. The United States must grow the skills it needs and discourage the development of skills that are not valued in a free market as a result of artificial increases in their monetary value.

Market supply and demand works—the substantial increase in pay for registered nurses over the last few years is one visible example. Also, because by 1995 more than half of the new entrants into the labor force will be women, women are moving and will continue to move into male-dominated jobs. People will be needed to fill these jobs, and more women are receiving training and education in male-dominated areas.

ENCOURAGE LONG-TERM PAY PROGRAMS. It is important for organizations to implement plans that ensure their sustained performance. Pay plans that encourage investment in the longer term are important to the competitiveness of American organizations. Pay plans that distribute variable pay based on sustained organizational performance should receive preferential tax treatment over variable pay that focuses only on short-term performance.

Organizations are too frequently managed from quarter to quarter without sufficient concern for the long term. Annual executive variable pay often rewards short-term financial results and encourages short-term thinking. This discourages organizations from making long-term investments in the future. If organizations are not encouraged to invest in the future, they will eventually lose their competitive advantage to foreign firms that invest strongly in the long term. Variable pay dollars that are paid out at the end of a three-year to five-year period for sustained performance should be tax-advantaged to the employee and to organizations that have tax obligations. Employees at the top of the organization should have the largest portion of their variable pay that is based on sustained results over a three-year to five-year period come to them at attractive tax terms.

Tax changes should provide a situation where benefits are taxed more than or equal to base pay, short-term variable pay is taxed less than base pay, and long-term variable pay is most preferentially taxed. This will encourage investment in the future. Using this approach requires modification of the tax structure to ensure that lower-income employees would not be at a tax disadvantage but would be encouraged to earn rewards based on sustained performance and results that help the U.S. economy.

Board Changes

Boards of directors and trustees should provide strategic guidance to total compensation programs to ensure they are consistent with the business, financial, and human resource strategies, culture, and values of the organization. The suggestions that follow represent some actions that can be taken by directors.

ASK FOR A TOTAL COMPENSATION STRATEGY. Directors should ask management to develop a total compensation strategy that defines the role pay plays in helping the organization meet its goals and objectives. In this way, directors can review the strategy and the resulting pay plans to ensure that they are properly aligned. Armed with a total compensation strategy, directors will have the opportunity to determine whether such programs as executive compensation plans within their purview are consistent with the goals of the organization. Organizations with a total compensation strategy are less likely to be "sold" programs that are not consistent with their long-term goals and objectives.

RESTRUCTURE EXECUTIVE PAY. Boards and executives are receiving negative press about unreasonable pay levels that are not related to how well, or how poorly, their organization is performing. This is being argued in the press to the detriment of executives, boards, shareholders, employees, and organizations.[4] The issue can only be resolved when executive pay is restructured so that it is principally variable pay based primarily on the long-term success of the organization and shareholders. This is consistent with our suggestion concerning preferential tax treatment for long-term forms of pay. The principles of the employee–organization partnership and a strong focus on variable pay rather than indirect pay and base pay apply to executives as much as they do to other employees in the organization. We do not isolate executives or managers for special treatment, because it is important to new pay that an organization's leaders set an example for other employees and have their total compensation directly vary based on organizational performance.

Rather than controlling executive total cash compensation as a multiple of the pay of some specific employee group, as is often suggested, it is the level of executive base pay that should be controlled. The board should strongly control the base pay of the top management group. Variable pay would not be controlled as a multiple of base pay, as is the traditional practice. Rather, variable pay would be based on a combination of sustained earnings, cash flow, stock price performance, and other measures that are either viewed by the financial community as representative of shareholder value or consistent with the organization's long-term strategic plan. High total pay levels could result from variable pay because of sustained levels of organizational performance rather than because of high base pay.

A larger portion of total executive pay could be awarded in the form of common stock. Executives and other investors should be treated more favorably from a tax standpoint only if shares are held for at least three to five years. On the other hand, executive stock gains would be taxed more aggressively than other elements of total compensation if stock is traded soon after it is awarded. This would cause executives to be more closely aligned with shareholder interests. It is important for executive pay to be more credible, and this is best accomplished if executive rewards are tied to the interests of the shareholder.

New pay organizations have many variable pay plans based on performance measures within the reach of employees. Boards should ensure that executive variable pay is linked to the awards earned by employees in variable pay plans so that the executives become partners with employees and the organization.

INCREASE EQUITY OWNERSHIP. Executives should own a substantial part of their organization on a sustained basis so that their decisions affect their own financial fortunes as well as those of other shareholders. Indeed, a good argument can be made for many employees owning common stock in their organization. The more an executive or other employee owns company stock, the more tax advantages should accrue to any long-term stock gains in order to link employees strongly with the success of the company. Where equity ownership is not possible, long-term cash variable pay plans should be designed to simulate ownership to the greatest extent possible. Rather than merely tenure restrictions, performance restrictions should be added to restricted stock plans to strengthen the relationship between pay and performance.

ENCOURAGE GROUP VARIABLE PAY. Because business practice has for so long emphasized individual results, it is sometimes difficult for directors who have experienced successful careers in this environment to perceive the value of new pay concepts. This often creates problems when organizations begin to move to new pay, where group measures of performance are used to encourage employees to help each other attain shared goals. However, in complex organizations, director encouragement is often important to getting teamwork and collaboration included in variable pay plans. Board focus should be on understanding the direction of the organization and ensuring that financial rewards are designed to supplement this direction strongly.

ENCOURAGE CONTROL OF FIXED BASE PAY AND BENEFITS. Directors can help organizations by discouraging high fixed base pay and benefits and encouraging new pay with moderate base pay, variable pay based on group results, and a strong focus on using pay as a communicator of organizational direction in the short and long term. Directors can ask what the organization gets from high levels of base pay and benefits in order to help the organization consider new pay as an alternative to traditional pay.

UNDERSTAND THE EMPLOYEE–ORGANIZATION PARTNERSHIP INITIA-TIVE. Employees who feel they have a stake in the success of the organization are more likely to identify with the goals, values, mission, and strategy of the organization than are employees who do not have a stake in the organization's future. New pay emphasizes that both the employee and the organization are rewarded when the organization succeeds. Directors can determine whether a partnership exists by seeing whether labor costs vary with the financial performance of the organization without negative actions such as layoffs. If labor costs increase without generating performance advantages to the organization, this may be a clue to ineffective total compensation management.

Predictions for the Future

A number of factors will create the need for organizations to change and to experiment aggressively in the area of employee performance. These factors include the following:

- continuing pressure on the financial success of organizations
- increasing global competition for market share
- increasing focus on quality of services and products
- increasing focus on responding to customer needs
- shortage of skilled and educated employees
- oversupply of unskilled and undereducated employees
- need for productivity improvements to make possible increases in real income for employees

In response to these forces for change, we predict an increasing recognition of the inability of traditional pay to meet organizational and employee needs, and a growing use and success of new pay. In part, this change is well under way.

Is there hope for American workers and organizations? Is there a positive message in all of this turmoil? We believe the future is positive principally because the United States has proven to be at its very best when strongly challenged. While our suggestions may seem somewhat dramatic at present, in ten years it will be seen that what we have labeled new pay dominates successful organizations. One reason that we believe this is true: in the early 1970s, one of us spoke at a management seminar and predicted that flexible benefit programs would be commonplace in the 1980s because they better match the needs and goals of employees and organizations. The individual who had introduced the presentation closed by making a joke of the flexible benefit prediction, saying, "This is something our children's children will be predicting." Flexible benefit programs, however, are no longer a prediction; they are a reality.

The future of employee–organization partnerships looks very positive and constructive to us, standing at the start of 1992 making predictions for the decade beginning with the year 2000:

- Employees and organizations will become more closely allied and increasingly willing to help each other succeed. The employee-organization partnership, too, will become a reality.
- Organizations will be taking a stronger role in helping employees

acquire the skills needed for gainful employment. Training will be a universal organizational priority.

- Employees will develop the ability to perform a wider range of needed skills in order to be of value to their organizations during times of change. Employees will become more flexible and more skilled.
- Communications and employee involvement will be a priority, and employees will be more willing to become informed stakeholders in the future of their organizations. Organizations will be more willing to acknowledge that employees at all levels can make a difference.
- Leaders will emerge who are better attuned with all the parties having a vested interest in their organization: customers, shareholders, employees, and the public. The "management by greed" that existed to some extent in the 1980s will be well behind us.
- Pay will be a positive force for organizational change and will facilitate making the time employees spend at work more challenging and interesting.

As these changes occur, some may say that new pay is already encompassed in traditional pay in order to save face for organizations that have been the champions of traditional pay. They will say that traditional pay has not become obsolete; rather, traditional pay has always had the flexibility to meet the needs of changing organizations and has now been called upon to meet the challenge and is doing so effectively. Regardless of the reasoning, new pay will become vital to U.S. industry within the next decade and beyond.

While the 1990s will be remembered as the time when American organizations *really* needed to change, the decade starting with the year 2000 will see the beginning of relationships between employees and organizations that help us forget the labels of *disenfranchised, adversarial,* and *we versus them* that are presently all too common. Although new pay is not likely to be the only factor that will help us move toward a more positive future, it is clearly the only way to make employee pay a constructive catalyst for this change.

Appendix

Guide to Total Compensation Strategy Development

Some organizations decide that it is timely to develop a contemporary and practical total compensation strategy involving both direct and indirect pay. A total compensation strategy can be meaningful only if it is developed by executives who have a knowledge of the organization in general as well as a specific understanding of the organization's short-term and long-term business, financial, and human resource strategies, and who have the opportunity to impact pay policy and practice. In this way the total compensation strategy can be integrated with other important corporate strategies. Unless this is the case, important human resource plans may not reflect the true goals of the organization.

The Strategic Role of Employee Pay

The following are sample questions that address the role the organization believes total employee compensation *should* play in assisting the organization to attain its business and financial goals and objectives. The objective is not to restate current practice but to set future strategy.

1. In general terms, what are the current business, financial, and human resource goals of the organization? In the next year? In the next three to five years? How should the business, financial, and human resource goals of the organization be integrated? What about the core businesses? What about new business ventures?

Any current businesses that will receive more emphasis? Less emphasis?

2. What role should total compensation play in helping the organization attain its business and financial goals?
3. How does the organization want to be viewed by employees? How does the organization want to be managed?
4. What should the organization expect from employees as a result of its total compensation programs?
5. What message to employees should the total compensation program communicate about their relationship with the organization?
6. What should be the balance between direct pay and indirect pay?
7. How should external labor market competition be defined for the organization?
8. What should be the total compensation policy as it relates to competitiveness?
9. What factors should be used to determine the level of direct pay and indirect pay?
10. Should all of the organization's employees be treated similarly as it relates to direct pay and indirect pay?
11. If a new element is added to a pay program or a program is modified, what justification should be required?

Role of Employee Involvement

These questions address the issue of employee involvement in reaching direct and indirect pay decisions that affect them.

1. What are the present experiences the organization has had with employee involvement? Were they viewed as successful? Why and how?
2. To what extent should employees be involved in decisions concerning direct and indirect pay?
3. If employees are to have no involvement in direct and indirect pay design, why is this the case?
4. If employees are to have some involvement in direct and indirect pay design, what will the organization gain from this involvement?
5. Using an example, what might employee involvement be like from a process standpoint?

6. What is too much or too little involvement?

Strategy Concerning Direct Pay

These sample questions address issues of direct pay. This involves base pay and variable pay.

Base Pay

1. What should the organization expect from employees in exchange for base pay?
2. What factors should determine the level of base pay paid within the organization? The labor market? Internal equity across the organization? Internal equity within broad functional areas? Job content? Skills? Individual performance? Organizational performance? Strategic value of jobs to business goals?
3. If competitive practice should play a role in determining the level of base pay, what should constitute competitive practice?
4. How should the value of jobs be determined using the elements defined in question number 2 above?
5. How should the organization determine how it benefits from base pay?
6. What should be the basis of any base pay increases granted?
7. If merit pay is to play a part in granting base pay increases, what role should it play?
8. What criteria and methodology should be used to appraise employee performance?

Variable Pay

1. What should be the role of variable pay (individual variable pay, group variable pay, gainsharing, lump-sum awards, long-term variable pay, etc.)?
2. How should the use of variable pay plans be determined?
3. What measures should be used to fund variable pay?
4. What measures should be used to distribute variable pay once variable pay is funded?
5. How should eligibility for variable pay participation be determined?

6. At what organizational unit should performance be measured? Organizational performance? Business unit performance? Team performance? Individual performance? Some other unit formed for a specific purpose? Other?
7. Should variable pay be at risk, added on, or put potential base pay increases at risk?
8. Where might long-term variable pay that measures performance over a period longer than a year be used?
9. To what extent should the organization use new pay variable pay programs (business plan gainsharing, group variable pay, winsharing, etc.)?
10. As a general rule, what posture should the organization have toward the use of variable pay?

Strategy Concerning Indirect Pay

These questions address the issue of indirect pay or benefits. These plans protect employees and their dependents against the major economic risks of sickness, disability, death, and aging and provide support to retirees. Indirect pay involves health care, life insurance, retirement, paid time off, and supplemental plans.

General Indirect Pay Issues

1. What should the organization expect from employees in exchange for indirect pay programs?
2. What level of income protection and replacement should be provided to employees?
3. To what extent should indirect pay programs vary based on tenure? Ability to pay? Type of job? Job level? Other?
4. What should be the organization's responsibility to pay for the costs of indirect pay? The employee's responsibility?
5. On what basis should external comparisons of indirect pay be made?
6. Once competitive practice is defined, how should the organization compare to this practice?
7. To what extent should indirect pay be consistent throughout the organization?

8. To what extent should the organization's employees have the opportunity to select indirect pay alternatives?

Health Care

1. What should be the responsibility of the organization to provide health care protection to employees?
2. If employees should share in the cost, how should this be accomplished?
3. To what extent and how should health care costs be contained?
4. What should be the policy of providing health care to retirees?

Disability Income

1. What should be the sick pay protection provided by the organization?
2. What should be the long-term disability provisions of the organization?

Life Insurance

1. What should be the purpose of life insurance?
2. What level of life protection should be provided?
3. What factors should play a role in survivor income protection?

Retirement/Capital Accumulation

1. What should be the organization's obligation to employees regarding retirement?
2. Should a defined benefit retirement program play a role in the organization's total compensation strategy? If so, how?
   a. What should be the levels of income replacement provided by retirement?
   b. What should be the basis of income replacement at retirement?
   c. What should be defined as the normal retirement age?
   d. What factors should be considered in determining retirement benefits? Years of service? Base pay? Variable pay?

3. Should profit sharing play a role in the organization's total compensation strategy?
   a. How should funding be determined?
   b. What should be the vesting schedule?
   c. What investment opportunities should be provided?
4. Should the organization provide a role for savings or thrift plans, employee stock-ownership plans, 401(k) plans, or capital accumulation plans?
5. How should retirement benefits be financed?
6. What benefits should be provided after retirement?

Paid Time Off

1. What should be the vacation policy?
2. What should be the holiday policy?
3. Should the organization have a paid time off program that combines different types of paid time off into a pool?

Other Benefits

This section covers other benefits, such as dental care, vision care, prescription drugs, employee assistance, dependent care, dependent life insurance, adoption benefits, educational assistance, relocation assistance, prepaid legal services, financial planning programs, employee recognition programs, severance, volunteerism, matching contribution programs, and executive benefits and perquisites.

1. What should be the criteria used to determine if additional indirect pay should be provided?
2. What criteria should be used to determine executive benefits/perquisites? Should executives be offered a choice in the selection of executive benefits/perquisites?

Strategy Concerning Flexible Benefits

This section is focused on the specific issues surrounding the design of a benefit program that provides choice making.

1. Why should choice making be considered as a strategy?
2. In planning flexible benefit programs, organizations often assess

their employees' needs and preferences to help determine which benefits and options to include. To what extent and how should employee input be gathered and used?

3. Which benefits should be included in the organization's flexible benefit program? Medical? Dental? Retirement? Vacation? Disability? Other?

4. Should a reimbursement account design be used for the flexible benefit program?

5. Should an additional allowance or "add-on" plan be used?

6. Should mix-and-match opportunities for choice making be used?

7. Should a core carve-out plan be used?

8. Should a modular plan be considered?

9. How can the organization prevent employees from making poor choices under a flexible benefit program?

10. How can adverse selection (i.e., employees selecting the most expensive alternatives) be avoided?

11. How can issues of administrative complexity be addressed in the program design?

12. How can the difficulty and expense of communications be effectively addressed?

13. How should flexible benefits be financed?

Notes

Preface

1. E.E. Lawler III, "The New Pay," CEO Publication G84-7(55) (Los Angeles: Center for Effective Organizations, University of Southern California, 1986).

Introduction

1. T. Peterson, W. Zellner & D. Woodruff, "All That Lean Isn't Turning into Green," *Business Week* (Nov. 18, 1991), pp. 39–40.
2. R.M. Kanter, "The Attack on Pay," *Harvard Business Review* (March/April 1987), 60–67.
3. M.E. Porter, *Competitive Advantage* (New York: Free Press, 1985).
4. J.R. Schuster, *Management Compensation in High Technology Companies: Assuring Corporate Excellence* (Lexington, MA: Lexington, 1984).

    J.R. Schuster, *Compensating Key Personnel in the Health Care Industry: The Path to Organizational Success* (Jamaica, NY: Spectrum, 1985).
5. American Compensation Association and M.J. Wallace, Jr., *Rewards and Renewal: America's Search for Competitive Advantage Through Alternative Pay Strategies* (Scottsdale, AZ: American Compensation Association, 1990).

Chapter 1. Socioeconomic Foundations of New Pay

1. F. Levy and R. Crandall, "America's Shrinking Middle Class," *Economist*, 12 Nov. 1988, pp. 84–85.
2. F. Levy and R. Crandall, "America's Shrinking Middle Class," *Economist*, 12 Nov. 1988, pp. 84–85.
3. "Two Trillion Dollars Is Missing," *New York Times*, 8 Jan. 1989.
4. "Human Decisions Give Technology Its Power," *Work in America*, Feb. 1990.

    M. Memmott, "Productivity Will Hold Down Living Standard," *USA Today*, 8 Nov. 1989.

    "To Involve Employees, You Must Involve Managers," *Work in America*, March 1990.

5. J. Seaberry, "Middle Class Dream Fades for Some," *Washington Post,* 4 Jan. 1987, p. 21.
6. S. Lehrman, "Middle Managers Face Squeeze as Firms Try New Structures," *Washington Post,* 4 Sept. 1988, p. 12.
7. "American Living Standards: Running to Stand Still," *Economist,* 10 Nov. 1990.
8. J. Seaberry, "Middle Class Dream Fades for Some," *Washington Post,* 4 Jan. 1987, p. 12.
9. A. Bernstein, "What Happened to the American Dream?", *Business Week,* 19 Aug. 1991, pp. 80–85.
10. J.R. Swinton, "Service-Sector Wages: The Importance of Education," *Economic Commentary* (Cleveland: Federal Reserve Bank of Cleveland, 15 Dec. 1988).
11. R.E. Litan, R.Z. Lawrence & C. Schultze, *America's Living Standards: Threats and Challenges* (Washington, DC: Brookings Institution, 1988).
12. S. Rich, "Female-Male Earnings Gap Narrows," *Washington Post,* Oct. 1990.
13. R.B. Reich, "New Economic Realities," *What's Next, a Newsletter of Emerging Issues and Trends,* 12, (2) (Summer 1990).
14. J.R. Swinton, "Service-Sector Wages: The Importance of Education," *Economic Commentary* (Cleveland: Federal Reserve Bank of Cleveland, 15 Dec. 1988).
15. F. Levy and R. Crandall, "America's Shrinking Middle," *Economist,* 12 Nov. 1988, pp. 84–85.
16. M.N. Baily and A.K. Chakrabarti, *Innovation and the Productivity Crisis* (New York: Brookings Institution, June 1988).
17. J.B. Quinn, J.J. Baruch and P. Paquette, "Technology in Services," *Scientific American,* Dec. 1987, pp. 50–58.
18. J.B. Quinn, J.J. Baruch and P. Paquette, "Technology in Services," *Scientific American,* Dec. 1987, pp. 50–58.
19. P. Behr, "The Case of the Missing Productivity," *Washington Post,* 21 Jan. 1990.
20. E. Pomice, "Shaping Up Services," *U.S. News and World Report,* 22 Jul. 1991, pp. 41–44.
21. B. Wysocki, Jr., "Overseas Calling: American Firms Send Office Work Abroad to Use Cheaper Labor," *Wall Street Journal,* 14 Aug. 1991, pp. A1, A6.
22. A. Bernstein, R.W. Anderson & W. Zellner, "Help Wanted," *Business Week,* 10 Aug. 1987, pp. 48–53.
23. R.E. Winter, "Scarcity of Workers Is Kindling Inflation: Labor Costs Stay High Despite Economic Slowdown," *Wall Street Journal,* 28 Mar. 1990.
   A. Freedman, "Help Wanted, Badly," *Across the Board,* Jan./Feb. 1989.
24. M.M. Hamilton, "U.S. Facing Severe Labor Shortage," *Washington Post,* 24 June 1988.
25. L. Mishel and R.A. Teixeira, *The Myth of the Coming Labor Shortage: Jobs, Skills, and Incomes of America's Workforce 2000* (Washington, DC: Economic Policy Institute, 1991).
26. W.B. Johnson, *Workforce 2000* (Indianapolis: Hudson Institute, 1987).
27. A. Packer, "Retooling the American Worker," *Washington Post,* 10 July 1988.

28. C. Gorman, "The Literacy Gap," *Time*, Dec. 1988, pp. 56–57.
29. N.J. Perry, "The Workers of the Future," *Fortune*, Spring/Summer 1991, pp. 68–72.
30. G. Edwards, "Bridging Schools & Skills," *Academy for Advanced & Strategic Studies*, 18 Nov. 1990.
31. J. Peterson, "Labor Department Panel Urges Teaching of New Skills for Jobs," *Los Angeles Times*, 3 July 1991, pp. D1–D5.

Chapter 2. Organizational Strategies and New Pay

1. E.L. Landon, Jr., "New Strategies for Bank Profitability," presented at Robert Morris Associates 1990 Spring Conference (San Antonio, TX, 19 April 1990).
2. T.J. Peters and R.H. Waterman, Jr., *In Search of Excellence: Lessons from America's Best Run Companies* (New York: Harper & Row, 1982).
3. P.S. Goodman (Ed.), *Change in Organizations* (San Francisco: Jossey-Bass, 1982).
4. E.E. Lawler III, *Pay and Organization Development* (Reading, MA: Addison-Wesley, 1981).
5. J.F. Sullivan, *The Components, Cost Structure and Objectives of a Total Compensation Program* (Phoenix, AZ: American Compensation Association, 1991).
6. L.W. Porter and E.E. Lawler III, *Managerial Attitudes and Performance* (Homewood, IL: Irwin, 1968).
7. J.G. Belcher, Jr., *Productivity Plus* (Houston, TX: Gulf, 1987).
8. E.E. Lawler III, *High-Involvement Management* (San Francisco: Jossey-Bass, 1986).
9. R.J. Doyle, *Gainsharing and Productivity: A Guide to Planning, Implementation and Development* (New York: AMACOM, 1983).
10. A. Kleingartner and C.S. Anderson, *Human Resource Management in High Technology Firms* (Lexington, MA: Lexington, 1987).
11. A.M. Mohrman, S.M. Resnick-West and E.E. Lawler III, *Designing Performance Appraisal Systems* (San Francisco: Jossey-Bass, 1989).
12. T.J. Peters and N.A. Austin, *A Passion for Excellence* (New York: Random House, 1985).
13. J.R. Schuster, *Management Compensation in High Technology Companies: Assuring Corporate Excellence* (Lexington, MA: Lexington, 1984).

Chapter 3. Designing New Pay Strategies

1. P.S. Goodman and J.W. Dean, Jr., "Creating Long-Term Organizational Change," *Change in Organizations*, Ed. P.S. Goodman (San Francisco: Jossey-Bass, 1982).
2. E.E. Lawler III, *Strategic Pay* (San Francisco: Jossey-Bass, 1990).
3. R.J. Schonberger, *Building a Chain of Customers: Linking Business Functions to Create the World Class Company* (New York: Free Press, 1990)

4. R.H. Waterman, Jr., *The Renewal Factor: How the Best Get and Keep the Competitive Edge* (Toronto: Bantam Books, 1987).

Chapter 5. From Strategy to Practice by Involvement

1. E.E. Lawler III, *High-Involvement Management* (San Francisco: Jossey-Bass, 1986).
2. A.M. Mohrman, Jr., S.M. Resnick-West and E.E. Lawler III, *Designing Performance Appraisal Systems* (San Francisco: Jossey-Bass, 1989).

Chapter 6. Principles of New Base Pay

1. U.S. Chamber Research Center, *Employee Benefits: Survey Data from Benefits Year 1989* (Washington, DC: U.S. Chamber of Commerce, 1990).
2. N.B. Winstanley, "Are Merit Increases Really Effective?", *Personnel Administrator,* 4 (1982), 37–41.
3. B. Baker, "SoCal Gas Sees the Light: Women's Pay Is on Par with Men," *Los Angeles Times,* 13 June 1991, pp. D1, D14.
4. "New SoCal Gas Policy on Equal Pay Questioned," *Los Angeles Times,* 7 July 1991, p. D3.

Chapter 7. Paying the Individual

1. G.E. Ledford, Jr., "The Design of Skill-Based Pay Plans," CEO Publication G89-15(158) (Los Angeles: Center for Effective Organizations, University of Southern California, Oct. 1989).
2. E.E. Lawler III and G.E. Ledford, "Skill-Based Pay: A Concept That's Catching On," *Personnel* 62 (9) (1985), 30–37.
3. N. Gupta et al., *Exploratory Investigations of Pay-for-Knowledge Systems,* Department of Labor Technical Report (BLMR 108) (Washington, DC: Bureau of National Affairs, 1990).
4. G.E. Ledford, Jr., "The Design of Skill-Based Pay Plans," CEO Publication G89-15(158) (Los Angeles: Center for Effective Organizations, University of Southern California, Oct. 1989).
5. N. Gupta, G.D. Jenkins, Jr., and W.P. Curington, "Paying for Knowledge: Myths and Realities," *National Productivity Review* 5 (2) (1986), 107–123.
6. R.J. Schonberger, *Building a Chain of Customers: Linking Business Functions to Create the World Class Company* (New York: Free Press, 1990).
7. E.E. Lawler III, *Strategic Pay* (San Francisco: Jossey-Bass, 1990).
8. J.H. Boyett and H.P. Conn, *Workplace 2000: The Revolution Reshaping American Business* (New York: Dutton, 1991).
9. N. Gupta et al., *Exploratory Investigations of Pay-for-Knowledge Systems,* Department of Labor Technical Report (BLMR 108) (Washington, DC: U.S. Department of Labor, 1986).

Chapter 8. Evaluating Jobs

1. A.O. Bellak, "The Hay Guide Chart-Profile Method of Job Evaluation," *Handbook of Wage and Salary Administration,* Ed. M. Rock (New York: McGraw-Hill, 1984).
2. L.R. Gomez-Mejia and R.C. Page, "Development and Implementation of a Computerized Job Evaluation System," *New Perspectives on Compensation,* Ed. D.B. Balkin and L.R. Gomez-Mejia (Englewood Cliffs, NJ: Prentice-Hall, 1987).
3. E.E. Lawler III, "What's Wrong with Point-Factor Job Evaluation?", *Compensation and Benefits Review, 18* (2) (1986), 20–28.
4. J.L. Otis and R.H. Leukart, *Job Evaluation,* 2nd. ed. (Englewood Cliffs, NJ: Prentice-Hall, 1954).
5. C.H. Lawshe, Jr., and G.A. Sattler, "Studies in Job Evaluation I: Factor Analyses of Point Ratings for Hourly-Paid Jobs in Three Industrial Plants," *Journal of Applied Psychology, 28* (3) (June 1944), 189–198.

   C.H. Lawshe, Jr., and A.A. Maleski, "Studies in Job Evaluation III: Analysis of Point Ratings for Salary-Paid Jobs in an Industrial Plant," *Journal of Applied Psychology, 30* (2) (April 1946), 117–128.
6. T.H. Patten, *Fair Pay* (San Francisco: Jossey-Bass, 1988).
7. J.R. Schuster, "How to Control Job Evaluation Inflation," *Personnel Administrator* (June 1985), 167–173.
8. J.R. Schuster, P.K. Zingheim and M.G. Dertien, "The Case for Computer-Assisted Market-Based Job Evaluation," *Compensation and Benefits Review, 22* (3) (May/June 1990), 44–54.

Chapter 9. Base Pay Adjustments

1. A.M. Mohrman, S.M. Resnick-West and E.E. Lawler III, *Designing Performance Appraisal Systems: Aligning Appraisals and Organizational Realities* (San Francisco: Jossey-Bass, 1989).
2. R.E. Kopelman, "Improving Productivity through Objective Feedback: A Review of the Evidence," *National Productivity Review* (Winter 1982–83), 43–55.

Chapter 10. Principles of New Variable Pay

1. J.G. Belcher, Jr., *Productivity Plus* (Houston: Gulf, 1987).
2. J.R. Schuster, "Toward a Direct-Contribution Reinforcement Pay System," *Management of Personnel Quarterly,* Spring, 1971, pp. 2–5.
3. U.S. Chamber Research Center, *Employee Benefits: Survey Data from Benefit Year 1989* (Washington, DC: U.S. Chamber of Commerce, 1989).
4. J.R. Schuster and P.K. Zingheim, "Tying Compensation to Top Performance Can Boost Profits," *Journal of Compensation and Benefits* (Sept./Oct. 1986), 69–73.
5. J.R. Schuster and P.K. Zingheim, "Sales Compensation Strategies at the Most Successful Companies," *Personnel Journal,* June 1986, pp. 112–116.

6. E.E. Lawler III, *High-Involvement Management* (San Francisco: Jossey-Bass, 1986).
7. T.E. Deal and A.L. Kennedy, *Corporate Cultures* (Menlo Park, CA: Addison-Wesley, 1982).
8. R. Johnson and P.R. Lawrence, "Beyond Vertical Integration: The Rise of the Value-Adding Partnership," *Harvard Business Review,* 66 (4) (1988), pp. 94–101.
9. J.R. Schuster and P.K. Zingheim, "Merit Pay: Is It Hopeless in the Public Sector?" *Personnel Administrator,* Oct. 1987, pp. 83–84.

Chapter 11. Types of Variable Pay

1. J. Nickel and S. O'Neal, "Small-Group Incentives: Gain Sharing in the Microcosm," *Compensation and Benefits Review,* Mar./Apr. 1990, pp. 5–12.
2. "Profit Sharing, Group Incentives Gaining Popularity with Firms, Study Finds," *Daily Labor Report,* No. 202, 20 Oct. 1989.
3. R.J. Doyle, *Gainsharing and Productivity: A Guide to Planning, Implementation and Development* (New York: AMACOM, 1983).
4. T.L. Ross and R.A. Ross, "Productivity Gainsharing: Resolving Some of the Measurement Problems," *National Productivity Review,* 3 (4) (Autumn 1984), 382–394.
5. E.E. Lawler III, *High-Involvement Management* (San Francisco: Jossey-Bass, 1986).
6. J.R. Schuster and P.K. Zingheim, "Improving Productivity Through Gainsharing: Can the Means Be Justified in the End?" *Compensation and Benefits Management,* 5 (3) (Spring 1989), 207–210.
7. S. Vittolino, "PepsiCo Designs Plans to Share and Share Alike," *HR News,* Aug. 1990.
8. P.F. Drucker, *The Frontiers of Management* (New York: Harper & Row, 1986).

Chapter 12. Variable Pay Design Issues

1. W.A. Band, *Creating Value for Customers: Designing and Implementing a Total Corporate Strategy* (New York: John Wiley & Sons, 1991).
2. F.F. Reichheld and W.E. Sasser, Jr., "Zero Defections: Quality Comes to Services," *Harvard Business Review,* Sept./Oct. 1990, pp. 105–111.

Chapter 13. Principles of New Indirect Pay

1. U.S. Chamber Research Center, *Employee Benefits: Survey Data from Benefit Year 1989* (Washington, DC: U.S. Chamber of Commerce, 1990).
2. J. Sutcliffe and J.R. Schuster, "Benefits Revisited, Benefits Predicted," *Personnel Journal,* Sept. 1985, pp. 62–68.

3. J.S. Rosenbloom (Ed.), *Employee Benefit Planning* (Englewood Cliffs, NJ: Prentice-Hall, 1986).

Chapter 14. Health Care Benefits Under New Pay

1. E. Chen, "The Health Care Crisis: Too Many Needs, Too Many Costs," *Los Angeles Times,* 21 July 1991.
2. R.M. McCaffery, *Employee Benefits Programs* (Boston: PWS-Kent, 1988).
3. T.B. Beam and J.J. McFadden, *Employee Benefits* (Homewood, IL: Irwin, 1985).
4. A. Bernstein, "Playing 'Pin the Insurance on the Other Guy'," *Business Week,* 19 Aug. 1991, pp. 104–105.
5. M.A. Verespej, "Health Care: Price Is Not the Problem," *Industry Week,* 17 Sept. 1990, pp. 22–30.
6. E. Chen, "The Health Care Crisis: Too Many Needs, Too Many Costs," *Los Angeles Times,* 21 July 1991.

Chapter 15. Other Employee Benefits Under New Pay

1. R.M. McCaffery, *Employee Benefits Programs* (Boston: PWS-Kent, 1988).
2. U.S. Chamber Research Center, *Employee Benefits: Survey Data from Benefit Year 1989* (Washington, DC: U.S. Chamber of Commerce, 1990).
3. U.S. Department of Labor, Bureau of Labor Statistics, *Employee Benefits in Medium to Large Firms, 1989* BLS Bulletin No. 2363 (Washington, DC: U.S. Government Printing Office, June 1990).

Chapter 16. Flexible Benefits

1. R.M. McCaffery, *Employee Benefits Programs* (Boston: PWS-Kent, 1988).
2. S.M. Nealy, "Pay and Benefit Preferences," *Industrial Relations, 3* (3) (1964), 135–144.
3. J.R. Schuster, "Another Look at Compensation Preferences," *Industrial Management Review,* Sloan School of Management, 7 (1969), 1–18.
4. J.R. Schuster, L.D. Hart and B. Clark. "EPIC: New Cafeteria Compensation Plan." *Datamation, 17* (3) (Feb. 1971), 28–30.
5. "Flexible-Benefit Plans Grow," *USA Today,* 21 Mar. 1989.
6. R.A. Rose, "Taking Control of Benefits," *Across the Board,* July/Aug. 1988.
7. D.E. Bloom and J.T. Trahan, *Flexible Benefits and Employee Choice* (Elmsford, NY: Pergamon Press, 1986).

Chapter 17. Survey of Pay Practices

1. J.R. Schuster, "Successful Hospitals Pay for Performance," *Hospitals,* 16 Mar. 1985, pp. 86–87.

J.R. Schuster, "Compensation Plan Design: The Power Behind the Best High-Tech Companies," *Management Review,* May 1985, pp. 21–25.

J.R. Schuster and P.K. Zingheim, "Designing Incentives for Top Financial Performance," *Compensation and Benefits Review,* May/June 1986, pp. 39–48.

2. J.R. Schuster and P.K. Zingheim, "New Compensation Planning Needed for Labor-Intensive Organizations," *Journal of Compensation and Benefits,* Nov./Dec. 1989, pp. 157–161.

3. J.R. Schuster and P.K. Zingheim, "Tying Compensation to Top Performance Can Boost Profits," *Journal of Compensation and Benefits,* Sept./Oct. 1986, pp. 69–73.

J.R. Schuster and P.K. Zingheim, "Incentives for Performance: How Much More Positive Proof Do We Need?" *Compensation and Benefits Management,* Autumn 1986, pp. 405–407.

Chapter 18. Linking Employees and Organizations

1. W.A. Band, *Creating Value for Customers: Designing and Implementing a Total Corporate Strategy* (New York: John Wiley & Sons, 1991).

2. M.L. Dertouzos et al., *Made in America: Regaining the Productive Edge* (Cambridge, MA: MIT Press, 1989).

3. B. Wysocki, Jr., "Southern Exposure: Canada Suffers Exodus of Jobs, Investment and Shoppers to U.S." *Wall Street Journal,* 20 June 1991, p. B1.

4. G.S. Crystal, "How Much CEOs Really Make," *Fortune,* 17 June 1991, pp. 72–74.

Bibliography

Adams, J. S. "Toward an Understanding of Inequity." *Journal of Abnormal and Social Psychology,* 1963, *67,* 422–436.

Adams, J. S. "Inequity in Social Exchange." *Advances in Experimental Social Psychology.* Ed. I. Berkowitz. Orlando, FL: Academic Press, 1965, 267–299.

Adizes, I. *Corporate Lifecycles: How and Why Organizations Grow and Die and What to Do About It.* Englewood Cliffs, NJ: Prentice-Hall, 1989.

American Compensation Association and M. J. Wallace, Jr. *Rewards and Renewal: America's Search for Competitive Advantage Through Alternative Pay Strategies.* Scottsdale, AZ: American Compensation Association, 1990.

"American Living Standards: Running to Stand Still." *Economist,* 10 Nov. 1990, p. 19.

Baily, M. N., and A. K. Chakrabarti. *Innovation and the Productivity Crisis.* New York: Brookings Institution, June 1988.

Band, W. A. *Creating Value for Customers: Designing & Implementing a Total Corporate Strategy.* New York: Wiley, 1991.

Barker, L. "Acquiring Competitive Information from Surveys: The Hay Compensation Information Center." *Handbook of Wage and Salary Administration.* Ed. M. Rock. 2nd ed. New York: McGraw-Hill, 1984.

Beam, T. B., and J. J. McFadden. *Employee Benefits.* Homewood, IL: Irwin, 1985.

Behr, P. "The Case of the Missing Productivity: Despite Computers, Faxes, Service Sector Output Lags." *Washington Post,* 21 Jan. 1990.

Belcher, D. W. *Compensation Administration.* Englewood Cliffs, NJ: Prentice-Hall, 1974.

Belcher, D. W., and T. J. Atchison. *Compensation Administration.* 2nd ed. Englewood Cliffs, NJ: Prentice-Hall, 1987.

Belcher, J. G., Jr. *Productivity Plus.* Houston, TX: Gulf, 1987.

Bellak, A. O. "The Hay Guide Chart Profile Method of Job Evaluation." *Handbook of Wage and Salary Administration.* Ed. M. Rock. New York: McGraw-Hill, 1984.

Benge, E. J., L. H. Burk, and E. N. Hay. *Manual of Job Evaluation.* New York: Harper & Brothers, 1941.

Bentson, M., and J. Schuster. "Executive Compensation and Employee Benefits." *Human Resource Management in the 1980's.* Washington, DC: Bureau of National Affairs, 1983, 6.1–6.33.

Bernstein, A. "Playing 'Pin the Insurance on the Other Guy'." *Business Week,* 19 Aug. 1991, pp. 104–105.

Bernstein, A. "What Happened to the American Dream?" *Business Week,* 19 Aug. 1991, pp. 80–85.

Bernstein, A., R. W. Anderson, and W. Zellner. "Help Wanted." *Business Week,* 10 Aug. 1987, pp. 48–53.

Berry, J. M. "Nation's Low Jobless Rate Belies Regional, Occupational Wastelands." *Washington Post,* 4 Sept. 1988.

Bloom, D. E., and J. T. Trahan. *Flexible Benefits and Employee Choice.* Elmsford, NY: Pergamon Press, 1986.

Boyett, J. H., and H. P. Conn. *Workplace 2000: The Revolution Reshaping American Business.* New York: Dutton, 1991.

Bullock, R. J., and E. E. Lawler III. "Gainsharing: A Few Questions, and Fewer Answers." *Human Resource Management,* 1984, 5, 197–212.

Bullock, R. J., and P. F. Bullock. "Gainsharing and Rubik's Cube: Solving System Problems." *National Productivity Review,* 1982, 2 (1), 396–407.

Bunning, R. L. "Skill-Based Pay." *Personnel Administrator,* June 1989, 34 (6), 65–70.

Bureau of National Affairs. *Changing Pay Practices: New Developments in Employee Compensation.* Washington, DC: Bureau of National Affairs, 1988.

Bureau of National Affairs. "Employee Award Programs." *Personnel Policies Forum (PPF) Survey No. 145.* Washington, DC: Bureau of National Affairs, Sept. 1987.

Burton, T. B., Jr., and J. J. McFadden. *Employee Benefits.* Homewood, IL: Irwin, 1985.

Cameron, K. S., and D. A. Whetten. "Perceptions of Organizational Life Cycles." *Administrative Science Quarterly,* 1981, 26, 525–544.

Campbell, J. P., and R. J. Campbell. *Productivity in Organizations.* San Francisco: Jossey-Bass, 1988.

Carroll, S. J., and C. E. Schneier. *Performance Appraisal and Review Systems.* Glenview, IL: Scott, Foresman, 1982.

Chen, E. "The Health Care Crisis: Too Many Needs, Too Many Costs." *Los Angeles Times,* 21 July 1991.

Cissel, M. J. "Designing Effective Reward Systems." *Compensation and Benefits Review,* Nov./Dec. 1987, 19 (6), 49–55.

Coch, L., and J. R. P. French, Jr. "Overcoming Resistance to Change." *Group Dynamics: Research and Theory.* Eds. D. Cartwright and A. Zander. New York: Harper & Row, 1968.

Cole, R. E. "Target Information for Competitive Performance." *Harvard Business Review,* 1985, 63 (3), 100–109.

Cook, B. M. "Flexible Manufacturing: Something That People Do." *Industry Week,* 5 Nov. 1990, pp. 36–43.

Crosby, P. B. *Quality Is Free.* New York: McGraw-Hill, 1979.

Crystal, G. S. *Executive Compensation.* Englewood Cliffs, NJ: Prentice-Hall, 1984.

Crystal, G. S. "How Much CEOs Really Make." *Fortune,* 17 June 1991, pp. 72–74.

Cummings, L. L. "Compensation, Culture, and Motivation: A Systems Perspective." *Organizational Dynamics,* Winter 1984.

Cyert, R., and J. A. March. *Behavioral Theory of the Firm.* Englewood Cliffs, NJ: Prentice-Hall, 1963.

Deal, T. E., and A. L. Kennedy. *Corporate Cultures.* Menlo Park, CA: Addison-Wesley, 1982.

DeBettignes, C. W. "Improving Organization-Wide Teamwork Through Gainsharing." *National Productivity Review,* Summer 1989, *8* (3), 287–394.

Deming, W. E. "The Merit System: The Annual Appraisal, Destroyer of People." Presented at "A Day with Dr. W. Edwards." University of Minnesota, 1987.

Dertouzos, M. L., et al. *Made in America: Regaining the Productive Edge.* Cambridge, MA: MIT Press, 1989.

Doyle, R. J. *Gainsharing and Productivity: A Guide to Planning, Implementation and Development.* New York: AMACOM, 1983.

Drucker, P. F. *Innovation and Entrepreneurship.* New York: Harper & Row, 1985.

Drucker, P. F. "If Earnings Aren't the Dial to Read," *Wall Street Journal,* 30 Oct. 1986.

Drucker, P. F. *The Frontiers of Management.* New York: Harper & Row, 1986.

Duffy, C. "Training: Expensive but Necessary for Business, Government." *Washington Technology,* 19 Dec. 1987.

Dunham, R. B., and R. A. Formisano. "Designing and Evaluating Employee Benefit Systems." *Personnel Administrator,* 4 Apr. 1982, *27,* 29–35.

Dyer, L., et al. "Managerial Perceptions Regarding Salary Increase Criteria." *Personnel Psychology,* 1976, *29,* 233–242.

Eberts, R. W. "Can State Employment Declines Foretell National Business Cycles?" *Economic Commentary.* Cleveland: Federal Reserve Bank of Cleveland, 15 Sept. 1990.

Edwards, G. "Bridging Schools & Skills." *Academy for Advanced & Strategic Studies,* 18 Nov. 1990.

Ellig, B. "Incentive Plans: Short-Term Design Issues." *Compensation Review,* Fall 1984, *16,* 26–36.

Ellis, R. J. "Improving Management Response in Turbulent Times." *Sloan Management Review,* Winter 1982, 3–12.

Evans, W. A. "Pay for Performance: Fact or Fable." *Personnel Journal,* Sept. 1970, 726–729.

Ewing, J. C. "Gainsharing Plans: Two Key Factors." *Compensation and Benefits Review,* Jan./Feb. 1989, *21* (1), 49–59.

Fein, M. "An Alternative to Traditional Managing." *Handbook of Industrial Engineering.* Ed. G. Savendy. New York: Wiley, 1981.

Festinger, L. A. *A Theory of Cognitive Dissonance.* New York: Harper & Row, 1957.

Feuer, D. "Paying for Knowledge." *Training,* May 1987, *24* (5), 57–66.

"Flexible-Benefits Plans Grow." *USA Today,* 21 Mar. 1989.

Florkowski, G. W. "The Organizational Impact of Profit Sharing." *Academy of Management Review,* 1987, *12* (4), 622–636.

Foster, K. E. "Measuring Overlooked Factors in Relative Job Worth and Pay." *Compensation Review,* 1983, *1,* 44–55.

Fragner, B. N. "Employees 'Cafeteria' Offers Insurance Options." *Harvard Business Review,* 1975, *53* (6), 2–4.

Freedman, A. "Help Wanted, Badly." *Across the Board,* Jan./Feb. 1989.

Freeman, R. R. *Labor Economics.* 2nd ed. Englewood Cliffs, NJ: Prentice-Hall, 1979.

Frost, C. F. "Participative Ownership: A Competitive Necessity." *New Management,* Spring 1986, *3* (4), 44–49.

Frost, C. F. "The Scanlon Plan: Anyone for Free Enterprise?" *MSU Business Topics,* Winter 1978, 26 (1), 25–33.

Frost, C. F., J. H. Wakely and R. A. Ruh. *The Scanlon Plan for Organizational Development: Identity, Participation, and Equity.* East Lansing, MI: Michigan State University Press, 1974.

Garland, S. B. "Help Wanted: America Faces an Era of Worker Scarcity That May Last to the Year 2000." *Business Week,* 10 Aug. 1987, pp. 48–53.

Gomez-Mejia, L. R., and R. C. Page. "Development and Implementation of a Computerized Job Evaluation System." *New Perspectives on Compensation.* Ed. D. B. Balkin and L. R. Gomez-Mejia. Englewood Cliffs, NJ: Prentice-Hall, 1987.

Goodman, P. S., ed. *Change in Organizations.* San Francisco: Jossey-Bass, 1982.

Goodman, P. S., and J. W. Dean, Jr. "Creating Long-Term Organizational Change." *Change in Organizations.* Ed. P. S. Goodman. San Francisco: Jossey-Bass, 1982.

Goett, P. "DuPont Fibers Weaves an Incentive Pay Plan in a Bold New Design." *Human Resources Professional,* Mar./Apr. 1989, *1* (3), 5–9.

Gorman, C. "The Literacy Gap." *Time,* 19 Dec. 1988, pp. 56–57.

Graham-Moore, B. E., and T. L. Ross. *Gainsharing: Plans for Improving Performance.* Washington, DC: Bureau of National Affairs, 1990.

Graham-Moore, B. E., and T. L. Ross. *Productivity Gainsharing.* Englewood Cliffs, NJ: Prentice-Hall, 1983.

Gupta, N., et al. *Exploratory Investigations of Pay-for-Knowledge Systems.* Department of Labor Technical Report (BLMR 108). Washington, DC: U.S. Department of Labor, 1986.

Gupta, N., and G. D. Jenkins, Jr. "The Payoffs of Paying for Knowledge." *National Productivity Review,* Spring 1985, *4* (2), 121–130.

Gupta, N., G. D. Jenkins, Jr., and W. P. Curington. "Paying for Knowledge: Myths and Realities." *National Productivity Review,* Spring 1986, *5* (2), 107–123.

Gupta, N., T. P. Schweizer and G. D. Jenkins, Jr. "Pay-for-Knowledge Compensation Plans: Hypotheses and Survey Results." *Monthly Labor Review,* Oct. 1987, *110* (10), 40–43.

Hackmann, J. R., and E. E. Lawler III. "Employee Reactions to Job Characteristics." *Journal of Applied Psychology,* 1971, *55,* 259–286.

Hamilton, M. M. "U.S. Facing Severe Labor Shortage." *Washington Post,* 24 June 1988.

Hammerstone, J. E. "How to Make Gainsharing Pay Off." *Training & Development Journal,* Apr. 1987.

Hatcher, L. L., and T. L. Ross. "Gainsharing Plans—How Managers Evaluate Them." *Business,* Oct./Nov./Dec. 1986, *36* (4), 30–37.

Hatcher, L. L., and T. L. Ross. "Organization Development Through Productivity Gainsharing." *Personnel,* Oct. 1985, *62* (10), 49–52.

Hatcher, L. L., T. L. Ross and R. A. Ross. "Gainsharing: Living Up to Its Name." *Personnel Administrator,* June 1987, *32* (6), 153–164.

Hauck, W. C., and T. L. Ross. "England's Approach to Increased Productivity: Added Value Schemes." *Industrial Management,* Mar./Apr. 1984, *26* (2), 15–21.

Hauck, W. C., and T. L. Ross. "Expanded Teamwork at Volvo Through Performance Gainsharing." *Industrial Management,* July/Aug. 1988, *30* (4), 17–20.

Hauck, W. C., and T. L. Ross. "Sweden's Experiment in Productivity Gainsharing: A Second Look." *Personnel,* Jan. 1987, *64* (1), 61–67.

Hay Group. "Survey of Incentive Practices in High-Technology Firms." *Ideals and Trends.* Chicago: Commerce Clearing House, 1985.

Hertzberg, F. "One More Time: How Do You Motivate Employees?" *Harvard Business Review,* Jan./Feb. 1968, 109–120.

Hertzberg, F. "Retrospective Commentary" [on his 1968 article]. *Harvard Business Review,* Sept./Oct. 1987, 118.

Hertzberg, F. *Work and the Nature of Man.* Cleveland: World, 1966.

Hewitt Associates. *On Flexible Compensation.* Lincolnshire, IL: Hewitt Associates, 1988.

Hewitt Associates. *Salaried Employee Benefits Provided by Major U.S. Employers: A Comparison Study.* Lincolnshire, IL: Hewitt Associates, 1985.

Hickmann, C. R., and M. Z. Silva. *Creating Excellence.* New York: New American Library, 1984.

Hills, F. S. "Comparable Worth: Implications for Compensation Managers." *Compensation and Benefits Review,* 1982, *14,* 33–43.

Horr, J. "The Payoff from Teamwork." *Business Week,* 10 July 1989, pp. 55–62.

Hufnagel, E. M. "Developing Strategic Compensation Plans." *Human Resource Management,* 1987, *26* (1), 93–108.

"Human Decisions Give Technology Its Power." *Work in America,* Feb. 1990.

Jenkins, G. D., and N. Gupta. "The Payoffs of Paying for Knowledge." *Labor-Management Cooperation Brief.* Washington, DC: U.S. Department of Labor, Bureau of Labor-Management Relations and Cooperative Programs, 1985.

Jensen, M. C., and K. J. Murphy. "CEO Incentives—It's Not How Much You Pay, But How." *Harvard Business Review,* May/June 1990, 138–149.

Johns, G. *Organizational Behavior: Understanding Life at Work.* Glenview, IL: Scott, Foresman, 1983.

Johnson, A. M. "How to Relate Long-Term Incentive Plans to Performance." *Topics in Total Compensation.* Ed. R. C. Ochsner. Greenvale, NY: Panel, 1986.

Johnson, R., and P. R. Lawrence. "Beyond Vertical Integration: The Rise of the Value-Adding Partnership." *Harvard Business Review,* 1988, *66* (4), 94–101.

Johnson, W. B. *Workforce 2000.* Indianapolis: Hudson Institute, 1987.

Kane, J. S., and E. E. Lawler III. "Performance Appraisal Effectiveness: Its Assessments and Detriments." *Research in Organizational Behavior.* Ed. B. Staw. Greenwich, CT: JAI Press, 1979.

Kanter, R. M. "The Attack on Pay." *Harvard Business Review,* Mar./Apr. 1987, *65* (2), 60–67.

Kanter, R. M. "From Status to Contribution: Some Organizational Implications of the Changing Basis for Pay." *Personnel,* 1987, *64,* 12–37.

Katz, D., and R. L. Kahn. *The Social Psychology of Organizations.* New York: Wiley, 1966.

Kendrick, J. W. *Improving Company Productivity.* Baltimore, MD: Johns Hopkins University Press, 1984.

Kiechel, W., III. "Corporate Strategy for the 1990s." *Fortune,* 29 Feb. 1988, pp. 34–42.

Kleingartner, A., and C. S. Anderson. *Human Resource Management in High Technology Firms.* Lexington, MA: Lexington, 1987.

Koenig, R. "DuPont Plan Linking Pay to Fibers Profit Unravels." *Wall Street Journal,* 25 Oct. 1990.

Kopelman, R. E. "Improving Productivity Through Objective Feedback: A Review of the Evidence." *National Productivity Review,* Winter 1982–83, 43–55.

Kopelman, R. E. "Job Redesign and Productivity: A Review of the Evidence." *National Productivity Review,* 1985, *4* (3), 237–255.

Kraus, D. "Executive Pay: Ripe for Reform?" *Harvard Business Review,* Mar./Apr. 1986, 78–85.

Krefting, L. A. "Differences in Orientation Toward Pay Increases." *Industrial Relations,* 1977, *19,* 81–87.

Krefting, L. A., and T. A. Mahoney. "Determining the Size of a Meaningful Pay Increase." *Industrial Relations,* 1977, 83–93.

Landon, E. L., Jr. "New Strategies for Bank Profitability." Presentation at Robert Morris Associates 1990 Spring Conference, San Antonio, TX, 19 Apr. 1990.

Latham, G. P., and E. A. Locke. "Goal Setting: A Motivational Technique That Works." *Organizational Dynamics,* 1979, 68–80.

Lawler, E. E., III. "Gainsharing Theory and Research: Findings and Future Directions." Eds. W. A. Pasamore and R. Woodman. *Research in Organizational Change and Development.* Vol. 2. Greenwich, CT: JAI Press, 1988.

Lawler, E. E., III. *High-Involvement Management.* San Francisco: Jossey-Bass, 1986.

Lawler, E. E., III. "Job Design and Employee Motivation." *Personnel Psychology,* 1969, *22,* 426–435.

Lawler, E. E., III. "The New Pay." CEO Publication G84-7(55), Los Angeles: Center for Effective Organizations, University of Southern California, 1986.

Lawler, E. E., III. "The Organizational Impact of Executive Compensation." *Executive Compensation.* Ed. F. K. Foulkes. Boston: Harvard Press, 1991.

Lawler, E. E., III. *Pay and Organizational Development.* Reading, MA: Addison-Wesley, 1981.

Lawler, E. E., III. *Pay and Organizational Effectiveness: A Psychological View.* New York: McGraw-Hill, 1971.

Lawler, E. E., III. "Pay for Performance: Making It Work." *Personnel,* Oct. 1988, *65* (10), 68–71.

Lawler, E. E., III. *Strategic Pay.* San Francisco: Jossey-Bass, 1990.

Lawler, E. E., III. "Whatever Happened to Incentive Pay?" *New Management,* 1984, 37–41.

Lawler, E. E., III. "What's Wrong with Point-Factor Job Evaluation?" *Compensation and Benefits Review*, Mar./Apr. 1986, *18* (2), 20–28.

Lawler, E. E., III, and G. E. Ledford. "Productivity and the Quality of Worklife." *National Productivity Review*, 1982, *1*, 23–36.

Lawler, E. E., III, and G. E. Ledford. "Skill-Based Pay: A Concept That's Catching On." *Personnel*, 1985, *62* (9), 30–37.

Lawler, E. E., III, G. E. Ledford and S. A. Mohrman. *Employee Involvement in America*. Houston: American Productivity and Quality Center, 1989.

Lawler, E. E., III, and S. A. Mohrman. "Quality Circles: After the Honeymoon." *Organizational Dynamics*, Spring 1987, *15* (4), 42–54.

Lawshe, C. H., Jr., and A. A. Maleski. "Studies in Job Evaluation III: An Analysis of Point Ratings for Salary-Paid Jobs in an Industrial Plant." *Journal of Applied Psychology*, Apr. 1946, *30* (2), 117–128.

Lawshe, C. H., Jr., and G. A. Sattler. "Studies in Job Evaluation I: Factor Analysis of Point Ratings for Hourly-Paid Jobs in Three Industrial Plants." *Journal of Applied Psychology*, June 1944, *28* (3), 189–198.

LeBlanc, P. V. "Fast Forward." CEO Publication G90-12(174). Los Angeles: Center for Effective Organizations, University of Southern California, June 1990.

Ledford, G. E., Jr. "The Design of Skill-Based Pay Plans." CEO Publication G89-15(158). Los Angeles: Center for Effective Organizations, University of Southern California, Oct. 1989.

Ledford, G. E., Jr., and G. Bergel. "Paying for Skills in Two Food Processing Plants." CEO Publication G90-13(175). Los Angeles: Center for Effective Organizations, University of Southern California, July 1990.

Lehrman, S. "Middle Managers Face Squeeze as Firms Try New Structures." *Washington Post*, 9 Sept. 1988, p. 12.

Lesieur, F. G., and E. S. Puckett. "The Scanlon Plan Has Proved Itself." *Harvard Business Review*, 1969, *47* (5), 109–118.

Lesieur, F. G., ed. *The Scanlon Plan*. Cambridge, MA: MIT Press, 1958.

Levy, F., and R. Crandall. "America's Shrinking Middle." *Economist*, 12 Nov. 1988, pp. 84–85.

Litan, R. E., R. Z. Lawrence and C. Schultze. *America's Living Standards: Threats and Challenges*. Washington, DC: Brookings Institution, 1988.

Locke, E. A., and D. M. Schweiger. "Participation in Decision-Making: One More Look." *Research in Organizational Behavior*. Greenwich, CT: JAI Press, 1979.

Locke, E. A. "Toward a Theory of Task Motivation and Incentives." *Organization Behavior and Human Performance*, 1968, *3*, 157–189.

London, M. *Change Agents: New Roles and Innovation Strategies for Human Resource Professionals*. San Francisco: Jossey-Bass, 1988.

"Lots of New Jobs—But Paychecks Are Still Shrinking." *Business Week*, 17 Oct. 1988.

Mahoney, T. A. *Compensation and Reward Perspectives*. Homewood, IL: Irwin, 1979.

Mahoney, T. A. "Organizational Hierarchy and Position Worth." *Academy of Management Journal*, 1979, *22*, 726–737.

Mamorsky, J. D. *Employee Benefit Handbook.* Revised ed. and updates. Boston: Warren, Gorham and Lamont, 1987.

March, J. G., and H. A. Simon. *Organizations.* New York: Wiley, 1963.

Maslow, A. H. *Motivation and Personality.* New York: Harper & Row, 1954.

McCaffery, R. M. *Employee Benefit Programs: A Total Compensation Perspective.* Boston: PWS-Kent, 1988.

McCaffery, R. M. *Managing the Employee Benefits Program.* New York: AMACOM, 1983.

McClenahen, J. S. "Now Do We Need a National Industrial Policy?" *Industry Week,* 18 Mar. 1991, pp. 56–62.

McCormick, E. J. *Job Analysis.* New York: AMACOM, 1979.

McGregor, D. *The Human Side of Enterprise.* New York: McGraw-Hill, 1960.

McGregor, D. "An Uneasy Look at Performance Appraisal." *Harvard Business Review,* May/June 1957, 89–94.

McIlroy, G. T. "Health Care Cost Containment in the 1980's." *Compensation Review,* Fourth Quarter 1983, 15–31.

McNamee, M. "High-Tech Can't Deliver on Jobs: Job Outlook 1995." *USA Today,* 16 Nov. 1983.

Memmott, M. "Productivity Will Hold Down Living Standard." *USA Today,* 8 Nov. 1989.

Metzger, B. L. *Profit Sharing in 38 Large Companies.* Evanston, IL: Profit Sharing Research Foundation, 1975.

Metzger, B. L., and J. A. Colletti. *Does Profit Sharing Pay?* Evanston, IL: Profit Sharing Research Foundation, 1971.

Meyer, H. "The Pay for Performance Dilemma." *Organizational Dynamics,* Winter 1975, 22–38.

Meyer, H. H., "How Can We Implement a Pay-for-Performance Policy Successfully?", *New Perspectives on Compensation.* Ed. D. B. Balkin and L. R. Gomez-Mejia. Englewood Cliffs, NJ: Prentice-Hall, 1987.

Meyer, H. H. "Self-Appraisal of Job Performance." *Personnel Psychology,* 1980, *33,* 291–296.

Meyer, M. *Flexible Employee Benefit Plans: 38 Companies' Experience.* New York: Conference Board, 1983.

Milkovich, G. T., and J. M. Newman. *Compensation.* Plano, TX: Business Publications, 1984.

Mishel, L., and R. A. Teixeira. *The Myth of the Coming Labor Shortage: Jobs, Skills and Incomes of America's Workforce 2000.* Washington, DC: Economic Policy Institute, 1991.

Mitchell, D. J. B., and E. E. Lawler III. "Alternative Pay Systems, Firm Performance, and Productivity." *Paying For Productivity.* Ed. A. S. Blinder. New York: Brookings Institution, 1990.

Mohrman, A. M. *Deming Versus Performance Appraisal: Is There a Resolution?"* Los Angeles: Center for Effective Organizations, University of Southern California, 1989.

Mohrman, A. M., S. M. Resnick-West and E. E. Lawler III. *Designing Performance*

Appraisal Systems: Aligning Appraisals and Organizational Realities. San Francisco: Jossey-Bass, 1989.

Moore, B. E., and T. L. Ross. *The Scanlon Way to Improved Productivity.* New York: Wiley, 1978.

Mount, M. K. "Coordinating Salary Action and Performance Appraisal." *New Perspectives on Compensation.* Ed. D. B. Balkin and L. R. Gomez-Mejia. Englewood Cliffs, NJ: Prentice-Hall, 1987.

Muczyk, J. P. "The Strategic Role of Compensation." *Human Resource Planning,* 1985, 2 (3), 225–239.

Murphy, K. J. "Top Executives Are Worth Every Nickel They Get." *Harvard Business Review,* Mar./Apr. 1986, 125–132.

Naisbitt, J. *Megatrends.* New York: Warner, 1982.

Naisbitt, J., and P. Aburdene. *Reinventing the Corporate Future.* New York: Warner, 1985.

Nealy, S. M. "Pay and Benefit Preferences." *Industrial Relations,* 1964, 3 (3), 135–144.

Newman, J. M. "Selecting Incentive Plans to Complement Organizational Strategy." *New Perspectives on Compensation.* Ed. D. B. Balkin and L. R. Gomez-Mejia. Englewood Cliffs, NJ: Prentice-Hall, 1987.

Nickel, J. E., and S. O'Neal. "Small-Group Incentives: Gain Sharing in the Microcosm." *Compensation and Benefits Review.* Mar./Apr. 1990, 5–12.

"'90 Productivity in Biggest Fall Since '82." *Los Angeles Times,* 5 Feb. 1991.

Nye, D. "Writing Off Older Assets." *Across the Board,* Sept. 1988.

Otis, J. L., and R. H. Leukart. *Job Evaluation.* 2nd ed. Englewood Cliffs, NJ: Prentice-Hall, 1954.

Ouchi, W. *Theory Z.* Reading, MA: Addison-Wesley, 1981.

O'Dell, C. *Gainsharing: Involvement, Incentives, and Productivity.* New York: AMACOM, 1981.

O'Dell, C., and C. J. Grayson, Jr. "Flex Your Pay Muscle." *Across the Board,* July/Aug. 1988, 43–48.

O'Dell, C., and J. McAdams. *People, Performance, and Pay.* Houston, TX: American Productivity Center, 1987.

O'Toole, J. *Vanguard Management.* New York: Doubleday, 1985.

O'Toole, J. *Work, Learning, and the American Future.* San Francisco: Jossey-Bass, 1977.

Packer, A. "Retooling the American Worker." *Washington Post,* 10 July 1988.

Pascale, R. T., and A. G. Athos. *The Art of Japanese Management.* New York: Simon and Schuster, 1981.

Patten, T. H. *Fair Pay.* San Francisco: Jossey-Bass, 1988.

Patten, T. H. "Merit Increases and the Facts of Organizational Life." *Management of Personnel Quarterly,* Summer 1969, 33–38.

Patten, T. H. "Pay Cuts: Will Employees Accept Them?" *National Productivity Review,* 1981, 1, 110–119.

Patten, T. H. *Pay: Employee Compensation and Incentive Plans.* New York: Free Press, 1977.

Patterson, T. T. *Job Evaluation: A New Method.* London: Camelot, 1972.

Pearce, J. L. "Why Merit Pay Doesn't Work: Implications from Organization Theory." *New Perspectives on Compensation.* Ed. D. B. Balkin and L. R. Gomez-Mejia. Englewood Cliffs, NJ: Prentice-Hall, 1987.

Pennar, K. "The New America: Economic Prospects for the Year 2000." *Business Week,* No. 3125 (Industrial/Technology Edition), 25 Sept. 1989, pp. 158–170.

Perry, G. L. "U.S. Economy Inefficiency, Inequity a Burden on Poor." *Los Angeles Times,* 14 Apr. 1991.

Perry, J. L., and J. C. Pearce. "Initial Reactions to Federal Merit Pay." *Personnel Journal,* 1983, 62, 230–237.

Perry, N. J. "The Workers of the Future." *Fortune,* Spring/Summer 1991, pp. 68–72.

Peters, T. J. *Thriving on Chaos: Handbook for Management Revolution.* New York: Knopf, 1987.

Peters, T. J., and N. A. Austin. *A Passion for Excellence.* New York: Random House, 1985.

Peters, T. J., and R. H. Waterman, Jr. *In Search of Excellence: Lessons from America's Best Run Companies.* New York: Harper & Row, 1982.

Peterson, J. "Labor Department Panel Urges Teaching of New Skills for Jobs." *Los Angeles Times,* 3 July 1991, pp. D1–D5.

Peterson, T., Z. Wellner, and D. Woodruff. "All That Lean Isn't Turning into Green." *Business Week,* 18 Nov. 1991, pp. 39–40.

Pomice, E. "Shaping Up Services." *U.S. News and World Report,* 22 July 1991, pp. 41–44.

Port, O. "Smart Factories: America's Turn?" *Business Week,* 8 May 1989, pp. 142–149.

Porter, L. W. and E. E. Lawler III. *Managerial Attitudes and Performance.* Homewood, IL: Irwin, 1968.

Porter, M. E. *Competitive Advantage.* New York: Free Press, 1985.

"Profit Sharing, Group Incentives Gaining Popularity with Firms, Study Finds." *Daily Labor Report,* No. 202, 20 Oct. 1989, pp. A1–A2.

Quinn, J. B., et al. "Technology in Services." *Scientific American,* Dec. 1987, pp. 50–58.

"Racing to Win on Costs." *Journal of Business Strategy,* Mar./Apr. 1989, 10 (2), 4–8.

Rappaport, A. "Executive Incentives vs. Corporate Growth." *Harvard Business Review,* 1978, 56 (4), 53–62.

Reich, R. B. "New Economic Realities." *What's New, a Newsletter of Emerging Issues and Trends,* Summer 1990, 12 (2).

Reichheld, F. F., and W. E. Sasser, Jr. "Zero Defections: Quality Comes to Services." *Harvard Business Review,* Sept./Oct. 1990, 105–111.

Rich, S. "Female-Male Earnings Gap Narrows." *Washington Post,* Oct. 1990.

Ringham, A. J. "Designing a Gainsharing Program to Fit a Company's Operations." *National Productivity Review,* Spring 1984, 3 (2), 131–144.

Rose, R. A. "Taking Control of Benefits." *Across the Board,* July/Aug. 1988.

Rosenbloom, J. S., ed. *Employee Benefit Planning.* Englewood Cliffs, NJ: Prentice-Hall, 1986.

Ross, T. L., and D. Collins. "Employee Involvement and the Perils of Democracy: Are

Management's Fears Warranted?" *National Productivity Review,* Autumn 1987, 6 (4), 348–359.

Ross, T. L., L. Hatcher and D. B. Adams. "How Unions View Gainsharing." *Business Horizons,* July/Aug. 1985, 28 (4), 15–22.

Ross, T. L., L. Hatcher and R. A. Ross. "The Incentive Switch: From Piecework to Companywide Gainsharing." *Management Review,* May 1989, 78 (5), 22–26.

Ross, T. L., and J. J. Keyser. "Gainsharing: Is It a Human Resource Strategy or a Group Incentive System?" *Business Quarterly (Canada),* Winter 1984/85, 49 (4), 92–96.

Ross, T. L. and R. A. Ross. "Productivity Gainsharing: Resolving Some of the Measurement Issues." *National Productivity Review,* Autumn 1984, 3 (4), 382–394.

Rothschild, W. E. *Strategic Alternatives.* New York: AMACOM, 1979.

Rynes, S. L., and G. T. Milkovich. "Wage Surveys: Dispelling Some Myths About the 'Market Wage'." *New Perspectives on Compensation.* Ed. D. B. Balkin and L. R. Gomez-Mejia. Englewood Cliffs, NJ: Prentice-Hall, 1987.

Salisbury, D. L., ed. *Why Tax Employee Benefits?* Washington, DC: Employee Benefits Research Institute, 1984.

Salter, M. "Tailor Incentive Compensation to Strategy." *Harvard Business Review,* 1973, 51, 94–102.

Scherer, W. O. "Communications." *Employee Benefit Programs: Management Planning and Control.* Ed. E. J. Griffes. Homewood, IL: Dow Jones-Irwin, 1983.

Schonberger, R. J. *Building a Chain of Customers: Linking Business Functions to Create the World Class Company.* New York: Free Press, 1990.

Schults, G. P. "Worker Participation on Production Problems: A Discussion of Experience with the Scanlon Plan." *Personnel,* Nov. 1951, 209–211.

Schuster, J. R. "Another Look at Compensation Preferences." *Industrial Management Review,* Sloan School of Management, 1969, 7, 1–18.

Schuster, J. R. "The Cafeteria Benefits Line." *Pension and Welfare News,* Oct. 1973, 8 (10), 57–59.

Schuster, J. R. *Compensating Key Personnel in the Health Care Industry: The Path to Organizational Success.* Jamaica, NY: Spectrum, 1985.

Schuster, J. R. "Compensation Plan Design: The Power Behind the Best High-Tech Companies." *Management Review,* May 1985, 21–25.

Schuster, J. R. "Flexible Compensation." *Personnel Administration and Public Personnel Review,* Nov./Dec. 1972, 1 (3), 12–16.

Schuster, J. R. "How to Control Job Evaluation Inflation." *Personnel Administrator,* June 1985, 167–173.

Schuster, J. R. *Management Compensation in High Technology Companies: Assuring Corporate Excellence.* Lexington, MA: Lexington, 1984.

Schuster, J. R. "The Relationship Between Perceptions Concerning Magnitudes of Pay and the Perceived Utility of Pay: Public and Private Organizations Compared." *Organization Behavior and Human Performance,* Feb. 1973, 9 (1), 110–119.

Schuster, J. R. "A Spectrum of Pay for Performance: How to Motivate Employees." *Management of Personnel Quarterly,* Fall 1969, 35–38.

Schuster, J. R. "Successful Hospitals Pay for Performance." *Hospitals,* Mar. 1985, 86–87.

Schuster, J. R. "Toward a Direct-Contribution Reinforcement Pay System." *Management of Personnel Quarterly,* Spring 1971, 2–5.

Schuster, J. R., B. Clark and M. Rogers. "Testing Portions of the Porter and Lawler Model Regarding the Motivational Role of Pay," *Journal of Applied Psychology,* 1971, *55* (3), 187–195.

Schuster, J. R., L. D. Hart and B. Clark. "EPIC: New Cafeteria Compensation Plan." *Datamation,* Feb. 1971, *17* (3), 28–30.

Schuster, J. R., and P. K. Zingheim. "Designing Incentives for Top Financial Performance." *Compensation and Benefits Review,* May/June 1986, 39–48.

Schuster, J. R., and P. K. Zingheim. "How Productivity-Based Pay Works in Retail Banking." *Bankers Magazine,* May/June 1989, 62–66.

Schuster, J. R., and P. K. Zingheim. "Improving Productivity Through Gainsharing: Can the Means Be Justified in the End?" *Compensation and Benefits Management,* Spring 1989, *5* (3), 207–210.

Schuster, J. R., and P. K. Zingheim. "Incentives for Performance: How Much More Positive Proof Do We Need?" *Compensation and Benefits Management,* Autumn 1986, 405–407.

Schuster, J. R., and P. K. Zingheim. "Incentive Plans That Work." *ABA Banking Journal,* Sept. 1988, 62–64.

Schuster, J. R., and P. K. Zingheim. "Managing Human Resources in a Merger." *Compensation and Benefits Management,* Spring 1990, 6 (3), 230–233.

Schuster, J. R., and P. K. Zingheim. "Merit Pay: Is It Hopeless in the Public Sector?" *Personnel Administrator,* Oct. 1987, 83–84.

Schuster, J. R., and P. K. Zingheim. "New Compensation Planning Needed for Labor-Intensive Organizations." *Journal of Compensation and Benefits,* Nov./Dec. 1989, 157–161.

Schuster, J. R., and P. K. Zingheim. "Sales Compensation Strategies at the Most Successful Companies." *Personnel Journal,* June 1986, 112–116.

Schuster, J. R., and P. K. Zingheim. "Tying Compensation to Top Performance Can Boost Profits." *Journal of Compensation and Benefits,* Sept./Oct. 1986, 69–73.

Schuster, J. R., P. K. Zingheim and M. G. Dertien. "The Case for Computer-Assisted Market-Based Job Evaluation." *Compensation and Benefits Review,* May/June 1990, *22* (3), 44–54.

Schuster, M. H. "Gainsharing: Do It Right the First Time." *Sloan Management Review Reprint Series,* Winter 1987.

Schuster, M. H., and C. S. Miller. "Gainsharing—a Productivity Tool." *Quality Circle Journal,* Sept. 1987, *10* (3), 24–28.

Schuster, M. H., and C. S. Miller. "Implementing Gainsharing into a Quality Circle Environment." *Quality Circle Journal,* 1984, *5* (3), 6–16.

Schwinger, P. *Wage Incentive Systems.* New York: Halsted, 1975.

Seaberry, J. "Middle-Class Dream Fades for Some." *Washington Post,* 4 Jan. 1987, p. 21.

Seaberry, J. "Typical Family's Income Has Fallen." *Washington Post,* 29 Nov. 1985, p. 46.

Sibson, R. E. *Compensation.* Revised ed. New York: AMACOM, 1981.

Sloma, R. S. *How to Measure Managerial Performance.* New York: Macmillan, 1980.

Smith, O. D. "PCs and Compensation Management in the 1990s." *HR/PC: Personnel Computing for Human Resource Management,* July/Aug. 1989, 4 (6), 7–8.

Snyder, D. P. "Compensation, Commitment and Productivity." Presented to the American Compensation Association, 18 July 1989.

Snyder, D. P. "Employees and Employers in the 1990s." Presented to the American Compensation Association, 18 July 1989.

Snyder, D. P. "Essential Knowledge for Managing the Future." Expert-research information base compiled and edited by G. Edwards and D. P. Snyder. Bethesda, MD: Snyder Family Enterprises, 1989.

Steers, R. M., and G. R. Ungson. "Strategic Issues in Executive Compensation Decisions." *New Perspectives on Compensation.* Ed. D. B. Balkin and L. R. Gomez-Mejia. Englewood Cliffs, NJ: Prentice-Hall, 1987.

Sutcliffe, J., and J. R. Schuster. "Benefits Revisited, Benefits Predicted." *Personnel Journal,* Sept. 1985, 62–68.

Svoboda, W. "Flunking Grade in Math." *Time,* 20 June 1988.

Swinton, J. R. "Service-Sector Wages: The Importance of Education." *Economic Commentary.* Cleveland: Federal Reserve Bank of Cleveland, 15 Dec. 1988.

Templin, N. "Young Workers Lack Skills." *USA Today,* 12 July 1988.

"To Involve Employees, You Must Involve Managers." *Work in America,* Mar. 1990.

Tosi, H., and L. Tosi. "What Managers Need to Know About Knowledge-Based Pay." *Organizational Dynamics,* Winter 1986, 14 (3), 52–59.

Tucker, S. A., and D. E. Strickland. "Role of Compensation in High-Commitment Organizations." *Perspectives in Total Compensation.* Published by American Compensation Association, June 1991, 2 (6), 1–8.

"Two Trillion Dollars Is Missing: Why Is U.S. Prosperity Eroding? It's No Mystery." *New York Times,* 8 Jan. 1989.

U.S. Chamber of Commerce. *Employee Benefits 1990.* Washington, DC: U.S. Chamber of Commerce, 1990.

U.S. Chamber Research Center. *Employee Benefits: Survey Data for Benefit Year 1989.* Washington, DC: U.S. Chamber of Commerce, 1990.

U.S. Department of Labor, Bureau of Labor Statistics. *Employee Benefits in Medium and Large Firms, 1989.* BLS Bulletin No. 2363. Washington, DC: U.S. Government Printing Office, June 1990.

Verespej, M. A. "Health Care: Price Is Not the Problem." *Industry Week,* 17 Sept. 1990, pp. 22–30.

Vittolino, S. "PepsiCo Designs Plan to Share and Share Alike." *HR News,* 14 Aug. 1990.

Vroom, V. H. *Work and Motivation.* New York: Wiley, 1964.

Wallace, M. J., Jr., and C. H. Fay. *Compensation Theory and Practice.* Boston: PWS-Kent, 1988.

Waterman, R. H., Jr. *The Renewal Factor: How the Best Get and Keep the Competitive Edge.* Toronto: Bantam Books, 1987.

Weber, S. "Help Wanted: Low-Skill Jobs Go Begging." *USA Today,* 6 May 1985.

Weidenbaum, M. "Filling in the Hollowed-Out Corporation: The Competitive Status of U.S. Manufacturing." *Business Economics,* Jan. 1990, 18–22.

Weiner, E., and A. Brown. "Human Factors: The Gap Between Humans and Machines." *Futurist,* May/June 1989, 9–11.

White, J. K. "The Scanlon Plan: Causes and Correlates of Success." *Academy of Management Journal,* June 1979, 292–312.

Winstanley, N. B. "Are Merit Increases Really Effective?" *Personnel Administrator,* 1982, *4,* 37–41.

Winter, R. E. "Scarcity of Workers Is Kindling Inflation: Labor Costs Stay High Despite Economic Slowdown." *Wall Street Journal,* 28 Mar. 1990.

Work in America. Report of a Special Task Force to the Secretary of Health, Education and Welfare. Cambridge, MA: MIT Press, 1973.

Wriston, W. B. "The State of American Management." *Harvard Business Review,* Jan./Feb. 1990, 78–83.

Wyatt Company, The. "A Survey of Human Resource Management Priorities." Presented to the American Compensation Association, June 1990.

Wysocki, B., Jr. "Overseas Calling: American Firms Send Office Work Abroad to Use Cheaper Labor." *Wall Street Journal,* 14 Aug. 1991, pp. A1, A6.

Wysocki, B., Jr. "Southern Exposure: Canada Suffers Exodus of Jobs, Investment and Shoppers to U.S." *Wall Street Journal,* 20 June 1991, p. 81.

Yoder, D., and H. G. Heneman, Jr. *ASPA Handbook of Personnel and Industrial Relations, Volume II, Motivation and Commitment.* Washington, DC: Bureau of National Affairs, 1975.

Ziskan, I. V. "Knowledge-Based Pay: A Strategic Analysis." *ILR Report,* Fall 1986, *24* (1), 16–22.

Index

About the
Authors

Jay R. Schuster is a partner in Schuster-Zingheim and Associates, Inc., a pay consulting firm in Los Angeles. He is an adviser to a wide range of prominent for-profit and not-for-profit organizations in linking employees and organizations through new pay strategies. A national leader in innovative pay with special emphasis on the use of variable or incentive pay, he works with organizations to investigate and introduce new pay where only traditional pay has been used. He works closely with executive teams and boards to develop total compensation strategies that emphasize performance during competitive times. His research interests include exploring the relationship between pay techniques and strategies and organizational performance. A frequent speaker on the subjects of pay and organization, he has written two previous books and many articles. He earned his B.B.A. and M.A. from the University of Minnesota and his Ph.D. from the University of Southern California.

Patricia K. Zingheim is a partner in Schuster-Zingheim and Associates, Inc. She advises a wide range of U.S. organizations in both capital- and labor-intensive industries in the areas of employee and management pay. She has worked with many major organizations in the development of pay strategies that are integrated with their business, financial, and human resource goals. She advises organizations on practical approaches to introducing new pay to facilitate not only financial performance but also quality and customer value. A recognized expert in many new variable or incentive pay technologies and in the development of market-based computer-assisted base pay programs, she is a member of the faculty of the American Compensation Association and a frequent speaker for management and business groups. She is the author of many articles and earned her A.B. from the University of Michigan and her M.A. and Ph.D. from Ohio State University.

———